Taste of Home
TEST KITCHEN
FAVORITES

TASTE OF HOME BOOKS • RDA ENTHUSIAST BRANDS, LLC • MILWAUKEE, WI

Taste *of* Home

International Standard Book Numbers:
D 978-1-62145-920-0
U 978-1-62145-921-7

Component Numbers:
D 119700120H
U 119700122H

Chief Content Officer, Home & Garden: Jeanne Sidner
Content Director: Mark Hagen
Associate Creative Director: Raeann Thompson
Senior Editor: Julie Schnittka
Senior Designer: Jazmin Delgado
Deputy Editor, Copy Desk: Dulcie Shoener
Copy Editor: Sara Strauss

Cover Photography: *Taste of Home* Photo Studio

Pictured on front cover:
Potato-Lentil Stew, p. 146
Peanut Butter Cookie Cups, p. 190
Rainbow Quiche, p. 47
Patriotic Ice Cream Cupcakes, p. 213
Chicken Tikka Meatballs with Ginger Rice, p. 109

Pictured on title page:
Chocolate-Strawberry Celebration Cake, p. 210

Pictured on back cover:
Roasted Red Pepper Bread, p. 72
Savory Roasted Chicken, p. 120
Prosciutto Egg Panini, p. 33
Creole Pasta with Sausage & Shrimp, p. 104
Berry-Patch Brownie Pizza, p. 176

Printed in China
1 3 5 7 9 10 8 6 4 2

More ways to connect with us:

Gathering for Goodies at the Food Bar

One of the things I love most about writing the letter for a *Test Kitchen Favorites* cookbook is taking a moment (okay, more like three big ol' coffee cups worth of moments) to really digest all the fantastic recipes, photos and tips in the book before I get to the writing part.

It's so fun to see what the Test Kitchen team members picked as their stand-out favorite recipes. And it brings back memories of those times when we worked on all those tasty dishes in the test kitchens and studios.

There's a magical place in the office known as the food bar. Really, it's just a centralized countertop where we put our finished recipes for the in-office team to eat and enjoy. It's not unusual to see two or three leftover strawberry cheesecakes—sauced, sliced and ready for the taking—at 8:00 a.m. (Cheesecake for breakfast? There's no judgment at the food bar!) Or maybe as folks leave for the day, a tray of fried chicken will arrive, still warm from the Test Kitchen. The team even has a group food chat where delicious deposits are announced to everyone throughout the day.

I'll often spot many of the recipes I had previously seen only on my laptop come to life on the food bar! It is the place that generates culinary excitement and gets the team buzzing about their favorite *Taste of Home* recipes.

And that's just what we've collected for you in this new cookbook— hundreds of tasty, inspiring and buzzworthy recipes enjoyed and recommended by *Taste of Home* staffers.

Check out Lisa Renshaw's impressive Beef Braciole on page 104. After preparing this recipe for a video shoot, word got out quickly once it landed on the food bar. This truly has become an all-time favorite entree of mine. It's incredibly flavorful, rich, robust and perfect for special occasions.

We included many everyday-easy recipes in this new cookbook too. If you're a fan of one-pot recipes, try Nora Rushev's One-Pot Black Bean Enchilada Pasta (page 132) or Julie Davis's One-Pot Spinach Beef Soup (page 95). In 30 minutes, you'll have dinner on the table!

Deanna Pietrowicz's Rainbow Gelatin Cubes (page 224) are an eye-catching dessert that adds a pop of pretty color (and fab flavor!) to any meal.

From breads and breakfasts to sweets and savories (with a few beverages and snacks in the mix too), we have you covered with this latest edition of *Test Kitchen Favorites*.

Wherever you gather around good food and good people, whether a dinner table, kitchen island, living room, patio or more unconventional spot like our uniquely inviting food bar, may your hearts (and bellies) be happy!

DISHING WITH

Sarah Farmer
Taste of Home
Executive Culinary Director

CATHERINE

ALICIA MAGGIE

SUZANNE

MARK

PEGGY

SARAH F.

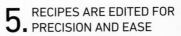

SHANNON

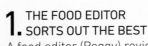

What "Test Kitchen Approved" Means

Our Test Kitchen staff (pictured on this page) puts every *Taste of Home* recipe through a rigorous approval process. It all starts with home cooks (like you!) who share recipes that have been tested in their own kitchens and approved by family and friends.

1. THE FOOD EDITOR SORTS OUT THE BEST

A food editor (Peggy) reviews recipes, looking for fresh ideas and spins on classics (or for dishes that sound irresistible). She also considers if a recipe uses everyday ingredients and is simple enough for home cooks to make.

2. PREP COOKS ASSEMBLE THE INGREDIENTS

In our Prep Kitchen, Catherine and Mark get the food ready for our recipe testers (and later for our food stylists).

3. EXPERT COOKS TEST EACH RECIPE

Test cooks (Alicia and Maggie) prepare each recipe, ensuring that the amounts, equipment, temperature and method are accurate, and making adjustments if needed.

4. TASTE TESTERS WEIGH IN

Taste testers evaluate the prepared recipes according to many factors, such as flavor, texture, appearance, overall appeal and level of difficulty.

5. RECIPES ARE EDITED FOR PRECISION AND EASE

Our recipe editors once again review the recipe's directions for clarity and conciseness.

6. THE PHOTO AND VIDEO TEAMS TAKE OVER

In the Photo Studio, food stylists (Shannon, Josh and Sarah F.) and a culinary producer (Sarah T.) work closely with art directors, photographers, and set and prop stylists on dishes, linens, surfaces and more.

Throughout the process, our culinary assistant (Ellen) and dishwasher (Suzanne) help keep the ship afloat!

JOSH

SARAH T.

ELLEN

PAGE 23

PAGE 226

PAGE 94

CONTENTS

FAVORITE...

APPETIZERS & BEVERAGES 6

BREAKFASTS...28

BREADS, ROLLS & MORE.............................52

SOUPS & SANDWICHES...............................76

MEATY MAIN DISHES..................................96

FISH, SEAFOOD & MEATLESS.......................122

SIDE DISHES & SALADS 148

COOKIES, BROWNIES & BARS 170

CAKES & PIES...192

DESSERTS..214

CUTTING TECHNIQUES 236

EQUIVALENTS & SUBSTITUTIONS 237

INDEX 238

BACON CHEDDAR
POTATO SKINS PAGE 16

Appetizers & Beverages

Like you, the *Taste of Home* Test Kitchen staff loves a good party! These mouthwatering munchies and satisfying sippers are the recipes they rely on the most when entertaining.

ARTICHOKE & SPINACH DIP PIZZA

When I have garlic oil in my pantry, I swap it for regular olive oil. The garlic adds a little something without being overpowering.
—Shelly Bevington, Hermiston, OR

Takes: 20 min. • **Makes:** 24 pieces

- 1 prebaked 12-in. pizza crust
- 1 Tbsp. olive oil
- 1 cup spinach dip
- 1 cup shredded part-skim mozzarella cheese
- 1 jar (7½ oz.) marinated quartered artichoke hearts, drained
- ½ cup oil-packed sun-dried tomatoes, patted dry and chopped
- ¼ cup chopped red onion

1. Preheat oven to 450°. Place the crust on an ungreased pizza pan; brush with oil. Spread spinach dip over top. Sprinkle with cheese, artichokes, tomatoes and onion.
2. Bake for 8-10 minutes or until the cheese is melted and edge is lightly browned. Cut into 24 pieces.
1 piece: 127 cal., 9g fat (2g sat. fat), 6mg chol., 213mg sod., 10g carb. (1g sugars, 0 fiber), 3g pro.

DIJON-BACON DIP FOR PRETZELS

With just four ingredients that you probably already have in your pantry, this quick appetizer comes together in a snap. If you like the zip of horseradish, start with 1 or 2 teaspoons and add more to your taste.
—Isabelle Rooney, Summerville, SC

Takes: 5 min. • **Makes:** 1½ cups

- 1 cup mayonnaise
- ½ cup Dijon mustard
- ¼ cup bacon bits or crumbled cooked bacon
- 1 to 3 tsp. prepared horseradish
  Pretzels or pretzel crisps

In a small bowl, combine mayonnaise, mustard, bacon and horseradish. Cover; chill until serving. Serve with pretzels.
2 Tbsp.: 154 cal., 16g fat (2g sat. fat), 8mg chol., 428mg sod., 1g carb. (0 sugars, 0 fiber), 2g pro.

ARTICHOKE & SPINACH DIP PIZZA

BIG-BATCH BLOODY MARYS

Tailgates, game-day parties and Sunday brunches call for a Bloody Mary recipe that caters to a bunch. This one has a little bit of a kick—just enough to get the crowd cheering. Have guests add their favorite garnishes.
—*Taste of Home* Test Kitchen

Takes: 20 min. • **Makes:** 8 servings

8   cups tomato juice
½   cup lemon juice
¼   cup lime juice
2   Tbsp. Worcestershire sauce
1   tsp. celery salt
1   tsp. pepper
1   tsp. hot pepper sauce
4   tsp. prepared horseradish, optional
2   cups vodka

OPTIONAL GARNISHES
Celery ribs, pickle spears, green and ripe olives, cucumber slices, pickled mushrooms, cubed cheese, beef sticks, cherry tomatoes, cocktail shrimp

In a pitcher, stir together first 7 ingredients. Stir in horseradish if desired. For each serving, pour about 1 cup over ice with ¼ cup vodka; add optional garnishes as desired.

1¼ cups: 180 cal., 1g fat (0 sat. fat), 0 chol., 817mg sod., 12g carb. (7g sugars, 1g fiber), 2g pro.

ASK SARAH

WHAT IS PREPARED HORSERADISH?
Prepared horseradish is made with freshly grated horseradish, vinegar and salt. Find it in the condiment aisle.

BIG-BATCH BLOODY MARYS

AIR-FRYER
CRISPY CHICKEN WINGS

AIR-FRYER CRISPY CHICKEN WINGS

You can't go wrong with air-fryer chicken wings. Our spice rub has a nice boost from the cayenne seasoning.
—*Taste of Home* Test Kitchen

Prep: 15 min. • **Cook:** 35 min./batch
Makes: 2 dozen

- 2 tsp. garlic powder
- 1 tsp. garlic salt
- 1 tsp. each ground mustard, ginger and nutmeg
- ½ tsp. pepper
- ½ tsp. ground allspice
- ½ tsp. baking soda
- ½ tsp. cayenne pepper
- 12 whole chicken wings (2½ lbs.)
  Optional: Ranch salad dressing, Buffalo sauce or barbecue sauce

1. Preheat the air fryer to 300°. In a large bowl, combine the garlic powder, garlic salt, mustard, ginger, nutmeg, pepper, allspice, baking soda and cayenne.
2. Cut the chicken wings into 3 sections; discard wing tip sections. Add to bowl with spices and stir to coat. In batches, arrange wings in a single layer on greased tray in air-fryer basket. Cook 15 minutes. Increase the temperature to 400°; cook until the chicken juices run clear and wings are golden brown, 20-25 minutes. Repeat with the remaining wings. Serve hot, with dressing or sauce if desired.
1 piece: 54 cal., 4g fat (1g sat. fat), 15mg chol., 102mg sod., 0 carb. (0 sugars, 0 fiber), 5g pro.

> "My husband enjoys chicken wings at restaurants, but I've never gotten into the habit of making them at home until now. This air-fryer version is a winner!"
>
> —PEGGY WOODWARD, SENIOR FOOD EDITOR

REUBEN WAFFLE POTATO APPETIZERS

REUBEN WAFFLE POTATO APPETIZERS

I love Reubens, so I turned the classic sammie into a fun appetizer with corned beef and sauerkraut on waffle fries.
—Gloria Bradley, Naperville, IL

Prep: 30 min. • **Bake:** 10 min./batch
Makes: about 4 dozen

- 1 pkg. (22 oz.) frozen waffle-cut fries
- 4 oz. cream cheese, softened
- 2 cups shredded fontina cheese, divided
- ⅓ cup Thousand Island salad dressing
- 3 Tbsp. chopped sweet onion
- 1½ tsp. prepared horseradish
- 12 oz. sliced deli corned beef, coarsely chopped
- 1 cup sauerkraut, rinsed, well drained and chopped
- 2 Tbsp. minced fresh chives

1. Prepare the waffle fries according to package directions for baking. Meanwhile, in a small bowl, beat cream cheese, 1 cup fontina cheese, salad dressing, onion and horseradish until blended.
2. Remove the fries from oven; set oven to 400°. Top each waffle fry with about ¼ oz. corned beef and 1 tsp. each cream cheese mixture, sauerkraut and remaining fontina cheese. Bake 8-10 minutes or until cheese is melted. Sprinkle with chives.
1 appetizer: 62 cal., 4g fat (2g sat. fat), 12mg chol., 168mg sod., 4g carb. (0 sugars, 0 fiber), 3g pro.

MARINATED CHEESE

This special appetizer always makes it to our neighborhood parties and is the first to disappear at the buffet table. It's attractive, delicious and so easy!
—Laurie Casper, Coraopolis, PA

Prep: 30 min. + marinating
Makes: about 2 lbs.

- 2 blocks (8 oz. each) white cheddar cheese
- 2 pkg. (8 oz. each) cream cheese
- ¾ cup chopped roasted sweet red peppers
- ½ cup olive oil
- ¼ cup white wine vinegar
- ¼ cup balsamic vinegar
- 3 Tbsp. chopped green onions
- 3 Tbsp. minced fresh parsley
- 2 Tbsp. minced fresh basil
- 1 Tbsp. sugar
- 3 garlic cloves, minced
- ½ tsp. salt
- ½ tsp. pepper
  Assorted crackers or toasted sliced French bread

1. Slice each block of cheddar cheese into twenty ¼-in. slices. Cut each block of cream cheese into 18 slices. Create four 6-in.-long blocks of stacked cheeses, sandwiching 9 cream cheese slices between 10 cheddar slices for each stack. Place in a 13x9-in. dish.
2. In a bowl, combine roasted peppers, oil, vinegars, onions, herbs, sugar, garlic, salt and pepper; pour over cheese stacks.
3. Cover and refrigerate overnight, turning the cheese blocks once. Drain the excess marinade. Serve the cheese slices with crackers or toasted bread.

1 oz. cheese: 121 cal., 11g fat (6g sat. fat), 30mg chol., 153mg sod., 1g carb. (0 sugars, 0 fiber), 5g pro.

SPARKLING RED WINE SANGRIA

Sangria is a Spanish drink of wine mixed with spices, cut fruit, and fruit juice, sherry or brandy. It's best to mix this and let it sit for an hour or more before serving so all the flavors of the fruit and wine blend together.
—*Taste of Home* Test Kitchen

Takes: 5 minutes • **Makes:** 6 servings

- 1 bottle (750 ml) dry red wine
- 1 cup sugar
- ½ cup orange liqueur
- ½ cup brandy
- 3 cups lemon-lime soda
- 1 cup sliced fresh strawberries
- 1 cup fresh blueberries
- 1 cup fresh raspberries
- 1 large navel orange, sliced

In a pitcher, stir the wine, sugar, orange liqueur and brandy until sugar dissolves. Stir in soda, berries and orange. Chill until ready to serve.

1 cup: 448 cal., 0 fat (0 sat. fat), 0 chol., 18mg sod., 69g carb. (61g sugars, 3g fiber), 1g pro.

MARINATED CHEESE

PARTY SHRIMP

ANTIPASTO KABOBS

My husband and I met at a cooking class. We have loved creating menus and entertaining ever since. These do-ahead appetizers are a favorite to serve.
—Denise Hazen, Cincinnati, OH

Prep: 35 min. + marinating
Makes: 40 appetizers

 1 pkg. (9 oz.) refrigerated
   cheese tortellini
40 pimiento-stuffed olives
40 large pitted ripe olives
¾ cup Italian salad dressing
40 thin slices pepperoni
20 thin slices hard salami, halved

1. Cook the tortellini according to package directions; drain and rinse in cold water. In a large bowl, combine the tortellini, olives and salad dressing. Toss to coat; cover and refrigerate for 4 hours or overnight.
2. Drain the mixture, discarding marinade. For each appetizer, thread a stuffed olive, a folded pepperoni slice, a tortellini, a folded salami piece and a ripe olive on a toothpick or short skewer.
1 kabob: 66 cal., 5g fat (1g sat. fat), 9mg chol., 315mg sod., 4g carb. (0 sugars, 0 fiber), 2g pro.

PARTY SHRIMP

The marinade for this dish makes the shrimp so flavorful that you won't need a dipping sauce. Even those who claim they don't like shellfish really dig this appetizer.
—Kendra Doss, Colorado Springs, CO

Prep: 15 min. + marinating • **Broil:** 10 min.
Makes: 2½ dozen

 1 Tbsp. olive oil
1½ tsp. brown sugar
1½ tsp. lemon juice
 1 garlic clove, thinly sliced
 ½ tsp. paprika
 ½ tsp. Italian seasoning
 ½ tsp. dried basil
 ¼ tsp. pepper
 1 lb. uncooked shrimp (26-30 per lb.),
   peeled and deveined

1. In a bowl or shallow dish, combine the first 8 ingredients. Add the shrimp; toss to coat. Refrigerate 2 hours.

2. Drain shrimp, discarding marinade. Place shrimp on an ungreased baking sheet. Broil 4 in. from heat until shrimp turn pink, 3-4 minutes on each side.
1 shrimp: 14 cal., 0 fat (0 sat. fat), 18mg chol., 18mg sod., 0 carb. (0 sugars, 0 fiber), 2g pro.

TEST KITCHEN TIP
To tell if your shrimp are done cooking, they should be curled into a nice C shape. Overcooked shrimp are curled tightly into an O shape.

TRIPLE TOMATO FLATBREAD

Tomatoes are the only reason I have a vegetable garden, and I developed this recipe as a way to show off my garden's plum, sun-dried and cherry tomatoes. The dish is easy and will impress.
—Rachel Kimbrow, Portland, OR

- -

Takes: 20 min. • **Makes:** 8 pieces

1	tube (13.8 oz.) refrigerated pizza crust
	Cooking spray
3	plum tomatoes, finely chopped (about 2 cups)
½	cup soft sun-dried tomato halves (not packed in oil), julienned
2	Tbsp. olive oil
1	Tbsp. dried basil
¼	tsp. salt
¼	tsp. pepper
1	cup shredded Asiago cheese
2	cups yellow and/or red cherry tomatoes, halved

1. Unroll and press dough into a 15x10-in. rectangle. Transfer dough to an 18x12-in. piece of heavy-duty foil coated with cooking spray; spritz the dough with cooking spray. In a large bowl, toss plum tomatoes and sun-dried tomatoes with oil and seasonings.

2. Carefully invert dough onto grill rack; remove foil. Grill, covered, over medium heat 2-3 minutes or until bottom is golden brown. Turn; grill 1-2 minutes longer or until second side begins to brown.

3. Remove from grill. Spoon plum tomato mixture over crust; top with cheese and cherry tomatoes. Return flatbread to grill. Grill, covered, 2-4 minutes or until crust is golden brown and cheese is melted.

1 piece: 235 cal., 9g fat (3g sat. fat), 12mg chol., 476mg sod., 29g carb. (7g sugars, 3g fiber), 8g pro.

Diabetic exchanges: 1½ starch, 1½ fat, 1 vegetable.

To bake flatbread: Preheat oven to 425°. Unroll and press dough onto bottom of a 15x10x1-in. baking pan coated with cooking spray. Bake for 6-8 minutes or until lightly browned. Assemble flatbread as directed. Bake 8-10 minutes longer or until crust is golden and cheese is melted.

TRIPLE TOMATO FLATBREAD

BAKED BABY POTATOES WITH OLIVE PESTO

These little cuties pack all the appeal of a dinner baked potato into a perfect bite-sized appetizer. I top each one with a dollop of sour cream and coarsely ground pepper.
—Sarah Shaikh, Mumbai, India

- -

Prep: 35 min. • **Bake:** 30 min.
Makes: about 3 dozen

- 3 lbs. baby red potatoes (1¾ in. wide, about 36)
- 6 Tbsp. olive oil, divided
- 2 tsp. salt
- 1½ cups pimiento-stuffed olives
- ½ cup chopped onion
- ¼ cup pine nuts, toasted
- 2 garlic cloves, minced
- ½ cup sour cream
  Coarsely ground pepper, optional

1. Preheat oven to 400°. Place potatoes in a large bowl. Add 2 Tbsp. oil and the salt; toss to coat. Transfer to a greased 15x10x1-in. baking pan. Bake potatoes for 30-35 minutes or until tender.

2. Meanwhile, place olives, onion, pine nuts and garlic in a food processor; pulse until chopped. Gradually add the remaining oil; process to reach desired consistency.

3. When the potatoes are cool enough to handle, cut thin slices off bottoms to allow potatoes to sit upright. Cut an "X" in the top of each potato; squeeze sides to open tops slightly. Place on a serving platter.

4. Spoon olive pesto onto potatoes; top with sour cream. If desired, sprinkle with pepper. Serve warm.

1 appetizer: 88 cal., 6g fat (1g sat. fat), 1mg chol., 303mg sod., 9g carb. (1g sugars, 1g fiber), 1g pro.

FROZEN MARGARITAS

One of my favorite summer drinks is a frozen margarita. What's not to love? This drink is perfect paired with tacos or chips and salsa.
—Caroline Stanko, Editor, *Taste of Home*

- -

Takes: 15 min. • **Makes:** 6 servings

- 6 lime wedges
  Kosher salt
- 1 cup tequila
- ½ cup Triple Sec
- ¼ cup lime juice (about 4 limes)
- ½ cup simple syrup or super fine sugar
- 6 to 9 cups ice cubes

1. Using lime wedges, moisten the rims of 6 margarita or cocktail glasses. Set aside lime wedges for garnish. Sprinkle salt on a plate; hold each glass upside down and dip rim into salt. Set aside. Discard remaining salt on plate.

2. In a blender, combine the tequila, Triple Sec, lime juice, simple syrup and enough ice to reach desired consistency; cover and process until blended. Pour into the prepared glasses. Garnish with lime wedges. Serve immediately.

1 cup: 214 cal., 0 fat (0 sat. fat), 0 chol., 34mg sod., 24g carb. (22g sugars, 0 fiber), 0 pro.

BAKED BABY POTATOES WITH OLIVE PESTO

BACON CHEDDAR POTATO SKINS

EASY EGG ROLLS

I've always loved egg rolls, but every recipe seemed too complicated. I decided to start with a packaged coleslaw mix. Now I can make these at a moment's notice.
—Samantha Dunn, Leesville, LA

Prep: 30 min. • **Cook:** 30 min.
Makes: 28 servings

- 1 lb. ground beef
- 1 pkg. (14 oz.) coleslaw mix
- 2 Tbsp. soy sauce
- ½ tsp. garlic powder
- ¼ tsp. ground ginger
- ⅛ tsp. onion powder
- 1 Tbsp. all-purpose flour
- 28 egg roll wrappers
   Canola oil for frying

1. In a large skillet, cook beef over medium heat until no longer pink, 5-7 minutes, breaking into crumbles; drain and cool slightly. In a bowl, combine beef, coleslaw mix, soy sauce, garlic powder, ginger and onion powder. In a small bowl, combine flour and enough water to make a paste.
2. With 1 corner of an egg roll wrapper facing you, place ¼ cup filling just below center of wrapper. (Cover remaining wrappers with a damp paper towel until ready to use.) Fold bottom corner over filling; moisten remaining wrapper edges with flour mixture. Fold the side corners toward center over filling. Roll egg roll up tightly, pressing at tip to seal. Repeat.
3. In an electric skillet or deep-fat fryer, heat oil to 375°. Fry egg rolls, a few at a time, until golden, 3-4 minutes, turning occasionally. Drain on paper towels.
1 egg roll: 185 cal., 9g fat (1g sat. fat), 13mg chol., 261mg sod., 20g carb. (1g sugars, 1g fiber), 6g pro.

BACON CHEDDAR POTATO SKINS

Both crisp and hearty, this restaurant-quality snack is one that is often requested by my family.
—Trish Perrin, Keizer, OR

Takes: 30 min.
Makes: 8 servings

- 4 large baking potatoes, baked
- 3 Tbsp. canola oil
- 1 Tbsp. grated Parmesan cheese
- ½ tsp. salt
- ¼ tsp. garlic powder
- ¼ tsp. paprika
- ⅛ tsp. pepper
- 8 bacon strips, cooked and crumbled
- 1½ cups shredded cheddar cheese
- ½ cup sour cream
- 4 green onions, sliced

1. Preheat oven to 475°. Cut potatoes in half lengthwise; scoop out pulp, leaving a ¼-in. shell (save pulp for another use). Place skins on a greased baking sheet.

2. Combine oil with next 5 ingredients; brush over both sides of skins.
3. Bake until crisp, about 7 minutes on each side. Sprinkle bacon and cheddar cheese inside the skins. Bake until the cheese is melted, about 2 minutes longer. Top with sour cream and green onions. Serve immediately.
1 potato skin: 350 cal., 19g fat (7g sat. fat), 33mg chol., 460mg sod., 34g carb. (2g sugars, 4g fiber), 12g pro.

TEST KITCHEN TIP
To bake potatoes, preheat the oven to 400°. Wash and dry the potatoes; prick each with a fork in a few places. Bake directly on the oven rack for 50-75 minutes or until fork tender.

EASY EGG ROLLS

BROCCOLI FRITTERS

These cute cakes offer a fun and kid-friendly way to use broccoli. They're tasty as a side dish paired with any meat, or serve them with salsa and a dollop of fat-free sour cream for a festive appetizer.
—Tracy Eubanks, Ewing, KY

- -

Prep: 20 min. • **Cook:** 10 min./batch
Makes: 12 servings

- 1 bunch broccoli, cut into florets
- 2 large eggs, lightly beaten
- 2 large egg whites
- ⅓ cup grated Parmesan cheese
- 2 Tbsp. all-purpose flour
- ½ tsp. salt
- ½ tsp. garlic powder
- ½ tsp. pepper
- 2 Tbsp. canola oil
  Salsa, optional

1. Place broccoli in a steamer basket; place basket in a small saucepan over 1 in. water. Bring to a boil; cover and steam until crisp-tender, 3-4 minutes. Coarsely chop broccoli and set aside.
2. In a large bowl, combine the eggs, egg whites, cheese, flour, salt, garlic powder and pepper. Stir in broccoli.
3. Heat 1 Tbsp. oil in a large cast-iron or other heavy skillet over medium heat. Drop the battered broccoli by heaping ⅛ cupfuls into oil; press lightly to flatten. Cook fritters in batches until golden brown, 3-4 minutes on each side, using remaining oil as needed. Drain on paper towels. If desired, serve with salsa .

1 fritter: 67 cal., 4g fat (1g sat. fat), 33mg chol., 176mg sod., 5g carb. (1g sugars, 1g fiber), 4g pro.

APRICOT KIELBASA SLICES

These satisfying sausage bites are coated in a thick, zesty sauce with just the right amount of sweetness. I know you're going to love 'em!
—Barbara McCalley, Allison Park, PA

- -

Takes: 15 min. • **Makes:** 12 servings

- 1 lb. fully cooked kielbasa or Polish sausage, cut into ¼-in. slices
- 1 jar (12 oz.) apricot preserves
- 2 Tbsp. lemon juice
- 2 tsp. Dijon mustard
- ¼ tsp. ground ginger

1. In a cast-iron or other heavy skillet, cook and stir sausage until browned. Remove from pan; discard drippings.
2. Add remaining ingredients to skillet; cook and stir over low heat until heated through, 2-3 minutes. Stir in sausage; heat through.

¼ cup: 47 cal., 3g fat (1g sat. fat), 6mg chol., 110mg sod., 5g carb. (4g sugars, 0 fiber), 1g pro.

TEST KITCHEN TIP
You can make this appetizer before guests arrive. Just transfer the sausage mixture to a slow cooker and keep warm on low heat.

BROCCOLI FRITTERS

SPINACH & FETA BOUREKAS

Light and soft, with a bit of crunch, these bourekas are one of my favorite appetizers for holidays. They can be filled with almost anything, but spinach and feta is one of my favorite fillings. These little triangles are out of this world!
—Alex Stepanov, Matawan, NJ

Prep: 25 min. • **Bake:** 25 min.
Makes: 8 servings

- 1 Tbsp. olive oil or avocado oil
- 1 lb. fresh spinach, trimmed
- ½ cup chopped shallots
- 1 Tbsp. minced garlic
- ½ tsp. salt
- ¼ tsp. pepper
- 1 pkg. (17.3 oz.) frozen puff pastry, thawed
- ½ cup crumbled feta cheese
- ½ cup whole-milk ricotta cheese
- 1 large egg, beaten
- 1 Tbsp. everything seasoning blend

1. Preheat oven to 400°. In a large skillet, heat oil over medium-high heat. Add the spinach, shallots and garlic; cook and stir until wilted, 2-3 minutes. Remove from heat; strain off any excess water. Stir in salt and pepper; set aside to cool to room temperature.

2. On a lightly floured surface, unfold puff pastry. Cut each sheet into 4 squares. In a small bowl, combine feta and ricotta; stir in spinach mixture. Spoon cheese mixture diagonally over half of each square to within ½ in. of edges. Brush pastry edges with egg. Fold 1 corner over filling to the opposite corner, forming a triangle; press the edges with a fork to seal. Place on parchment-lined baking sheets. Brush remaining egg over pastries; sprinkle with seasoning blend. Bake until golden brown, 25-30 minutes.

Freeze option: Freeze unbaked pastries on a parchment-lined baking sheet until firm. Transfer to an airtight container; return to freezer. To use, cook frozen pastries as directed until golden brown and heated through, increasing time to 30-32 minutes, covering with foil if pastries begin to brown too quickly.

1 pastry: 383 cal., 21g fat (6g sat. fat), 22mg chol., 635mg sod., 39g carb. (2g sugars, 6g fiber), 9g pro.

SPINACH & FETA BOUREKAS

"This is such a flavorful appetizer idea! The everything seasoning on top is the crowning touch. I appreciate the fact that these can be made when time allows and then popped into the freezer until I'm ready to use them."
—SARAH FISCHER, ASSOCIATE FOOD STYLIST

CHOCOLATE CHIP CHEESE BALL

Your guests are in for a sweet surprise when they try this unusual cheese ball that tastes just like cookie dough! Rolled in chopped pecans, the chip-studded spread is terrific on regular or chocolate graham crackers. I especially like the recipe because it can be assembled in a wink.
—Kelly Glascock, Syracuse, MO

- -

Prep: 15 min. + chilling
Makes: 16 servings

- 1   pkg. (8 oz.) cream cheese, softened
- ½   cup butter, softened
- ¼   tsp. vanilla extract
- ¾   cup confectioners' sugar
- 2   Tbsp. brown sugar
- ¾   cup miniature semisweet chocolate chips
- ¾   cup finely chopped pecans
       Graham crackers

1. In a large bowl, beat cream cheese, butter and vanilla until smooth; beat in the sugars just until blended. Stir in the chocolate chips. Refrigerate, covered, until firm enough to shape, about 2 hours.
2. Shape mixture into a ball. Wrap and refrigerate at least 1 hour.
3. To serve, roll cheese ball in pecans. Serve with graham crackers.
2 Tbsp.: 203 cal., 17g fat (8g sat. fat), 30mg chol., 92mg sod., 14g carb. (12g sugars, 1g fiber), 2g pro.

TEST KITCHEN TIP

This indulgent spread can be made with reduced-fat cream cheese, but it will be too soft to shape into a ball. Instead, serve it in a shallow dish and sprinkle it with the chips and pecans. It's still completely delicious but with fewer calories and less fat.

BUFFALO WING POPPERS

The taste of Buffalo wings and pepper poppers pair up in this appealing appetizer. It will disappear fast—so make a double batch and have copies of the recipe handy.
—Barbara Nowakowski, Mesa, AZ

- -

Prep: 20 min. • **Bake:** 20 min.
Makes: 40 appetizers

- 20   jalapeno peppers
- 1   pkg. (8 oz.) cream cheese, softened
- 1½   cups shredded part-skim mozzarella cheese
- 1   cup diced cooked chicken
- ½   cup blue cheese salad dressing
- ½   cup Buffalo wing sauce

1. Preheat oven to 325°. Cut peppers in half lengthwise, leaving stems intact; discard the seeds. In a small bowl, combine the remaining ingredients. Pipe or stuff into pepper halves.
2. Place in a greased 15x10x1-in. baking pan. Bake, uncovered, 20 minutes for spicy flavor, 30 minutes for medium and 40 minutes for mild.
1 popper: 57 cal., 5g fat (2g sat. fat), 12mg chol., 159mg sod., 1g carb. (1g sugars, 0 fiber), 2g pro.

CHOCOLATE CHIP
CHEESE BALL

RED LENTIL HUMMUS
WITH BRUSSELS
SPROUT HASH

RED LENTIL HUMMUS WITH BRUSSELS SPROUT HASH

Instead of chickpeas, this spicy dip uses lentils to create a hearty, healthful appetizer. The Brussels sprout topping makes this feel more special than plain hummus, but you can serve the dip without the topping too.
—Carolyn Manning, Seattle, WA

- -

Prep: 20 min. + cooling • **Cook:** 15 min.
Makes: 10 servings

- 1   cup dried red lentils, rinsed
- ¼   cup tahini
- 2   Tbsp. lemon juice
- 1   Tbsp. olive oil
- 3   garlic cloves, halved
- 1   tsp. ground cumin
- 1   tsp. curry powder
- ½   tsp. salt
- ½   tsp. ground ginger
- ⅛   tsp. white pepper
- ⅛   tsp. cayenne pepper

BRUSSELS SPROUT HASH
- 1   Tbsp. olive oil
- 1   shallot, minced
- ½   lb. fresh Brussels sprouts, thinly sliced
- 1   cup canned diced tomatoes
- ¼   tsp. salt
- ¼   tsp. crushed red pepper flakes
      Assorted fresh vegetables

1. Place lentils in a small saucepan; add water to cover. Bring to a boil; reduce heat. Simmer, covered, until lentils are tender, 12-15 minutes. Drain; cool for 10 minutes. Transfer to a food processor. Add tahini, lemon juice, oil, garlic and seasonings. Process until smooth.
2. For hash, in a large skillet, heat oil over medium heat. Add shallot; cook and stir until tender, 3-4 minutes. Add Brussels sprouts and tomatoes; cook until sprouts are crisp-tender, 12-15 minutes longer. Remove from heat; stir in salt and pepper flakes. Spread hummus on a serving plate; top with hash. Serve with vegetables.
1 serving: 154 cal., 7g fat (1g sat. fat), 0 chol., 226mg sod., 18g carb. (2g sugars, 4g fiber), 7g pro. **Diabetic exchanges:** 1½ fat, 1 starch.

GARLIC TOMATO BRUSCHETTA

I drew inspiration from my grandma's recipe for this bruschetta. The tomato goodness says welcome to the party, or serve it as a complement to your favorite Italian entree.
—Jean Franzoni, Rutland, VT

- -

Prep: 30 min. + chilling • **Makes:** 2 dozen

- ¼   cup olive oil
- 3   Tbsp. chopped fresh basil
- 3   to 4 garlic cloves, minced
- ½   tsp. salt
- ¼   tsp. pepper
- 4   medium tomatoes, diced
- 2   Tbsp. grated Parmesan cheese
- 1   loaf (1 lb.) unsliced French bread

1. In a large bowl, combine the oil, basil, garlic, salt and pepper. Add tomatoes and toss gently. Sprinkle with cheese. Refrigerate at least 1 hour.
2. Bring to room temperature before serving. Cut bread into 24 slices; toast under broiler until lightly browned. Top with tomato mixture. Serve immediately.
1 piece: 77 cal., 3g fat (0 sat. fat), 0 chol., 172mg sod., 11g carb. (1g sugars, 1g fiber), 2g pro. **Diabetic exchanges:** ½ starch, ½ fat.

HOT WING DIP

HOT WING DIP

Since I usually have all the ingredients on hand for this recipe, this is a terrific go-to snack when entertaining friends and family.
—Coleen Corner, Grove City, PA

- -

Prep: 10 min. • **Cook:** 1 hour
Makes: 4½ cups

- 2 cups shredded cooked chicken
- 1 pkg. (8 oz.) cream cheese, cubed
- 2 cups shredded cheddar cheese
- 1 cup ranch salad dressing
- ½ cup Louisiana-style hot sauce
   Minced fresh parsley, optional
   Tortilla chips and celery sticks

In a 3- or 4-qt. slow cooker, mix the first 5 ingredients. Cook, covered, on low for 1-2 hours or until the cheese is melted. If desired, sprinkle with parsley. Serve with tortilla chips and celery.

¼ cup: 186 cal., 16g fat (7g sat. fat), 43mg chol., 235mg sod., 2g carb. (1g sugars, 0 fiber), 8g pro.

Baked Hot Wing Dip: Preheat oven to 350°. Spread dip mixture into an ungreased 9-in. square baking dish. Bake, uncovered, for 20-25 minutes or until heated through.

MARGARITA CHICKEN QUESADILLAS

Quesadillas have never tasted as good as when they are filled with slightly sweet onions and peppers and topped with lime butter and salt. It's the perfect balance of sweet and savory. This version is just the recipe for a summer party—or a fantastic way to bring a little bit of summer into the cold winter months.
—Stephanie Bright, Simpsonville, SC

- -

Prep: 35 min. + marinating
Cook: 5 min./batch
Makes: 16 wedges

- 4 boneless skinless chicken breast halves (5 oz. each)
- ¾ cup thawed frozen limeade concentrate
- 1 large onion, sliced
- 1 medium sweet orange pepper, julienned
- 1 medium sweet yellow pepper, julienned
- 1 Tbsp. canola oil
- ¼ tsp. salt

MARGARITA CHICKEN QUESADILLAS

- ¼ tsp. pepper
- 4 flour tortillas (10 in.)
- 1 cup shredded Monterey Jack cheese
- 1 cup shredded cheddar cheese
- 2 Tbsp. butter, melted
- 1 Tbsp. lime juice
- 1 Tbsp. chopped fresh cilantro
   Lime wedges, optional

1. Place chicken in a large bowl. Add limeade concentrate and turn to coat. Cover bowl; refrigerate for 6 hours or overnight.

2. In a large nonstick skillet, saute onion and sweet peppers in oil until tender; season with salt and pepper. Remove and set aside; wipe out skillet. Drain chicken, discarding marinade.

3. Grill chicken, covered, on a greased rack over medium heat or broil 4 in. from the heat for 5-8 minutes on each side or until a thermometer reads 165°. Cut the chicken into ¼-in. strips; set aside. On half of each tortilla, layer the Monterey Jack cheese, chicken, pepper mixture and cheddar cheese; fold over. Combine butter and lime juice; brush over tortillas.

4. In same skillet used to cook vegetables, cook quesadillas over medium heat until cheese is melted, 2-3 minutes per side. Keep warm in the oven while cooking the remaining quesadillas. Cut each quesadilla into 4 wedges. Sprinkle with cilantro; serve with lime wedges if desired.

1 wedge: 204 cal., 9g fat (4g sat. fat), 37mg chol., 288mg sod., 18g carb. (8g sugars, 1g fiber), 12g pro.

CHEESE LOVER'S FONDUE

French bread cubes and apples are the perfect dippers for this classic fondue, made with white wine and Swiss and Gruyere cheeses. It's a crowd pleaser.
—Linda Vogel, Elgin, IL

- -

Prep: 15 min. • **Cook:** 20 min.
Makes: 2 cups

- 4 tsp. cornstarch, divided
- 1 Tbsp. plus 1 cup dry white wine, divided
- 1½ cups shredded Gruyere cheese
- 1½ cups shredded Swiss cheese
- 1 garlic clove, peeled and halved
- 1½ tsp. lemon juice
- ⅛ tsp. garlic powder
- ⅛ tsp. dried oregano
- ⅛ tsp. Worcestershire sauce
- 3 drops hot pepper sauce
  Miniature smoked sausages, dill pickles and pretzels

1. In a bowl, combine 2 tsp. cornstarch with 1 Tbsp. wine; set aside. Combine the cheeses and remaining cornstarch; set aside.
2. Rub the sides of a large saucepan with cut sides of garlic; discard the garlic. Add remaining wine to the pan and heat over medium heat until bubbles form around sides of pan. Stir in lemon juice.
3. Reduce the heat to medium-low; add a handful of cheese mixture. Stir constantly, using a figure-8 motion, until almost completely melted. Continue adding the cheese, a handful at a time, allowing cheese to almost completely melt between additions. Stir in garlic powder, oregano, Worcestershire sauce and pepper sauce. Stir cornstarch mixture; gradually add to the pan. Cook and stir until the mixture is thickened and smooth. Keep warm. Serve with sausages, pickles and pretzels.
¼ cup: 196 cal., 12g fat (8g sat. fat), 42mg chol., 127mg sod., 3g carb. (1g sugars, 0 fiber), 12g pro.

"I'm a Wisconsin girl, so I love anything with cheese. In addition to bread cubes and mini smoked sausages, I serve this dip with avocado cubes, celery sticks and crispy bacon slices. Feel free to get creative!"
—AMY GLANDER, EDITOR

WATERMELON CUPS

This lovely appetizer is almost too pretty to eat! Sweet watermelon cubes hold a refreshing topping that showcases cucumber, red onion and fresh herbs.
—*Taste of Home* Test Kitchen

- -

Takes: 25 min. • **Makes:** 16 appetizers

- 16 seedless watermelon cubes (1 in.)
- ⅓ cup finely chopped cucumber
- 5 tsp. finely chopped red onion
- 2 tsp. minced fresh mint
- 2 tsp. minced fresh cilantro
- ½ to 1 tsp. lime juice

1. Using a small melon baller or measuring spoon, scoop out the center of each melon cube, leaving a ¼-in. shell (save centers for another use).
2. In a small bowl, combine the remaining ingredients; spoon into watermelon cubes.
1 piece: 7 cal., 0 fat (0 sat. fat), 0 chol., 1mg sod., 2g carb. (2g sugars, 0 fiber), 0 pro.

CHEESE LOVER'S FONDUE

BACON-WRAPPED SPAM BITES

ITALIAN MEATBALL BUNS

These soft little rolls come with a pleasant surprise inside—savory Italian meatballs. The apps are wonderful dipped in marinara sauce, which makes them fun for my grandkids—and adults too. I love how easy they are to put together.
—Trina Linder-Mobley, Clover, SC

- -

Prep: 30 min. + rising • **Bake:** 15 min.
Makes: 2 dozen

- 12 frozen bread dough dinner rolls
- 1 pkg. (12 oz.) frozen fully cooked Italian meatballs, thawed
- 2 Tbsp. olive oil
- ¼ cup grated Parmesan cheese
- ¼ cup minced fresh basil
- 1½ cups marinara sauce, warmed

1. Let dough stand at room temperature until softened, 25-30 minutes.
2. Cut each roll in half. Wrap each portion around a meatball, enclosing meatball completely; pinch dough firmly to seal. Place on greased baking sheets, seam side down. Cover with kitchen towel; let rise in a warm place until almost doubled, 1½-2 hours.
3. Preheat oven to 350°. Bake buns until golden brown, 12-15 minutes. Brush tops with oil; sprinkle with cheese and basil. Serve with marinara sauce.
1 bun with 1 Tbsp. sauce: 98 cal., 4g fat (1g sat. fat), 13mg chol., 253mg sod., 12g carb. (2g sugars, 1g fiber), 5g pro.

BACON-WRAPPED SPAM BITES

These sweet and savory bites use Spam in a fun new way. Bet you can't stop at just one!
—*Taste of Home* Test Kitchen

- -

Prep: 20 min. • **Bake:** 15 min.
Makes: 32 pieces

- 16 bacon strips
- 1 can (12 oz.) reduced-sodium SPAM, cut into 32 cubes
- 32 wooden toothpicks
- ⅓ cup yellow mustard
- ¼ cup maple syrup
- 1 garlic clove, minced

1. Preheat oven to 400°. Cut bacon strips crosswise in half. In a large skillet, cook bacon over medium heat until partially cooked but not crisp. Remove to paper towels to drain; keep warm.

2. Wrap a bacon piece around each Spam cube; secure with a toothpick. Place in a 15x10x1-in. ungreased baking pan. Bake 10 minutes. In a bowl, combine mustard, syrup and garlic; drizzle over the bacon-wrapped Spam. Bake until bacon is crisp, 5-10 minutes longer.
1 appetizer: 60 cal., 4g fat (1g sat. fat), 12mg chol., 211mg sod., 2g carb. (2g sugars, 0 fiber), 3g pro.

TEST KITCHEN TIP
To make ahead, wrap Spam cubes with bacon and secure each with a toothpick. Store bites, covered, in the refrigerator for up to 2 days.

EASY DEVILED EGGS

This recipe comes from the Durbin Inn, a well-known restaurant in Rushville, Indiana, from the 1920s until it closed in the late '70s. The eggs are delicious, and it's easy to make more for larger gatherings.
—Margaret Sanders, Indianapolis, IN

- -

Takes: 15 min. • **Makes:** 1 dozen

- 6 hard-boiled large eggs
- 2 Tbsp. mayonnaise
- 1 tsp. sugar
- 1 tsp. white vinegar
- 1 tsp. prepared mustard
- ½ tsp. salt
  - Paprika

Slice the eggs in half lengthwise; remove yolks and set whites aside. In a small bowl, mash yolks with a fork. Add mayonnaise, sugar, vinegar, mustard and salt; mix well. Stuff or pipe into egg whites. Sprinkle with paprika. Refrigerate until serving.

1 egg half: 55 cal., 4g fat (1g sat. fat), 94mg chol., 146mg sod., 1g carb. (1g sugars, 0 fiber), 3g pro.

Santa Fe Deviled Eggs: To the mashed yolks, add 3 Tbsp. each mayonnaise and canned chopped green chiles, 1½ tsp. chipotle pepper in adobo sauce and ¼ tsp. garlic salt. Stuff as directed. Garnish each with 1 tsp. salsa and a sliver of ripe olive.

FETA CHEESE & POMEGRANATE GUACAMOLE

Want to add a little festive flair to your bowl of guac? Top it off with chunks of feta and fresh pomegranate seeds. Since the cheese is briny, we recommend cutting back on the amount of salt you use in the guacamole recipe or using reduced-sodium chips.
—*Taste of Home* Test Kitchen

- -

Takes: 15 min. • **Makes:** 6 servings

- 3 medium ripe avocado, peeled and cubed
- 2 to 3 Tbsp. fresh lime juice
- ½ to 1 tsp. kosher salt
- ½ cup pomegranate seeds
- ½ cup crumbled feta cheese

In a bowl, mash avocados until almost smooth. Stir in lime juice and ½ tsp. salt. Let stand 10 minutes to allow flavors to blend. Adjust seasoning with additional lime juice and salt if desired. Top with pomegranate seeds and feta.

¼ cup: 146 cal., 12g fat (2g sat. fat), 5mg chol., 256mg sod., 9g carb. (2g sugars, 5g fiber), 3g pro. **Diabetic exchanges:** 2 fat, ½ starch.

HERBED CHEESE STICKS

We love the breadsticks we get hot from the oven at our local pizza parlor. Now I can serve that same wonderful goodness at home.
—Heather Bates, Athens, ME

- -

Takes: 30 min. • **Makes:** 16 cheese sticks

- 1 pkg. (6½ oz.) pizza crust mix
- 1½ tsp. garlic powder
- 1 Tbsp. olive oil
- 1 cup shredded part-skim mozzarella cheese
- ¼ cup shredded Parmesan cheese
- 1 tsp. Italian seasoning
  - Pizza sauce

1. Preheat oven to 450°. In a bowl, mix the pizza dough according to package directions, adding garlic powder to dry mix. Cover; let rest 5 minutes.
2. Knead dough 4-5 times or until easy to handle. On a greased baking sheet, press dough into an 8-in. square. Brush top with oil; sprinkle with cheeses and Italian seasoning.
3. Bake 6-8 minutes or until cheese is lightly browned. Cut square in half; cut each half crosswise into 8 strips. Serve with pizza sauce.

1 cheese stick: 72 cal., 3g fat (1g sat. fat), 5mg chol., 117mg sod., 8g carb. (1g sugars, 0 fiber), 3g pro.

BAKED CHIPS

These basic, crispy baked chips are the perfect canvas for almost any meal. They are awesome for snacking.
—Mary Lou Kelly, Scottdale, PA

- -

Takes: 25 min. • **Makes:** 2 servings

- 2 medium potatoes
- ¼ cup olive oil
- ½ tsp. salt

1. Preheat oven to 425°. Cut potatoes into ⅛-in. slices; arrange in a single layer on 2 greased baking sheets. In a bowl, mix oil and salt; brush over both sides of potatoes.
2. Roast until the potatoes are tender, golden brown and crisp, 15-20 minutes, turning occasionally.
1 cup: 403 cal., 27g fat (4g sat. fat), 0 chol., 603mg sod., 37g carb. (2g sugars, 4g fiber), 4g pro.

MANGO ORANGE QUENCHER

Serve this beautiful beverage at your next brunch in place of mimosas. Just chill the base an hour before adding the club soda.
—*Taste of Home* Test Kitchen

- -

Prep: 10 min. + chilling
Makes: 13 servings (2½ qt.)

- 4 cups mango nectar
- 2 cups orange juice
- 2 Tbsp. lime juice
- 1 bottle (1 liter) club soda, chilled
  Lime slices, optional

1. In a large pitcher, combine the nectar and juices. Refrigerate for at least 1 hour.
2. Just before serving, stir in the club soda. Serve in champagne flutes or wine glasses. Garnish with lime slices if desired.
¾ cup: 58 cal., 0 fat (0 sat. fat), 0 chol., 19mg sod., 14g carb. (12g sugars, 0 fiber), 0 pro.
Diabetic exchanges: 1 fruit.

SAUSAGE CHIVE PINWHEELS

These spirals are simple to make but look special on a buffet. Our guests eagerly help themselves—sometimes the eye-catching pinwheels don't even make it to their plates!
—Gail Sykora, Menomonee Falls, WI

- -

Takes: 30 min. • **Makes:** 1 dozen

- 1 tube (8 oz.) refrigerated crescent rolls
- ½ lb. uncooked bulk pork sausage
- 2 Tbsp. minced chives

1. Preheat oven to 375°. Unroll the crescent dough on a lightly floured surface; press the perforations to seal. Roll into a 14x10-in. rectangle.
2. Spread sausage to within ½ in. of edges. Sprinkle with chives. Roll up carefully jelly-roll style, starting with a long side; pinch seam to seal. Cut into 12 slices; place 1 in. apart in an ungreased 15x10x1-in. pan.
3. Bake until golden brown and sausage is cooked through, 12-16 minutes.
1 pinwheel: 132 cal., 9g fat (3g sat. fat), 13mg chol., 293mg sod., 8g carb. (1g sugars, 0 fiber), 4g pro.

Breakfasts

It's time to rise and shine! The most important meal of the day calls for done-right dishes to guarantee a good morning.

HASH BROWN EGG BAKE

Frozen hash browns make this yummy recipe simple to prepare. Featuring bacon and cheddar cheese, it's tasty breakfast or brunch fare. You can even make it the night before, keep it in the fridge and bake it the next morning.
—Cheryl Johnson, Plymouth, MN

- -

Prep: 20 min. • **Bake:** 45 min.
Makes: 8 servings

- 1 pkg. (30 oz.) frozen cubed hash brown potatoes, thawed
- 1 lb. bacon strips, cooked and crumbled
- 1 cup shredded cheddar cheese, divided
- ¼ to ½ tsp. salt
- 8 large eggs
- 2 cups 2% milk
  Paprika

1. In a large bowl, combine hash browns, bacon, ½ cup cheese and salt. Spoon into a greased 13x9-in. baking dish. In another large bowl, beat the eggs and milk until blended; pour over hash brown mixture. Sprinkle with paprika.

2. Bake at 350°, uncovered, 45-50 minutes or until a knife inserted in center comes out clean. Sprinkle with remaining cheese.

Note: Dish may be prepared in advance, covered and refrigerated overnight. Remove from refrigerator 30 minutes before baking.

1 cup: 354 cal., 19g fat (8g sat. fat), 227mg chol., 649mg sod., 23g carb. (4g sugars, 1g fiber), 21g pro.

> "I substituted turkey bacon for regular bacon and added an onion for a bit of extra flavor. The result was a hearty, protein-packed slice of ooey-gooey goodness!"
> —SAMMI DIVITO, ASSISTANT EDITOR

MINI HAM QUICHES

These adorable quiches are delightful for an after-church brunch when you don't want to fuss. Replace the ham with bacon, sausage, chicken or shrimp, or substitute chopped onion, red pepper or zucchini for the olives if you'd like.
—Marilou Robinson, Portland, OR

- -

Prep: 15 min. • **Bake:** 20 min.
Makes: 1 dozen

- ¾ cup diced fully cooked ham
- ½ cup shredded sharp cheddar cheese
- ½ cup chopped ripe olives
- 3 large eggs, lightly beaten
- 1 cup half-and-half cream
- ¼ cup butter, melted
- 3 drops hot pepper sauce
- ½ cup biscuit/baking mix
- 2 Tbsp. grated Parmesan cheese
- ½ tsp. ground mustard

1. In a bowl, combine ham, cheddar cheese and olives; divide among 12 greased muffin cups. In another bowl, combine remaining ingredients just until blended.

2. Pour over ham mixture. Bake at 375° until a knife inserted in the center comes out clean, 20-25 minutes. Let stand for 5 minutes before serving.

1 quiche: 141 cal., 11g fat (6g sat. fat), 84mg chol., 332mg sod., 5g carb. (1g sugars, 0 fiber), 6g pro.

HASH BROWN
EGG BAKE

YOGURT BERRY PARFAITS

Homemade granola layered with fresh fruit and yogurt makes a superb breakfast. Sometimes I skip the parfait step to enjoy the granola on hikes or picnics.
—Donna Speirs, Kennebunk, ME

Prep: 30 min. • **Bake:** 35 min. + cooling
Makes: 8 servings

- 2 cups old-fashioned oats
- ½ cup pecan halves
- ½ cup sliced almonds
- ¼ cup sunflower kernels
- ½ cup packed brown sugar
- ½ tsp. salt
- ¼ cup butter, cubed
- ¼ cup honey
- ½ tsp. ground cinnamon
- 1 tsp. vanilla extract
- ½ cup dried cherries
- ½ cup dried blueberries

PARFAITS
- 2 cups fresh blueberries
- 2 cups fresh raspberries
- 2 cups chopped fresh strawberries
- 4 cups honey Greek yogurt

1. Preheat oven to 350°. In a large bowl, combine first 6 ingredients. In a small saucepan, mix the butter, honey and cinnamon. Cook over medium heat until blended, 3-4 minutes. Remove from heat; stir in vanilla. Pour over the oat mixture; stir to coat.

2. Spread mixture evenly into a greased 15x10x1-in. baking pan. Bake until crisp and dark golden brown, 35-40 minutes, stirring every 10 minutes. Cool completely on a wire rack. Stir in dried fruit.

3. In a small bowl, combine the berries. Layer ¼ cup each berries, yogurt and granola in 8 parfait glasses. Repeat layers. Top with remaining berries.

1 parfait: 590 cal., 27g fat (11g sat. fat), 42mg chol., 294mg sod., 81g carb. (55g sugars, 9g fiber), 10g pro.

YOGURT BERRY
PARFAITS

PROSCIUTTO
EGG PANINI

PROSCIUTTO EGG PANINI

Change up the usual bacon and egg sandwich by piling on prosciutto instead. It's a breakfast worth waking up for!
—Erin Mylroie, Santa Clara, UT

Takes: 30 min. • Makes: 8 servings

- 3   large eggs
- 2   large egg whites
- 6   Tbsp. fat-free milk
- 1   green onion, thinly sliced
- 1   Tbsp. Dijon mustard
- 1   Tbsp. maple syrup
- 8   slices sourdough bread
- 8   thin slices prosciutto or deli ham
- ½   cup shredded
     sharp cheddar cheese
- 8   tsp. butter

1. In a small bowl, whisk the eggs, egg whites, milk and onion. Coat a large skillet with cooking spray and place over medium heat. Add egg mixture; cook and stir over medium heat until completely set.
2. Combine mustard and syrup; spread over 4 bread slices. Layer with scrambled eggs, prosciutto and cheese; top with the remaining bread. Butter the outsides of the sandwiches.
3. Cook on a panini maker or indoor grill for 3-4 minutes or until bread is browned and cheese is melted. Cut each panini in half to serve.

½ sandwich: 228 cal., 10g fat (5g sat. fat), 111mg chol., 640mg sod., 21g carb. (3g sugars, 1g fiber), 13g pro. **Diabetic exchanges:** 1½ starch, 1½ fat, 1 lean meat.

TEST KITCHEN TIP
To separate eggs without an egg separator, set a slotted spoon over a bowl and crack the eggs into the spoon. The whites will slide right through, leaving the yolks in the spoon.

FLUFFY PANCAKES

FLUFFY PANCAKES

I found this fluffy pancake recipe among our old family favorites and adapted it to make a small amount. It's quick and easy to prepare, but we still consider it a special treat.
—Eugene Presley, Council, VA

Takes: 15 min. • Makes: 8 pancakes

- 1   cup all-purpose flour
- 1   Tbsp. sugar
- 2   tsp. baking powder
- ½   tsp. salt
- 1   large egg, room temperature
- ¾   cup 2% milk
- ¼   cup shortening or butter, melted

1. In a small bowl, combine flour, sugar, baking powder and salt. Combine egg, milk and shortening; stir into dry ingredients just until moistened.
2. Pour batter by ¼ cupfuls onto a greased hot griddle. Turn when bubbles form on top of pancakes; cook until the second side is golden brown.

2 pancakes: 274 cal., 15g fat (9g sat. fat), 82mg chol., 664mg sod., 29g carb. (5g sugars, 1g fiber), 6g pro.

TRUE BELGIAN WAFFLES

It was during a visit to my husband's relatives in Europe that I was given this recipe. These homemade waffles are fantastic with any kind of topping: blueberries, strawberries, raspberries, fried apples or powdered sugar.
—Rose Delemeester, St. Charles, MI

- -

Takes: 30 min.
Makes: 10 waffles (about 4½ in.)

- 2 cups all-purpose flour
- ¾ cup sugar
- 3½ tsp. baking powder
- 2 large eggs, separated, room temperature
- 1½ cups whole milk
- 1 cup butter, melted
- 1 tsp. vanilla extract
  Sliced fresh strawberries or syrup

1. In a bowl, combine flour, sugar and baking powder. In another bowl, lightly beat egg yolks. Add the milk, butter and vanilla; mix well. Stir into dry ingredients just until combined. Beat egg whites until stiff peaks form; fold into batter.
2. Bake in preheated waffle maker until golden, according to manufacturer's directions. Serve with berries or syrup.
2 waffles: 696 cal., 41g fat (25g sat. fat), 193mg chol., 712mg sod., 72g carb. (34g sugars, 1g fiber), 10g pro.

APPLE DUTCH BABY

APPLE DUTCH BABY

This dish has been a longtime family favorite for Christmas morning. It is light, airy, and filled with eggs and juicy apple. I like to serve it alongside bacon or sausage.
—Teeny McCloy, Red Deer, AB

- -

Prep: 15 min. • **Bake:** 30 min.
Makes: 8 servings

- ¼ cup butter, cubed
- 3 to 4 medium tart apples, peeled and sliced
- ¼ cup packed brown sugar
- 1 tsp. ground cinnamon
- 6 large eggs, separated, room temperature
- ⅔ cup all-purpose flour
- ⅓ cup 2% milk
- 1 tsp. baking powder
- ½ tsp. salt
- ¼ cup sugar
  Confectioners' sugar, optional

1. Preheat oven to 400°. Place butter in a 13x9-in. baking dish. Heat until melted, 5-8 minutes. Stir in apples, brown sugar and cinnamon. Bake until apples are tender, 15-18 minutes.
2. Meanwhile, in a small bowl, whisk egg yolks, flour, milk, baking powder and salt until smooth. In a large bowl, beat egg whites on medium speed until soft peaks form. Gradually add sugar, 1 Tbsp. at a time, beating on high until stiff peaks form.
3. Fold egg whites into egg yolk mixture. Spread over apples. Bake until set and golden, 12-15 minutes. If desired, sprinkle with confectioners' sugar.
1 piece: 223 cal., 10g fat (5g sat. fat), 156mg chol., 313mg sod., 28g carb. (19g sugars, 1g fiber), 6g pro.

ITALIAN BRUNCH TORTE

We always pair this impressive layered breakfast bake with a salad of mixed greens and tomato wedges. Served warm or cold, it's one of our most requested dishes.
—Danny Diamond, Farmington Hills, MI

Prep: 50 min. • **Bake:** 1 hour + standing
Makes: 10 servings

- 2 tubes (8 oz. each) refrigerated crescent rolls, divided
- 1 tsp. olive oil
- 1 pkg. (6 oz.) fresh baby spinach
- 1 cup sliced fresh mushrooms
- 7 large eggs, divided use
- 1 cup grated Parmesan cheese
- 2 tsp. Italian seasoning
- ⅛ tsp. pepper
- ½ lb. thinly sliced deli ham
- ½ lb. thinly sliced hard salami
- ½ lb. sliced provolone cheese
- 2 jars (12 oz. each) roasted sweet red peppers, drained, sliced and patted dry

1. Preheat oven to 350°. Place a greased 9-in. springform pan on a double thickness of heavy-duty foil (about 18 in. square). Securely wrap foil around pan. Unroll 1 tube of crescent dough and separate into triangles. Press onto bottom of prepared pan to form a crust, sealing seams well. Bake until set, 10-15 minutes.

2. Meanwhile, in a large skillet, heat the oil over medium-high heat. Add the spinach and mushrooms; cook and stir until the mushrooms are tender. Drain on several layers of paper towels, blotting well. In a large bowl, whisk 6 eggs, Parmesan cheese, Italian seasoning and pepper.

3. Layer the crust with half each of the following: ham, salami, provolone cheese, red peppers and spinach mixture. Pour half the egg mixture over top. Repeat layers; top with remaining egg mixture.

4. On a work surface, unroll and separate remaining crescent dough into triangles. Press together to form a circle and seal seams; place over filling. Whisk remaining egg; brush over top.

5. Bake, uncovered, for 1-1¼ hours or until a thermometer reads 160°, covering loosely with foil if needed to prevent overbrowning. Carefully loosen sides from pan with a knife; remove rim from pan. Let stand 20 minutes.

1 piece: 480 cal., 29g fat (13g sat. fat), 191mg chol., 1674mg sod., 25g carb. (8g sugars, 0 fiber), 26g pro.

CHORIZO & GRITS BREAKFAST BOWLS

While growing up, I bonded with my dad over chorizo and eggs. My fresh approach combines them with grits and black beans. You can even add a spoonful of pico de gallo.
—Jenn Tidwell, Fair Oaks, CA

Takes: 30 min. • **Makes:** 6 servings

- 2 tsp. olive oil
- 1 pkg. (12 oz.) fully cooked chorizo chicken sausages or flavor of choice, sliced
- 1 large zucchini, chopped
- 3 cups water
- ¾ cup quick-cooking grits
- 1 can (15 oz.) black beans, rinsed and drained
- ½ cup shredded cheddar cheese
- 6 large eggs
  Optional: Pico de gallo and chopped fresh cilantro

1. In a large skillet, heat oil over medium heat. Add sausage; cook and stir until lightly browned, 2-3 minutes. Add zucchini; cook and stir until tender, 4-5 minutes longer. Remove from pan; keep warm.

2. Meanwhile, in a large saucepan, bring water to a boil. Slowly stir in grits. Reduce heat to medium-low; cook, covered, until thickened, stirring occasionally, about 5 minutes. Stir in beans and cheese until blended. Remove from heat.

3. Wipe skillet clean; coat with cooking spray and place over medium heat. In batches, break eggs, 1 at a time, into pan. Immediately reduce heat to low; cook until whites are completely set and yolks begin to thicken but are not hard, about 5 minutes.

4. To serve, divide grits mixture among 6 bowls. Top with chorizo mixture, eggs and, if desired, pico de gallo and cilantro.

1 serving: 344 cal., 14g fat (5g sat. fat), 239mg chol., 636mg sod., 30g carb. (4g sugars, 4g fiber), 24g pro. **Diabetic exchanges:** 3 medium-fat meat, 2 starch.

ITALIAN BRUNCH TORTE

**TROPICAL
SMOOTHIE BOWL**

TROPICAL SMOOTHIE BOWL

*This wake-me-up smoothie bowl with fruit,
oats and cinnamon helps me start the day
feeling satisfied. Sometimes I top it with
granola and berries or cherries.*
—Jonelle Dansie, Murray, UT

- -

Takes: 10 min. • **Makes:** 2 servings

2   Tbsp. frozen orange juice
    concentrate, thawed
¾   cup peeled fresh or frozen
    mango chunks, thawed
¾   cup (½ lb.) fresh or frozen
    pineapple cubes
¼   cup quick-cooking oats
¼   cup vanilla soy or
    whey protein powder
2   Tbsp. ground flaxseed
¼   tsp. ground cinnamon
¼   tsp. ground nutmeg
1   cup cold water
    Optional: Granola, chopped
    mango and pineapple

Place the orange juice concentrate in a
blender. Add fruit, oats, protein powder,
flax, seasonings and water. Cover and
process until smooth. If desired, garnish
with optional toppings. Serve immediately.
1¼ cups: 239 cal., 5g fat (1g sat. fat), 5mg
chol., 70mg sod., 43g carb. (28g sugars,
6g fiber), 10g pro.
Note: If desired, 1½ cups fresh or thawed
frozen pitted sweet cherries may be
substituted for the mango and pineapple.
Top with additional cherries and granola.

ASK SARAH

DO I HAVE TO USE
QUICK-COOKING OATS
IN THIS RECIPE?

Nope! Feel free to use whatever
kind of oats you have on hand
or whatever kind you enjoy.

SAUSAGE CHEESE PUFFS

People are always surprised when I tell them there are only four ingredients in these tasty bite-sized puffs. Cheesy and spicy, the golden morsels are a fun novelty at a breakfast or brunch, and they also make yummy party appetizers.
—Della Moore, Troy, NY

- -

Takes: 25 min. • **Makes:** about 4 dozen

1	lb. bulk Italian sausage
3	cups biscuit/baking mix
4	cups shredded cheddar cheese
¾	cup water

1. Preheat oven to 400°. In a large skillet, cook sausage over medium heat until no longer pink, 5-7 minutes, breaking sausage into crumbles; drain.
2. In a large bowl, combine the biscuit mix and cheese; stir in sausage. Add water and toss with a fork until moistened. Shape into 1½-in. balls. Place 2 in. apart on ungreased baking sheets.
3. Bake for 12-15 minutes or until puffed and golden brown. Cool on wire racks.
1 appetizer: 89 cal., 6g fat (3g sat. fat), 14mg chol., 197mg sod., 6g carb. (0 sugars, 0 fiber), 4g pro.

BLT WAFFLE SLIDERS

Craving a BLT for breakfast? Try a deliciously different version that features crisp bacon and fresh tomatoes between two golden cornmeal waffles. Prepare the waffles ahead of time and reheat in the toaster for quick assembly.
—Stacy Joura, Stoneboro, PA

- -

Takes: 30 min.
Makes: 12 servings

¾	cup all-purpose flour
¾	cup cornmeal
3	tsp. baking powder
1	Tbsp. sugar
1	tsp. salt
2	large eggs, separated, room temperature
1	cup 2% milk
3	Tbsp. butter, melted
½	cup shredded cheddar cheese
6	Tbsp. mayonnaise
12	bacon strips, cooked and drained
2	small tomatoes, sliced
6	lettuce leaves
	Salt and pepper to taste

1. Preheat waffle maker. Whisk together the first 5 ingredients. In another bowl, whisk the egg yolks, milk and butter. Stir into dry ingredients just until moistened. Stir in cheese.
2. In a separate bowl, beat egg whites until stiff but not dry. Fold into the batter. Drop 1 heaping Tbsp. of batter in the center of each waffle maker quadrant; bake according to manufacturer's directions until golden brown, about 5 minutes. Cool on wire rack. Repeat with remaining batter.
3. Spread mayonnaise evenly over half the waffle pieces; top with bacon, tomatoes, lettuce, seasonings and remaining waffle pieces to make sliders. Serve immediately.
1 slider: 224 cal., 14g fat (5g sat. fat), 54mg chol., 574mg sod., 17g carb. (3g sugars, 1g fiber), 7g pro.

For regular-size Cornmeal Waffle Sandwiches: Prepare batter as instructed. Bake 3 waffles according to manufacturer's directions until golden brown. Cut waffles into fourths. Spread the mayonnaise on 6 pieces; top with bacon, tomatoes, seasonings and remaining waffle pieces to make sandwiches. Serve immediately.

BLT WAFFLE SLIDERS

PRESSURE-COOKER HAWAIIAN
BREAKFAST HASH

MONTE CRISTO CASSEROLE WITH RASPBERRY SAUCE

My husband likes the ham and cheese sandwich known as the Monte Cristo, so I came up with a baked casserole.
—Mary Steiner, Parkville, MD

Prep: 20 min. + chilling
Bake: 30 min. + standing
Makes: 10 servings (1¾ cups sauce)

- 1 loaf (1 lb.) French bread, cut into 20 slices
- 2 Tbsp. Dijon mustard
- ½ lb. sliced deli ham
- ½ lb. sliced Swiss cheese
- ½ lb. sliced deli turkey
- 6 large eggs
- 1½ cups 2% milk
- 2 tsp. sugar
- 2 tsp. vanilla extract

TOPPING
- ½ cup packed brown sugar
- ¼ cup butter, softened
- ½ tsp. ground cinnamon

RASPBERRY SAUCE
- ⅓ cup sugar
- 1 Tbsp. cornstarch
- ¼ cup cold water
- ¼ cup lemon juice
- ¼ cup maple syrup
- 2 cups fresh or frozen raspberries

1. Line a greased 13x9-in. baking dish with half the bread. Spread the mustard over bread. Layer with ham, cheese, turkey and remaining bread (dish will be full).
2. In a large bowl, whisk eggs, milk, sugar and vanilla; pour over top. Refrigerate, covered, overnight.
3. Preheat oven to 375°. Remove casserole from refrigerator while oven heats. In a small bowl, mix the topping ingredients; sprinkle over casserole. Bake, uncovered, until golden brown, 30-40 minutes.
4. Meanwhile, in a saucepan, combine the sugar and cornstarch. Stir in the water, lemon juice and maple syrup until smooth. Add the raspberries. Bring to a boil; cook and stir until thickened, about 2 minutes. Cool slightly.
5. Let casserole stand 10 minutes before cutting. Serve with sauce.
1 piece with about 3 Tbsp. sauce: 476 cal., 17g fat (8g sat. fat), 167mg chol., 906mg sod., 55g carb. (29g sugars, 3g fiber), 25g pro.

PRESSURE-COOKER HAWAIIAN BREAKFAST HASH

Breakfast is our favorite meal, and we love a wide variety of dishes. This hash brown recipe is full of flavor and possibilities. Top with some eggs or spinach for another twist!
—Courtney Stultz, Weir, KS

Prep: 30 min. • **Cook:** 5 min.
Makes: 6 servings

- 4 bacon strips, chopped
- 1 Tbsp. canola or coconut oil
- 2 large sweet potatoes (about 1½ lbs.), peeled and cut into ½-in. pieces
- 2 cups cubed fresh pineapple (½-in. cubes)
- ½ tsp. salt
- ¼ tsp. chili powder
- ¼ tsp. paprika
- ¼ tsp. pepper
- ⅛ tsp. ground cinnamon

1. Select the saute or browning setting on a 6-qt. electric pressure cooker; adjust for medium heat. Add bacon; cook and stir until crisp. Remove with a slotted spoon; drain on paper towels. Discard drippings.
2. Add oil to pressure cooker. When oil is hot, brown potatoes in batches. Remove from pressure cooker. Add 1 cup water to pressure cooker. Cook 1 minute, stirring to loosen browned bits from pan. Press cancel. Place the steamer basket in the pressure cooker.
3. Stir the pineapple and seasonings into potatoes; transfer to a steamer basket. Lock lid; close pressure-release valve. Adjust to pressure-cook on high for 2 minutes. Quick-release the pressure. Sprinkle with bacon.
⅔ cup: 194 cal., 5g fat (1g sat. fat), 6mg chol., 309mg sod., 35g carb. (17g sugars, 4g fiber), 4g pro. **Diabetic exchanges:** 2 starch, 1 fat.

MONTE CRISTO CASSEROLE
WITH RASPBERRY SAUCE

OVERNIGHT FRUIT SALAD

I first tasted this rich fruit salad at my wedding reception almost 40 years ago. The ladies who did the cooking wouldn't share the recipe at the time, but I eventually got it from them. I've made it for many meals, and our daughters copied the recipe when they married.

—Eileen Duffeck, Lena, WI

- -

Prep: 30 min. + chilling
Makes: 16 servings

- 3 large eggs, beaten
- ¼ cup sugar
- ¼ cup white vinegar
- 2 Tbsp. butter
- 2 cups green grapes
- 2 cups miniature marshmallows
- 1 can (20 oz.) pineapple chunks, drained
- 1 can (15 oz.) mandarin oranges, drained
- 2 medium firm bananas, sliced
- 2 cups heavy whipping cream, whipped
- ½ cup chopped pecans

1. In a double boiler over medium heat, cook and stir eggs, sugar and vinegar until mixture is thickened and reaches 160°. Remove from heat; stir in butter. Cool.
2. In a large serving bowl, combine grapes, marshmallows, pineapple, oranges and bananas; add cooled dressing and stir to coat. Refrigerate for 4 hours or overnight. Just before serving, fold in whipped cream and pecans.
½ cup: 244 cal., 16g fat (8g sat. fat), 84mg chol., 44mg sod., 24g carb. (21g sugars, 1g fiber), 3g pro.

SHAKSHUKA BREAKFAST PIZZA

I turned traditional shakshuka into a fun brunch pizza. Its sweet, spicy and crunchy ingredients make it perfect for morning, noon or night.

—Phillipe Sobon, Harwood Heights, IL

- -

Prep: 35 min. • **Bake:** 15 min.
Makes: 6 servings

- 1 Tbsp. olive oil
- 1 large onion, thinly sliced
- 1 Tbsp. ground cinnamon
- 1 Tbsp. paprika
- 2 tsp. ground cumin
- 2 garlic cloves, minced
- ⅛ tsp. cayenne pepper
- 1 can (14½ oz.) whole plum tomatoes, undrained
- 1 tsp. hot pepper sauce
- ½ tsp. salt
- ¼ tsp. pepper
- 1 loaf (1 lb.) frozen pizza dough, thawed
- 6 large eggs
- ½ cup crumbled feta cheese

1. Preheat the oven to 400°. In a large saucepan, heat oil over medium-high heat. Add the onion; cook and stir until tender, 4-5 minutes. Add the cinnamon, paprika, cumin, garlic and cayenne; cook 1 minute longer. Stir in tomatoes, hot sauce, salt and pepper; cook and stir over medium heat until thickened, about 10 minutes.
2. Meanwhile, grease a 12-in. pizza pan. Roll the dough to fit pan. Pinch edge to form a rim. Bake until edge is lightly browned, 10-12 minutes.
3. Spread crust with tomato mixture. Using a spoon, make 6 indentations in tomato mixture; carefully break an egg into each. Sprinkle with feta. Bake until egg whites are completely set and yolks begin to thicken but are not hard, 12-15 minutes.
1 serving: 336 cal., 12g fat (3g sat. fat), 191mg chol., 654mg sod., 41g carb. (4g sugars, 5g fiber), 16g pro.

SHAKSHUKA BREAKFAST PIZZA

SAUSAGE & CRESCENT ROLL CASSEROLE

I made this tasty casserole for a baby shower. It saved me! Preparing it ahead gave me more time to finish decorating for the party.
—Melody Craft, Conroe, TX

Prep: 15 min. • **Bake:** 35 min.
Makes: 12 servings

- 1 lb. bulk pork sausage
- 1 tube (8 oz.) refrigerated crescent rolls
- 2 cups shredded part-skim mozzarella cheese
- 8 large eggs
- 2 cups 2% milk
- ½ tsp. salt
- ¼ tsp. pepper

1. Preheat oven to 375°. In a large skillet, cook the sausage over medium heat until no longer pink, 6-8 minutes, breaking it into crumbles; drain. Unroll crescent roll dough into a greased 13x9-in. baking dish. Seal seams and perforations. Sprinkle with sausage and cheese.
2. In a large bowl, whisk the eggs, milk, salt and pepper. Pour over the sausage and cheese.
3. Bake, uncovered, 35-40 minutes or until a knife inserted in center comes out clean. Let stand 5-10 minutes before serving.
To make ahead: Refrigerate unbaked casserole, covered, several hours or overnight. To use, preheat oven to 375°. Remove casserole from refrigerator while oven heats. Bake as directed, increasing time as necessary until a knife inserted in the center comes out clean. Let stand 5-10 minutes before serving.
1 piece: 283 cal., 19g fat (6g sat. fat), 160mg chol., 662mg sod., 12g carb. (4g sugars, 0 fiber), 15g pro.

SAUSAGE & CRESCENT ROLL CASSEROLE

TEST KITCHEN TIP
It's usually cheaper to buy cheese in blocks rather than already shredded. So purchase large quantities of cheddar, Monterey Jack and mozzarella, then use your food processor to shred it. Store the shredded cheese in the freezer so you have it when needed.

BISCUITS & SAUSAGE GRAVY

This is an old southern recipe that I've adapted. It's the kind of hearty breakfast that will warm you right up.
—Sue Baker, Jonesboro, AR

Takes: 15 min. • **Makes:** 2 servings

- ¼ lb. bulk pork sausage
- 2 Tbsp. butter
- 2 to 3 Tbsp. all-purpose flour
- ¼ tsp. salt
- ⅛ tsp. pepper
- 1¼ to 1⅓ cups whole milk
  Warm biscuits

In a small skillet, cook sausage over medium heat until no longer pink, 3-5 minutes, breaking it into crumbles; drain. Add butter, and heat until melted. Add the flour, salt and pepper; cook and stir until blended. Gradually add the milk, stirring constantly. Bring to a boil; cook and stir until thickened, about 2 minutes. Serve with biscuits.

¾ cup: 337 cal., 27g fat (14g sat. fat), 72mg chol., 718mg sod., 14g carb. (8g sugars, 0 fiber), 10g pro.

TEST KITCHEN TIP
Make a double or triple batch of the sausage gravy and refrigerate any extra. Reheat in a saucepan over low temperature, whisking vigorously once it comes to a boil.

OH-SO-GOOD OATMEAL

I add even more nutrition to fiber-rich oatmeal with chopped almonds and apples with the peel left on. My two boys demand seconds! What's not to love?
—Danielle Pepa, Elgin, IL

Takes: 20 min. • **Makes:** 4 servings

- 3 cups water
- 2 medium tart apples, chopped
- 1½ cups old-fashioned oats
  Dash salt
- ¼ cup packed brown sugar
- ½ tsp. ground cinnamon
- ½ tsp. vanilla extract
- ¼ cup chopped almonds
  Optional: Maple syrup and fat-free milk

1. In a large saucepan over medium heat, bring water to a boil. Add apples, oats and salt; cook and stir for 5 minutes.
2. Remove from the heat; stir in brown sugar, cinnamon and vanilla. Cover and let stand for 2 minutes. Sprinkle each serving with almonds. If desired, serve with syrup and milk.

1½ cups: 253 cal., 7g fat (1g sat. fat), 0 chol., 42mg sod., 46g carb. (22g sugars, 6g fiber), 6g pro.

BISCUITS & SAUSAGE GRAVY

CREAMY STRAWBERRY CREPES

Wrap summer-ripe strawberries and creamy filling into these delicate crepes for an elegant brunch entree.
—Kathy Kochiss, Huntington, CT

- -

Prep: 15 min. + chilling • **Cook:** 35 min.
Makes: 7 servings

- 4 **large eggs**
- 1 **cup 2% milk**
- 1 **cup water**
- 2 **Tbsp. butter, melted**
- 2 **cups all-purpose flour**
- ¼ **tsp. salt**

FILLING
- 1 **pkg. (8 oz.) cream cheese, softened**
- 1¼ **cups confectioners' sugar**
- 1 **Tbsp. lemon juice**
- 1 **tsp. grated lemon zest**
- ½ **tsp. vanilla extract**
- 4 **cups fresh strawberries, sliced, divided**
- 1 **cup heavy whipping cream, whipped**

1. In a large bowl, whisk eggs, milk, water and butter. In another bowl, mix flour and salt; add to the egg mixture and mix well. Refrigerate, covered, 1 hour.

2. Heat a lightly greased 8-in. nonstick skillet over medium heat. Stir batter. Fill a ¼-cup measure halfway with batter; pour into center of pan. Quickly lift and tilt pan to coat bottom evenly. Cook until top appears dry; turn crepe over and cook until bottom is cooked, 15-20 seconds longer. Remove to a wire rack. Repeat with remaining batter, greasing pan as needed. When cool, stack crepes between pieces of waxed paper or paper towels.

3. For filling, in a small bowl, beat cream cheese, confectioners' sugar, lemon juice and zest, and vanilla until smooth. Fold in 2 cups strawberries and the whipped cream. Spoon about ⅓ cup filling down center of each crepe; roll up. Garnish with remaining strawberries and, if desired, additional confectioner's sugar. Cover and refrigerate or freeze remaining crepes in an airtight container, unfilled, for another use.

2 crepes: 415 cal., 26g fat (16g sat. fat), 115mg chol., 163mg sod., 40g carb. (28g sugars, 2g fiber), 7g pro.

CREAMY
STRAWBERRY CREPES

EGGS BENEDICT CASSEROLE

EGGS BENEDICT CASSEROLE

Here's a casserole as tasty as eggs Benedict but without the hassle. Simply assemble the ingredients ahead, and bake the next morning for an elegant breakfast or brunch.
—Sandie Heindel, Liberty, MO

Prep: 25 min. + chilling • **Bake:** 45 min.
Makes: 12 servings (1⅔ cups sauce)

- 12 oz. Canadian bacon, chopped
- 6 English muffins, split and cut into 1-in. pieces
- 8 large eggs
- 2 cups 2% milk
- 1 tsp. onion powder
- ¼ tsp. paprika

HOLLANDAISE SAUCE
- 4 large egg yolks
- ½ cup heavy whipping cream
- 2 Tbsp. lemon juice
- 1 tsp. Dijon mustard
- ½ cup butter, melted
   Minced chives, optional

1. Place half the Canadian bacon in a greased 3-qt. or 13x9-in. baking dish; top with English muffins and remaining bacon. In a large bowl, whisk the eggs, milk and onion powder; pour over top. Refrigerate, covered, overnight.
2. Preheat oven to 375°. Remove casserole from the refrigerator while oven heats. Sprinkle top with paprika. Bake, covered, 35 minutes. Uncover; bake 10-15 minutes longer or until a knife inserted in center comes out clean.
3. In top of a double boiler or metal bowl over simmering water, whisk egg yolks, cream, lemon juice and mustard until blended; cook until the mixture is just thick enough to coat a metal spoon and temperature reaches 160°, whisking constantly. Reduce heat to very low. Very slowly drizzle in the warm melted butter, whisking constantly. Serve sauce immediately with casserole. If desired, sprinkle with chives.
1 piece: 286 cal., 19g fat (10g sat. fat), 256mg chol., 535mg sod., 16g carb. (4g sugars, 1g fiber), 14g pro.

BANANAS FOSTER
BAKED FRENCH TOAST

BANANAS FOSTER BAKED FRENCH TOAST

This yummy baked French toast serves up all the taste of the spectacular dessert in fine fashion.
—Laurence Nasson, Hingham, MA

Prep: 20 min. + chilling • **Bake:** 35 min.
Makes: 6 servings

- ½ cup butter, cubed
- ⅔ cup packed brown sugar
- ½ cup heavy whipping cream
- ½ tsp. ground cinnamon
- ½ tsp. ground allspice
- ¼ cup chopped pecans, optional
- 3 large bananas, sliced
- 12 slices egg bread or challah (about ¾ lb.)
- 1½ cups 2% milk
- 3 large eggs
- 1 Tbsp. sugar
- 1 tsp. vanilla extract

1. Place the butter in a microwave-safe bowl; microwave, covered, until melted, 30-45 seconds. Stir in brown sugar, cream, cinnamon, allspice and, if desired, pecans. Add bananas; toss gently to coat.
2. Transfer to a greased 13x9-in. baking dish. Arrange bread over top, trimming to fit as necessary.
3. Place the remaining ingredients in a blender; process just until blended. Pour over bread. Refrigerate, covered, 8 hours or overnight.
4. Preheat oven to 375°. Remove the French toast from refrigerator while oven heats. Bake, uncovered, until a knife inserted in center comes out clean, 35-40 minutes. Let stand 5-10 minutes. Invert to serve.
1 piece: 658 cal., 31g fat (17g sat. fat), 218mg chol., 584mg sod., 84g carb. (39g sugars, 4g fiber), 14g pro.

POWER BERRY SMOOTHIE BOWL

While you can't taste the spinach in these smoothies, you get all its nutrients with big berry flavor.
—Christine Hair, Odessa, FL

Takes: 10 min. • **Makes:** 3 servings

- ½ cup orange juice
- ½ cup pomegranate juice
- 1 container (6 oz.) mixed berry yogurt
- 1 cup frozen unsweetened strawberries
- 1 cup fresh baby spinach
- ½ medium ripe frozen banana, sliced
- ½ cup frozen unsweetened blueberries
- 2 Tbsp. ground flaxseed
  Optional: Sliced fresh strawberries, fresh blueberries, flaxseed and granola

In a blender, combine first 8 ingredients; cover and process for 30 seconds or until smooth. Pour into chilled bowls; top as desired. Serve immediately.
1 cup: 172 cal., 3g fat (0 sat. fat), 3mg chol., 47mg sod., 35g carb. (28g sugars, 4g fiber), 5g pro.

SPICY BREAKFAST LASAGNA

SPICY BREAKFAST LASAGNA

It's fun to cook up something new for family and friends—especially when it gets rave reviews. When I took this dish to our breakfast club at work, people said it really woke up their taste buds!
—Guthrie Torp Jr., Highland Ranch, CO

Prep: 20 min. + chilling • **Bake:** 35 min.
Makes: 16 servings

- 3 cups 4% cottage cheese
- ½ cup minced chives
- ¼ cup sliced green onions
- 18 large eggs
- ⅓ cup 2% milk
- ½ tsp. salt
- ¼ tsp. pepper
- 1 Tbsp. butter
- 8 lasagna noodles, cooked and drained
- 4 cups frozen shredded hash browns, thawed
- 1 lb. bulk pork sausage, cooked and crumbled
- 8 oz. sliced Monterey Jack cheese with jalapeno peppers
- 8 oz. sliced Muenster cheese

1. In a bowl, combine the cottage cheese, chives and onions. In another bowl, whisk eggs, milk, salt and pepper until blended. In a large skillet, heat butter over medium heat. Pour in egg mixture; cook and stir until eggs are thickened and no liquid egg remains. Remove from heat.
2. Place 4 lasagna noodles in a greased 13x9-in. baking dish. Layer with 2 cups hash browns, scrambled eggs, sausage and half the cottage cheese mixture. Cover with Monterey Jack cheese. Top with the remaining 4 lasagna noodles, hash browns and cottage cheese mixture. Cover with Muenster cheese. Refrigerate, covered, 8 hours or overnight.
3. Remove the dish from the refrigerator 30 minutes before baking. Preheat oven to 350°. Bake, uncovered, until a knife inserted in the center comes out clean, 35-40 minutes. Let stand for 5 minutes before cutting.
1 piece: 366 cal., 23g fat (11g sat. fat), 256mg chol., 640mg sod., 16g carb. (3g sugars, 1g fiber), 23g pro.

"This egg bake has it all—pasta, potatoes, sausage and lots of cheese! The recipe is perfect for morning entertaining because it's assembled the night before."
—JULIE SCHNITTKA, SENIOR EDITOR

RAINBOW QUICHE

With plenty of veggies and a creamy egg-cheese filling, this tasty quiche gets rave reviews every time I make it!
—Lilith Fury, Adena, OH

- -

Prep: 30 min. • **Bake:** 40 min. + standing
Makes: 8 servings

- 1 sheet refrigerated pie crust
- 2 Tbsp. butter
- 1 small onion, finely chopped
- 1 cup sliced fresh mushrooms
- 1 cup small fresh broccoli florets
- ½ cup finely chopped sweet orange pepper
- ½ cup finely chopped sweet red pepper
- 3 large eggs, lightly beaten
- 1⅓ cups half-and-half cream
- ¾ tsp. salt
- ½ tsp. pepper
- 1 cup shredded Mexican cheese blend, divided
- 1 cup fresh baby spinach

1. Preheat oven to 425°. Unroll pie crust onto a lightly floured surface, roll to a 12-in. circle. Transfer to a 9-in. deep-dish pie plate; trim and flute edge. Refrigerate while preparing filling.

2. In a large skillet, heat the butter over medium-high heat; saute the onion, mushrooms, broccoli and peppers until the mushrooms are lightly browned, 6-8 minutes. Cool slightly.

3. Whisk together eggs, cream, salt and pepper. Sprinkle ½ cup cheese over crust; top with spinach and vegetable mixture. Sprinkle with remaining cheese. Pour in egg mixture.

4. Bake quiche on a lower oven rack for 15 minutes. Reduce oven setting to 350°; bake until a knife inserted in the center comes out clean, 25-30 minutes. (Cover the edge loosely with foil if necessary to prevent overbrowning.) Let stand for 10 minutes before cutting.

1 piece: 295 cal., 20g fat (10g sat. fat), 115mg chol., 482mg sod., 18g carb. (4g sugars, 1g fiber), 9g pro.

Italian Sausage Quiche: Omit broccoli and butter. Substitute Italian cheese blend for the Mexican cheese blend. In a large skillet, saute 1 lb. bulk Italian sausage, onion, mushrooms and peppers until tender; drain. Add ½ tsp. dried basil, ½ tsp. dried parsley and ⅛ tsp. crushed red pepper to the egg mixture.

DID YOU KNOW?

Baby spinach leaves are simply spinach leaves that have been harvested before they are fully mature. They are more tender and sweet than regular spinach.

RAINBOW QUICHE

BROCCOLI-MUSHROOM BUBBLE BAKE

BROCCOLI-MUSHROOM BUBBLE BAKE

I got bored with the same old breakfast casseroles served at our monthly moms' meeting, so I decided to create something new. Judging by the reactions of the other moms, this one's a keeper.
—Shannon Koene, Blacksburg, VA

- -

Prep: 20 min. • **Bake:** 25 min.
Makes: 12 servings

 1 tsp. canola oil
 ½ lb. fresh mushrooms,
     finely chopped
 1 medium onion, finely chopped
 1 tube (16.3 oz.) large
     refrigerated flaky biscuits
 1 pkg. (10 oz.) frozen broccoli
     with cheese sauce
 3 large eggs
 1 can (5 oz.) evaporated milk
 1 tsp. Italian seasoning
 ½ tsp. garlic powder
 ½ tsp. salt
 ¼ tsp. pepper
 1½ cups shredded Colby-
     Monterey Jack cheese

1. Preheat oven to 350°. In a large skillet, heat oil over medium-high heat. Add the mushrooms and onion; cook and stir until tender, 4-6 minutes.
2. Cut each biscuit into 8 pieces; place in a greased 13x9-in. baking dish. Top with mushroom mixture.
3. Cook the broccoli with cheese sauce according to package directions. Spoon over mushroom mixture.
4. In a large bowl, whisk the eggs, milk and seasonings; pour over top. Sprinkle with cheese. Bake until golden brown, 25-30 minutes.
1 serving: 233 cal., 13g fat (6g sat. fat), 64mg chol., 648mg sod., 21g carb. (6g sugars, 1g fiber), 9g pro.

BERRY PUFF PANCAKE

Breakfast is my husband's favorite meal of the day. I use our homegrown blueberries in this sweet morning treat.
—Cecilia Morgan, Milwaukie, OR

- -

Takes: 25 min. • **Makes:** 6 servings

  1 **Tbsp. butter**
  3 **large eggs, room temperature**
  ¾ **cup 2% milk**
  ¾ **cup all-purpose flour**
  ½ **tsp. salt**
BERRY TOPPING
  1 **cup fresh raspberries**
  1 **cup fresh blueberries**
  1 **cup sliced fresh strawberries**
  ⅓ **cup orange marmalade**
  2 **Tbsp. confectioners' sugar**
      Whipped cream, optional

1. Place the butter in a 9-in. pie plate; place in a 400° oven 4-5 minutes or until melted. Tilt pie plate to evenly coat bottom and sides with butter.
2. In a small bowl, whisk eggs and milk. In another small bowl, combine flour and salt; whisk in the egg mixture until smooth. Pour batter into prepared pie plate. Bake until sides are crisp and golden brown, 15-20 minutes.
3. Meanwhile, in a large bowl, gently combine the berries and marmalade. Sprinkle pancake with confectioners' sugar; fill with berry mixture. Serve immediately. If desired, serve with whipped cream.
1 piece: 215 cal., 6g fat (3g sat. fat), 116mg chol., 273mg sod., 36g carb. (21g sugars, 3g fiber), 6g pro.

PINEAPPLE SMOOTHIES

I got this recipe more than 30 years ago. I've tried several diabetic recipes, and this is one of the best.
—Margery Bryan, Moses Lake, WA

- -

Prep: 5 min. + freezing
Makes: 5 servings

  1 **can (20 oz.) unsweetened pineapple chunks, undrained**
  1 **cup buttermilk**
  2 **tsp. vanilla extract**
  2 **tsp. sugar or sugar substitute**

Drain pineapple, reserving ½ cup juice. Freeze pineapple chunks. Place juice, buttermilk, vanilla, sugar and frozen pineapple in a blender; cover and process until smooth. Serve immediately.
¾ cup: 96 cal., 0 fat (0 sat. fat), 2mg chol., 93mg sod., 19g carb. (18g sugars, 1g fiber), 3g pro. **Diabetic exchanges:** 1 starch.

TEST KITCHEN TIP
No buttermilk? Use 1 Tbsp. lemon juice or distilled white vinegar plus enough milk to measure 1 cup. Stir and then let stand for 5 minutes.

BERRY PUFF
PANCAKE

FOUR-FRUIT COMPOTE

A beautiful side dish, this compote spotlights bananas, apples, oranges and pineapple. I like that it can be made at any time of the year. I'm sure you'll get as many smiles as I do when I bring out this refreshing salad.
—Donna Long, Searcy, AR

- -

Prep: 15 min. + chilling
Makes: 16 servings

- 1 can (20 oz.) pineapple chunks
- ½ cup sugar
- 2 Tbsp. cornstarch
- ⅓ cup orange juice
- 1 Tbsp. lemon juice
- 1 can (11 oz.) mandarin oranges, drained
- 3 to 4 medium apples, chopped
- 2 to 3 medium bananas, sliced

1. Drain pineapple, reserving ¾ cup juice. In a large saucepan, combine sugar and cornstarch. Whisk in the orange, lemon and pineapple juices until smooth. Cook and stir over medium heat until thickened and bubbly; cook and stir 1 minute longer. Remove from the heat; set aside.
2. In a large bowl, combine fruits. Pour warm sauce over the fruit; stir gently to coat. Cover and refrigerate.
1 cup: 93 cal., 0 fat (0 sat. fat), 0 chol., 4mg sod., 24g carb. (20g sugars, 1g fiber), 0 pro.

LEMON BREAKFAST PARFAITS

I serve these refreshing parfaits as a lively start to a day. You can make the couscous mixture ahead, then cover and chill it overnight.
—Janelle Lee, Appleton, WI

- -

Prep: 25 min. + cooling
Makes: 6 servings

- ¾ cup fat-free milk
  Dash salt
- ⅓ cup uncooked couscous
- ½ cup reduced-fat sour cream
- ½ cup lemon yogurt
- 1 Tbsp. honey
- ¼ tsp. grated lemon zest
- 1 cup sliced peeled kiwifruit
- 1 cup fresh blueberries
- 1 cup fresh raspberries
  Chopped crystallized ginger and minced fresh mint

1. In a saucepan, bring milk and salt to a boil. Stir in couscous. Remove from heat; cover and let stand 5-10 minutes or until milk is absorbed. Fluff with a fork; cool.
2. In a small bowl, combine sour cream, yogurt, honey and lemon zest. Stir in the couscous.
3. Combine the kiwi, blueberries and raspberries; spoon ¼ cup into each of 6 parfait glasses. Layer with couscous mixture and remaining fruit. Garnish with ginger and mint.
1 parfait: 146 cal., 2g fat (1g sat. fat), 8mg chol., 64mg sod., 27g carb. (16g sugars, 3g fiber), 5g pro. **Diabetic exchanges:** 1 starch, ½ fruit.

CHEESY VEGETABLE EGG DISH

I'm a cook at a Bible camp, and this is one of my most popular recipes with the youngsters. What touched me the most was when a 10-year-old boy asked me for the recipe so he could have his mother make it at home.
—Elsie Campbell, Dulzura, CA

- -

Prep: 20 min. • **Bake:** 35 min.
Makes: 10 servings

- 1 medium zucchini, diced
- 1 medium onion, chopped
- 1 can (4 oz.) mushroom stems and pieces, drained
- ¼ cup chopped green pepper
- ½ cup butter, cubed
- ½ cup all-purpose flour
- 1 tsp. baking powder
- ½ tsp. salt
- 10 large eggs, lightly beaten
- 2 cups 4% cottage cheese
- 4 cups shredded Monterey Jack cheese

1. In a large skillet, saute the zucchini, onion, mushrooms and green pepper in butter until tender. Stir in the flour, baking powder and salt until blended.
2. In a large bowl, combine the eggs and cottage cheese. Stir in vegetables and Monterey Jack cheese.
3. Transfer to a greased 2½-qt. baking dish. Bake, uncovered, at 350° for 35-45 minutes or until a thermometer reads 160°.
1 piece: 407 cal., 30g fat (17g sat. fat), 287mg chol., 759mg sod., 10g carb. (4g sugars, 1g fiber), 24g pro.

PEANUT BUTTER & JELLY FRENCH TOAST

I've always tried to make cooking fun—for myself, my daughters and my grandchildren. Cooking teaches children the importance of following directions and being organized. This recipe is easy to make, and kids really like it.
—Flo Burtnett, Gage, OK

- -

Takes: 20 min. • **Makes:** 6 servings

- ¾ cup peanut butter
- 12 slices bread
- 6 Tbsp. jelly or jam
- 3 large eggs
- ¾ cup 2% milk
- ¼ tsp. salt
- 2 Tbsp. butter

1. Spread the peanut butter on 6 slices of bread; spread jelly on remaining 6 slices of bread. Put 1 slice of each together to form sandwiches. In a large bowl, whisk eggs, milk and salt. Dip both sides of sandwiches in egg mixture.
2. In a skillet, melt butter over medium heat. Cook sandwiches for 2-3 minutes on each side or until golden brown.
1 piece: 450 cal., 22g fat (5g sat. fat), 96mg chol., 567mg sod., 50g carb. (20g sugars, 3g fiber), 16g pro.

SAUTEED APPLES

Here's a sweet side dish my family loves. You can use it to top pancakes or French toast, but it's wonderful with pork or chicken too.
—Shirley Heston, Pickerington, OH

- -

Takes: 30 min. • **Makes:** 6 servings

- ¼ cup butter, cubed
- 5 medium Golden Delicious apples, peeled and thinly sliced
- ¼ cup water
- ½ cup sugar
- ½ tsp. ground cinnamon

In a large cast-iron or other heavy skillet, heat butter over medium-high heat; saute apples 1 minute. Add water; bring to a boil. Stir in sugar and cinnamon. Reduce heat; simmer, covered, until apples are tender, 10-12 minutes, stirring occasionally.
⅔ cup: 185 cal., 8g fat (5g sat. fat), 20mg chol., 61mg sod., 31g carb. (28g sugars, 2g fiber), 0 pro.

LEAN GREEN SMOOTHIE

Kids love the unusual color of this frosty and flavorful smoothie. It's fine-tuned to their liking with bananas, creamy yogurt and spinach.
—Madison Mayberry, Ames, IA

- -

Takes: 10 min. • **Makes:** 4 servings

- ¾ cup fat-free milk
- 1½ cups fat-free vanilla yogurt
- 1 cup ice cubes
- 1 cup fresh spinach
- 1 ripe medium banana
- 2 Tbsp. lemon juice

In a blender, combine all ingredients; cover and process for 30 seconds or until smooth. Pour into chilled glasses; serve immediately.
1 cup: 99 cal., 0 fat (0 sat. fat), 4mg chol., 24mg sod., 19g carb. (12g sugars, 1g fiber), 5g pro. **Diabetic exchanges:** 1 fat-free milk, ½ fruit.

"My friend introduced me to green smoothies with this recipe, and now I'm hooked! Instead of lemon juice, I toss in a handful of frozen cranberries."
—CHRISTINE RUKAVENA, SENIOR EDITOR

MANGO BREAD
PAGE 57

FAVORITE

Breads, Rolls & More

The aroma of bread baking in the oven is one of life's greatest pleasures. Turn the page and take a peek at what our Test Kitchen staff whips up in their own homes!

GREEN CHILE CORN FRITTERS

I usually have all the ingredients on hand for these fritters. They are a crispy side dish, appetizer or snack to add to a Mexican meal—but go equally well with chili or soup.
—Johnna Johnson, Scottsdale, AZ

Prep: 20 min. • **Cook:** 5 min./batch
Makes: 2 dozen

- 1 cup yellow cornmeal
- ½ cup all-purpose flour
- 1½ tsp. baking powder
- ¾ tsp. salt
- ½ tsp. garlic powder
- ½ tsp. onion powder
- ½ tsp. paprika
- ½ tsp. pepper
- 1 large egg, room temperature
- ⅔ cup whole milk
- 1 can (8¾ oz.) whole kernel corn, drained
- 1 can (4 oz.) chopped green chiles, drained
  Oil for deep-fat frying
  Optional: Sriracha mayonnaise or condiment of your choice

1. In a large bowl, whisk first 8 ingredients. In another bowl, whisk egg and milk until blended. Add to dry ingredients, stirring just until moistened. Let stand 5 minutes. Fold in corn and green chiles.
2. In a deep cast-iron or electric skillet, heat the oil to 375°. Drop the batter by tablespoonfuls, a few at a time, into hot oil. Fry until golden brown, 1-1½ minutes on each side. Drain on paper towels. Serve with desired condiments.
1 fritter: 74 cal., 4g fat (0 sat. fat), 8mg chol., 159mg sod., 9g carb. (1g sugars, 1g fiber), 1g pro.

MOIST PINEAPPLE BANANA BREAD

Our four kids like slices of this moist and tropical-tasting banana bread for breakfast. I sometimes bake it in mini loaf pans, then freeze the loaves so we can enjoy a small portion at a time.
—Mary Watkins, Chaska, MN

Prep: 15 min. • **Bake:** 1 hour + cooling
Makes: 2 loaves (16 pieces each)

- 3 cups all-purpose flour
- 2 cups sugar
- 1 tsp. salt
- 1 tsp. baking soda
- 1 tsp. ground cinnamon
- 3 large eggs, room temperature
- 1¼ cups canola oil
- 2 tsp. vanilla extract
- 1 can (8 oz.) crushed pineapple, drained
- 2 cups mashed ripe bananas (4 to 5 medium)

1. Preheat oven to 350°. In a large bowl, combine flour, sugar, salt, baking soda and cinnamon. In another bowl, whisk eggs, oil and vanilla; add pineapple and bananas. Stir into the dry ingredients just until moistened. Pour into 2 greased 9x5-in. loaf pans.
2. Bake until a toothpick comes out clean, 60-65 minutes. Cool 10 minutes before removing from pans to wire racks.
1 piece: 191 cal., 9g fat (1g sat. fat), 20mg chol., 120mg sod., 26g carb. (16g sugars, 1g fiber), 2g pro.

"These loaves turn out delicious and moist every time. We line our pans with parchment to make it easier to lift out the loaves."
—RAEANN THOMPSON, ASSOCIATE CREATIVE DIRECTOR

GREEN CHILE CORN FRITTERS

ANGEL BISCUITS

These light, airy biscuits are always a treat, especially when you serve them with butter and honey.
—Faye Hintz, Springfield, MO

- -

Prep: 20 min. + rising • **Bake:** 10 min.
Makes: 2½ dozen

2	pkg. (¼ oz. each) active dry yeast
¼	cup warm water (110° to 115°)
2	cups warm buttermilk (110° to 115°)
5	to 5½ cups all-purpose flour
⅓	cup sugar
2	tsp. salt
2	tsp. baking powder
1	tsp. baking soda
1	cup shortening
	Melted butter

1. In a small bowl, dissolve yeast in warm water. Let stand 5 minutes. Stir in warm buttermilk; set aside.

2. In a large bowl, combine the flour, sugar, salt, baking powder and baking soda. Cut in shortening with a pastry blender until mixture resembles coarse crumbs. Stir in yeast mixture.

3. Turn onto a lightly floured surface; knead lightly 3-4 times. Roll out to ½-in. thickness; cut with a 2½-in. biscuit cutter. Place 2 in. apart on lightly greased baking sheets. Cover with kitchen towels and let rise in a warm place until almost doubled, about 1 hour.

4. Bake at 450° for 8-10 minutes or until golden brown. Lightly brush tops with melted butter. Serve warm.

1 biscuit: 150 cal., 7g fat (2g sat. fat), 1mg chol., 244mg sod., 19g carb. (3g sugars, 1g fiber), 3g pro.

ANGEL
BISCUITS

MANGO BREAD

MANGO BREAD

When it's mango season in Maui, everyone shares their crop, so you get to try different varieties. I like the Hayden because it's big, but other mangoes or diced mangoes from the refrigerated or frozen sections work too.
—Lillian Takaki, Wailuku, HI

- -

Prep: 20 min.
Bake: 1 hour 15 min. + cooling
Makes: 24 servings

- 4 cups all-purpose flour
- 2½ cups sugar
- 4 tsp. ground cinnamon
- 3 tsp. baking soda
- 1 tsp. salt
- 6 large eggs, room temperature
- 1½ cups canola oil
- 2 tsp. vanilla extract
- 4 cups chopped peeled mango
- 1 cup chopped walnuts, optional
- 1 cup raisins, optional

1. Preheat oven to 325°. In a large bowl, whisk the flour, sugar, cinnamon, baking soda and salt. In another bowl, whisk the eggs, oil and vanilla until blended. Add to flour mixture; stir just until moistened. Fold in mangoes and, if desired, walnuts and raisins.

2. Transfer to a greased 13x9-in. baking dish lined with parchment. Bake until a toothpick comes out clean, 1¼-1½ hours Cool completely in dish on a wire rack.

1 piece: 317 cal., 16g fat (1g sat. fat), 47mg chol., 274mg sod., 42g carb. (25g sugars, 1g fiber), 4g pro.

DID YOU KNOW?
Using room temperature eggs will help the ingredients blend more uniformly.

MINI SWEET POTATO SCONES WITH ROSEMARY & BACON

MINI SWEET POTATO SCONES WITH ROSEMARY & BACON

I grow my own sweet potatoes, so I'm always trying to think of new ways to use them. I created this recipe on a whim and am thrilled with the results—everyone who tries these scones thinks they're delicious!
—Sue Gronholz, Beaver Dam, WI

- -

Prep: 30 min. • **Bake:** 15 min.
Makes: 16 scones

- 2½ cups all-purpose flour
- ½ cup sugar
- 2½ tsp. baking powder
- 1½ tsp. pumpkin pie spice or ground cinnamon
- 1½ tsp. minced fresh rosemary or ½ tsp. dried rosemary, crushed
- ½ tsp. salt
- ¼ tsp. baking soda
- ½ cup cold butter
- 4 bacon strips, cooked and crumbled
- ½ cup mashed sweet potatoes
- ¼ cup plain Greek yogurt
- 1 large egg, room temperature
- 2 Tbsp. maple syrup

TOPPING
- 1 Tbsp. 2% milk
- 1 Tbsp. sugar

1. Preheat oven to 425°. In a large bowl, whisk the first 7 ingredients. Cut in butter until mixture resembles coarse crumbs. Stir in bacon. In another bowl, whisk sweet potatoes, yogurt, egg and maple syrup until blended; stir into crumb mixture just until combined.

2. Turn onto a floured surface; knead gently 10 times. Divide dough in half. Pat each half into a 6-in. circle. Cut each into 8 wedges. Place wedges on a greased baking sheet. Brush with milk; sprinkle with sugar. Bake until golden brown, 12-14 minutes. Serve warm.

Freeze option: Freeze cooled scones in freezer containers. To use, thaw before serving or, if desired, reheat on a baking sheet in a preheated 350° oven until warmed, 3-4 minutes.

1 scone: 184 cal., 7g fat (4g sat. fat), 30mg chol., 261mg sod., 26g carb. (9g sugars, 1g fiber), 3g pro.

40-MINUTE HAMBURGER BUNS

Here on our ranch, I cook for three men who love burgers. These fluffy hamburger buns are just right for their big appetites. The buns are so good that I also serve them plain with a meal.
—Jessie McKenney, Twodot, MT

- -

Prep: 20 min. + resting • **Bake:** 10 min.
Makes: 1 dozen

- 2 Tbsp. active dry yeast
- 1 cup plus 2 Tbsp. warm water (110° to 115°)
- ⅓ cup vegetable oil
- ¼ cup sugar
- 1 large egg, room temperature
- 1 tsp. salt
- 3 to 3½ cups all-purpose flour

1. In a large bowl, dissolve yeast in warm water. Add the oil and sugar; let stand for 5 minutes. Add the egg, salt and enough flour to form a soft dough.
2. Turn onto a floured surface; knead until smooth and elastic, 3-5 minutes. Do not let rise. Divide into 12 pieces; shape each into a ball. Place 3 in. apart on greased baking sheets. Preheat oven to 425°.
3. Cover and let rest for 10 minutes. Bake until golden brown, 8-12 minutes. Remove from pans to wire racks to cool.
1 bun: 195 cal., 7g fat (1g sat. fat), 18mg chol., 204mg sod., 29g carb. (5g sugars, 1g fiber), 5g pro.

LEMON BLUEBERRY BREAD

LEMON BLUEBERRY BREAD

Of all the quick breads we had growing up, this beautifully glazed, berry-studded loaf is the best! The lemon glaze locks in moisture and adds a beautiful finish.
—Julianne Johnson, Grove City, MN

- -

Prep: 15 min.
Bake: 1 hour + cooling
Makes: 1 loaf (16 pieces)

- ⅓ cup butter, melted
- 1 cup sugar
- 3 Tbsp. lemon juice
- 2 large eggs, room temperature
- 1½ cups all-purpose flour
- 1 tsp. baking powder
- ½ tsp. salt
- ½ cup 2% milk
- 1 cup fresh or frozen blueberries
- ½ cup chopped nuts
- 2 Tbsp. grated lemon zest

GLAZE
- 2 Tbsp. lemon juice
- ¼ cup sugar

1. In a large bowl, beat the butter, sugar, lemon juice and eggs. Combine the flour, baking powder and salt; stir into the egg mixture alternately with milk, beating well after each addition. Fold in the blueberries, nuts and lemon zest.
2. Transfer to a greased 8x4-in. loaf pan. Bake at 350° for 60-70 minutes or until a toothpick inserted in the center comes out clean. Cool for 10 minutes before removing from pan to a wire rack.
3. Combine glaze ingredients; drizzle over warm bread. Cool completely.
1 piece: 181 cal., 7g fat (3g sat. fat), 38mg chol., 149mg sod., 27g carb. (17g sugars, 1g fiber), 3g pro.

> "When I need to make something for a bake sale, this is the recipe I reach for. I sometimes use raspberries for the blueberries— or a combination of the two."
> —JULIE SCHNITTKA, SENIOR EDITOR

TOFFEE APPLE CINNAMON BUNS

This recipe was my dad's favorite growing up. He would sit and watch his mom sprinkle the dough with sweet filling, carefully roll it up and cut it into rounds. The anticipation waiting for them to come out of the oven was almost more than he could bear.
—Jeanne Holt, St. Paul, MN

- -

Prep: 30 min.
Bake: 25 min.
Makes: 8 cinnamon buns

- 1   medium Granny Smith apple, peeled and chopped
- 1   Tbsp. thawed apple juice concentrate
- ⅔   cup plus 2 Tbsp. sugar, divided
- 1½ tsp. ground cinnamon
- 3¼ cups all-purpose flour
- 1¼ tsp. baking powder
- ½   tsp. baking soda
- ½   tsp. salt
- 1¼ cups buttermilk
- 6   Tbsp. butter, melted, divided
- ¼   cup brickle toffee bits

GLAZE
- 1½ cups confectioners' sugar
- 3   Tbsp. thawed apple juice concentrate
- 2   Tbsp. brickle toffee bits

1. Preheat oven to 400°. In a microwave-safe bowl, combine apple and apple juice concentrate; microwave, covered, on high for 1-2 minutes or until tender. Drain; cool slightly. In a small bowl, mix ⅔ cup sugar and cinnamon.

2. In a large bowl, whisk the flour, baking powder, baking soda, salt and remaining sugar. Stir in buttermilk and 2 Tbsp. melted butter just until moistened. Turn onto a lightly floured surface; knead until smooth, 2-4 minutes.

3. Roll the dough into a 12x9-in. rectangle. Brush with 2 Tbsp. melted butter to within ½ in. of edges; sprinkle with sugar mixture, apple and toffee bits. Roll up jelly-roll style, starting with a long side; pinch the seam to seal. Cut into 8 slices.

4. Place in a greased 9-in. square or round baking pan, cut side down. Brush with the remaining melted butter. Bake until golden brown, 22-28 minutes.

5. Cool for 5 minutes on a wire rack. In a small bowl, mix the confectioners' sugar and apple juice concentrate until smooth. Spread over buns; sprinkle with toffee bits. Serve warm.

1 bun: 525 cal., 13g fat (7g sat. fat), 28mg chol., 498mg sod., 96g carb. (56g sugars, 2g fiber), 7g pro.

TOFFEE APPLE CINNAMON BUNS

TEST KITCHEN TIP
Braeburn, Golden Delicious and Jonagold can be substituted for the Granny Smith apples.

BLT MUFFINS

BLT MUFFINS

These muffins prove the classic combo of bacon, lettuce and tomato is good for so much more than a sandwich. They're winners at both breakfast and dinner.
—Katie Koziolek, Hartland, MN

Prep: 15 min. • **Bake:** 20 min. + cooling
Makes: 1 dozen

- 2 cups all-purpose flour
- 1 Tbsp. baking powder
- 1 Tbsp. sugar
- 1 cup 2% milk
- ½ cup mayonnaise
- ¾ cup crumbled cooked bacon (about 12 strips)
- ½ cup chopped seeded plum tomatoes
- 2 Tbsp. minced fresh parsley
  Shredded lettuce, optional

1. In a large bowl, combine flour, baking powder and sugar. In a small bowl, whisk milk and mayonnaise until smooth. Stir mixture into the dry ingredients just until moistened. Fold in the bacon, tomatoes and parsley.
2. Fill 12 greased or paper-lined muffin cups two-thirds full. Bake at 400° for 20-25 minutes or until a toothpick inserted in the center of a muffin comes out clean. Cool 5 minutes before removing from pan to a wire rack to cool completely. If desired, sprinkle with lettuce.
1 muffin: 185 cal., 10g fat (2g sat. fat), 11mg chol., 385mg sod., 18g carb. (3g sugars, 1g fiber), 6g pro.

BEST BRAN MUFFINS

Having these muffins for breakfast provides a good start to a busy day. My husband loves pineapple, which makes these muffins moist and delicious!
—Suzanne Smith, Framingham, MA

- -

Takes: 30 min. • **Makes:** 18 muffins

- ½ cup old-fashioned oats
- 1 cup all-purpose flour
- 1 cup whole wheat flour
- ½ cup all-bran cereal
- ½ tsp. salt
- 1 tsp. baking powder
- 1 tsp. baking soda
- 1 large egg, beaten
- ¼ cup vegetable oil
- ½ cup molasses
- ¾ cup buttermilk
- 1 can (8 oz.) crushed pineapple in natural juice, undrained
- ½ cup chopped nuts, dates or raisins

1. In a bowl, combine first 7 ingredients. Make a well in the center. Combine the egg, oil, molasses, buttermilk and pineapple with juice. Pour into well; mix just until dry ingredients are moistened. Stir in the nuts, dates or raisins.
2. Fill 18 greased muffin cups two-thirds full. Bake at 400° for 12 minutes or until golden brown.
1 muffin: 151 cal., 6g fat (1g sat. fat), 11mg chol., 194mg sod., 22g carb. (9g sugars, 2g fiber), 4g pro. **Diabetic exchanges:** 1½ starch, 1 fat.

MILK-AND-HONEY WHITE BREAD

Honey adds special flavor to this traditional white bread. My dad's a wheat farmer, so this recipe represents our region and our family well.
—Kathy McCreary, Goddard, KS

- -

Prep: 15 min. + rising • **Bake:** 30 min.
Makes: 2 loaves (16 pieces each)

- 2 pkg. (¼ oz. each) active dry yeast
- 2½ cups warm whole milk (110° to 115°)
- ⅓ cup honey
- ¼ cup butter, melted
- 2 tsp. salt
- 7 to 8½ cups all-purpose flour

1. In a large bowl, dissolve yeast in warm milk. Add honey, butter, salt and 5 cups flour; beat until smooth. Add enough remaining flour, in ½-cup increments, to form a soft dough.
2. Turn onto a floured board; knead until smooth and elastic, 6-8 minutes. Place in a greased bowl, turning once to grease top. Cover and let rise in a warm place until doubled, about 1 hour.
3. Punch the dough down and shape into 2 loaves. Place in greased 9x5-in. loaf pans. Cover and let rise until doubled, about 30 minutes.
4. Bake at 375° 30-35 minutes or until golden brown. Cover loosely with foil if tops brown too quickly. Remove from pans and cool on wire racks.
1 piece: 149 cal., 2g fat (1g sat. fat), 6mg chol., 172mg sod., 28g carb. (4g sugars, 1g fiber), 4g pro.

TEST KITCHEN TIP
Coat the measuring cup with cooking spray before measuring honey, and it will slide right out!

MILK-AND-HONEY WHITE BREAD

HERBED ONION BAGELS

GARLIC KNOTS

Here's a handy bread that can be made in no time flat. Refrigerated biscuits make preparation simple. The classic Italian flavors complement a variety of meals.
—Jane Paschke, University Park, FL

Takes: 30 min. • **Makes:** 2½ dozen

- 1 tube (12 oz.) refrigerated buttermilk biscuits
- ¼ cup canola oil
- 3 Tbsp. grated Parmesan cheese
- 1 tsp. garlic powder
- 1 tsp. dried oregano
- 1 tsp. dried parsley flakes

1. Preheat oven to 400°. Cut each biscuit into thirds. Roll each piece into a 4-in. rope and tie into a knot; tuck ends under. Place 2 in. apart on a greased baking sheet. Bake until golden brown, 8-10 minutes.
2. In a large bowl, combine the remaining ingredients; add warm knots and gently toss to coat.
1 knot: 46 cal., 2g fat (0 sat. fat), 0 chol., 105mg sod., 6g carb. (0 sugars, 0 fiber), 1g pro.

ASK SARAH

HOW DO I PREVENT MY HANDS FROM STICKING TO THE DOUGH WHEN SHAPING BAGELS?
Before shaping the dough into balls, moisten your hands with a little water first.

HERBED ONION BAGELS

I created my bagels with elements from several recipes. I like toast them and then spread them with plain or onion and chive cream cheese.
—Pam Kaiser, Mansfield, MO

Prep: 30 min. + chilling
Bake: 15 min.
Makes: 9 bagels

- ½ cup finely chopped sweet onion
- 2 Tbsp. butter
- 1 pkg. (¼ oz.) active dry yeast
- ¾ cup warm water (110° to 115°)
- ¼ cup sour cream
- 3 Tbsp. sugar, divided
- 3½ tsp. salt, divided
- 1½ tsp. minced chives
- 1½ tsp. dried basil
- 1½ tsp. dried parsley flakes
- ¾ tsp. dried oregano
- ¾ tsp. dill weed
- ¾ tsp. dried minced garlic
- 3 cups bread flour
- 2 Tbsp. yellow cornmeal

1. In a large skillet, saute onion in butter until tender; set aside.

2. Dissolve yeast in warm water. In small bowl, combine sour cream and 2 Tbsp. sugar. In a large bowl, combine onion mixture, 1½ tsp. salt, herbs, garlic and flour. Add yeast mixture, sour cream mixture and enough water to form a soft dough. Turn onto a floured surface; knead for 8-10 minutes or until a smooth, firm dough forms. Shape into 9 balls. Push thumb through centers to form a 1½-in. hole. Place on parchment-lined baking sheets. Cover and let rest for 30 minutes in a warm place. Refrigerate overnight.
3. Let stand at room temperature for 30 minutes; flatten bagels slightly. In a non-aluminum Dutch oven, bring 3 qt. water to a boil with remaining sugar and salt. Drop the bagels, 1 at a time, into the water. Cook for 30 seconds; turn and cook 30 seconds longer. Remove with a slotted spoon; drain well on paper towels.
4. Sprinkle 2 greased baking sheets with cornmeal; place bagels 2 in. apart on prepared pans. Bake at 425° until golden brown, 12-15 minutes. Remove to wire racks to cool.
1 bagel: 195 cal., 4g fat (2g sat. fat), 11mg chol., 415mg sod., 35g carb. (3g sugars, 2g fiber), 6g pro

GARLIC KNOTS

CINNAMON SWIRL QUICK BREAD

While cinnamon bread is a natural for breakfast, we love it any time of the day. This one is a nice twist on traditional cinnamon swirl yeast breads.
—Helen Richardson, Shelbyville, MI

Prep: 15 min. • **Bake:** 45 min. + cooling
Makes: 16 pieces

- 2 cups all-purpose flour
- 1½ cups sugar, divided
- 1 tsp. baking soda
- ½ tsp. salt
- 1 cup buttermilk
- 1 large egg, room temperature
- ¼ cup canola oil
- 3 tsp. ground cinnamon

GLAZE
- ¼ cup confectioners' sugar
- 1½ to 2 tsp. 2% milk

1. Preheat oven to 350°. In a large bowl, combine flour, 1 cup sugar, baking soda and salt. Combine the buttermilk, egg and oil; stir into dry ingredients just until moistened. In a small bowl, combine cinnamon and remaining ½ cup sugar.

2. Grease the bottom only of a 9x5-in. loaf pan. Pour half the batter into pan; sprinkle with half the cinnamon sugar. Carefully spread with remaining batter and sprinkle with the remaining cinnamon sugar; cut through batter with a knife to swirl.

3. Bake 45-50 minutes or until a toothpick inserted in center comes out clean. Cool 10 minutes before removing from pan to a wire rack to cool completely. For the glaze, combine confectioners' sugar and enough milk to reach desired consistency; drizzle over the loaf.

1 piece: 179 cal., 4g fat (1g sat. fat), 14mg chol., 173mg sod., 34g carb. (21g sugars, 1g fiber), 3g pro.

FRUITY PULL-APART BREAD

Who doesn't love to start the day with monkey bread? This skillet version is packed with bright berries and topped with irresistibly rich cream cheese. A sprinkle of basil brings it together.
—Darla Andrews, Boerne, TX

Prep: 15 min. • **Bake:** 35 min.
Makes: 8 servings

- 1 tube (16.3 oz.) large refrigerated flaky honey butter biscuits
- ½ cup packed dark brown sugar
- ½ cup sugar
- ⅓ cup butter, melted
- 1 cup fresh blueberries
- 1 cup chopped fresh strawberries
- 4 oz. cream cheese, softened
- 1 Tbsp. minced fresh basil

1. Preheat oven to 350°. Separate dough into 8 biscuits; cut biscuits into fourths.

2. In a shallow bowl, combine sugars. Dip the biscuits in melted butter, then in sugar mixture. Place the biscuits in a greased 10¼-in. cast-iron skillet. Top with berries; dollop with cream cheese. Bake until biscuits are golden brown and cooked through, 35-40 minutes. Sprinkle with the fresh basil.

1 serving: 383 cal., 20g fat (9g sat. fat), 30mg chol., 641mg sod., 49g carb. (28g sugars, 2g fiber), 5g pro.

CINNAMON SWIRL QUICK BREAD

SOFT GARLIC BREADSTICKS

I rely on the convenience of my bread machine to mix the dough for buttery golden breadsticks that are mildly seasoned with garlic and basil. I like to use this dough when making pizza, too. The recipe will yield two 12-inch crusts.
—Charles Smith, Baltic, CT

Prep: 30 min. + rising • **Bake:** 20 min.
Makes: 20 breadsticks

SOFT GARLIC BREADSTICKS

1 cup plus 2 Tbsp. water (70° to 80°)
2 Tbsp. olive oil
3 Tbsp. grated Parmesan cheese
2 Tbsp. sugar
3 tsp. garlic powder
1½ tsp. salt
¾ tsp. minced fresh basil
  or ¼ tsp. dried basil
3 cups bread flour
2 tsp. active dry yeast
1 Tbsp. butter, melted
  Additional grated Parmesan
  cheese, optional

1. In bread machine pan, place the first 9 ingredients in the order suggested by manufacturer. Select dough setting (check dough after 5 minutes of mixing; add 1-2 Tbsp. water or flour if needed).
2. When the cycle is completed, turn dough onto a lightly floured surface. Divide into 20 portions. Shape each into a ball; roll each into a 9-in. rope. Place on greased baking sheets. Cover; let rise in a warm place for 40 minutes or until doubled.
3. Bake at 350° for 18-22 minutes or until golden brown. Remove to wire racks to cool. Brush warm breadsticks with butter. If desired, sprinkle with additional grated Parmesan cheese.
1 breadstick: 88 cal., 2g fat (1g sat. fat), 2mg chol., 196mg sod., 15g carb., 1g fiber), 3g pro.

TEST KITCHEN TIP
Store garlic breadsticks at room temperature wrapped in foil. Use within 4 days.

GARLIC BUBBLE LOAF

GARLIC BUBBLE LOAF

Complete your next spaghetti dinner with this eye-catching loaf. Family and friends will have fun pulling off each rich and buttery piece.
—Lynn Nichols, Bartlett, NE

- -

Prep: 35 min. + rising
Bake: 35 min. + cooling
Makes: 2 loaves (12 pieces each)

- 2 pkg. (¼ oz. each) active dry yeast
- ¼ cup warm water (110° to 115°)
- 2 cups warm whole milk (110° to 115°)
- 2 Tbsp. sugar
- 1 Tbsp. shortening
- 2 tsp. salt
- 6¼ to 6½ cups all-purpose flour
- ½ cup butter, melted
- 1 Tbsp. dried parsley flakes
- 2 tsp. garlic powder

1. In a large bowl, dissolve yeast in warm water. Add the milk, sugar, shortening, salt and 2 cups flour; beat until smooth. Stir in enough of the remaining flour to form a soft dough. Turn out dough on a floured surface; knead until smooth and elastic, 6-8 minutes. Place in a greased bowl, turning once to grease the top. Cover and let rise in a warm place until doubled, about 1 hour.
2. Punch dough down. Turn onto a lightly floured surface; divide into fourths. Divide each portion into 12 pieces. In a shallow bowl, combine the butter, parsley and garlic powder. Shape each piece into a ball; dip in butter mixture. Place in 2 greased 9x5-in. loaf pans. Pour any remaining butter mixture over dough. Cover and let rise until doubled, about 30 minutes.
3. Bake at 375° 35-40 minutes or until golden brown. Cool 10 minutes. Remove from pans to wire racks. Serve warm.
1 piece: 176 cal., 5g fat (3g sat. fat), 12mg chol., 237mg sod., 27g carb. (2g sugars, 1g fiber), 4g pro.

TEST KITCHEN TIP
You can tailor the flavors of this loaf to your meal. Add taco seasoning on Mexican night, Old Bay on seafood night, and more!

CINNAMON
TEA ROLLS

CINNAMON TEA ROLLS

Refrigerated crescent roll dough makes it a snap to whip up these oven-fresh goodies. The glaze has a hint of orange.
—*Taste of Home* Test Kitchen

- -

Takes: 20 min. • **Makes:** 4 rolls

- 1 tube (4 oz.) refrigerated crescent rolls
- 1 Tbsp. sugar
- ⅛ tsp. ground cinnamon
- ¼ cup confectioners' sugar
- 1¼ tsp. orange juice

1. Preheat oven to 375°. Unroll crescent dough into 1 rectangle; seal perforations. Combine sugar and cinnamon; sprinkle over dough. Roll up jelly-roll style, starting with a short side; pinch seam to seal. Using a serrated knife, cut into 4 pieces.
2. Place rolls, cut side down, in ungreased muffin cups. Bake for 10-12 minutes or until golden brown. Cool for 5 minutes before removing from the pan to a wire rack. In a small bowl, combine confectioners' sugar and orange juice; drizzle over rolls.
1 roll: 144 cal., 5g fat (0 sat. fat), 0 chol., 213mg sod., 23g carb. (14g sugars, 0 fiber), 2g pro.

GRAHAM STREUSEL COFFEE CAKE

I use this sweet coffee cake recipe often. It's quick and easy to make.
—Blanche Whytsell, Arnoldsburg, WV

- -

Prep: 20 min. • **Bake:** 40 min. + cooling
Makes: 16 servings

- 1½ cups graham cracker crumbs
- ¾ cup packed brown sugar
- ¾ cup chopped pecans
- 1½ tsp. ground cinnamon
- ⅔ cup butter, melted
- 1 pkg. yellow cake mix (regular size)
- ½ cup confectioners' sugar
- 1 Tbsp. 2% milk

1. In a small bowl, combine the graham cracker crumbs, brown sugar, pecans and cinnamon. Stir in the butter; set aside. Prepare cake mix batter according to package directions.
2. Pour half of the batter into a greased 13x9-in. baking pan. Sprinkle with half the graham cracker mixture. Carefully spoon remaining batter on top. Sprinkle with the remaining graham cracker mixture.
3. Bake at 350° for 40-45 minutes or until a toothpick inserted in center comes out clean. Cool on a wire rack. Combine the confectioners' sugar and milk; drizzle over coffee cake.
1 piece: 329 cal., 15g fat (6g sat. fat), 21mg chol., 332mg sod., 46g carb. (30g sugars, 2g fiber), 3g pro.

ORANGE ZUCCHINI MUFFINS

Orange juice and zest infuse these moist muffins with a pleasant citrus flavor. We enjoy them fresh from the oven.
—Chris Snyder, Boulder, CO

- -

Prep: 15 min. • **Bake:** 20 min.
Makes: 10 muffins

- 1 cup shredded zucchini
- 1¼ cups all-purpose flour
- ¾ tsp. ground nutmeg, divided
- ½ tsp. baking powder
- ½ tsp. baking soda
- ½ tsp. ground cinnamon
- ¼ tsp. salt
- 2 large eggs
- ¾ cup packed brown sugar
- ⅓ cup canola oil
- 2 Tbsp. orange juice
- 1 tsp. grated orange zest
- 1 tsp. vanilla extract
- ½ cup raisins
- 1 Tbsp. sugar

1. Squeeze zucchini until dry; set aside. In a large bowl, combine the flour, ½ tsp. nutmeg, baking powder, baking soda, cinnamon and salt. In another bowl, whisk the eggs, brown sugar, oil, orange juice, orange zest and vanilla. Stir into the dry ingredients just until moistened. Fold in raisins and reserved zucchini.
2. Fill paper-lined muffin cups two-thirds full. Combine the sugar and remaining nutmeg; sprinkle over batter. Bake at 350° 18-22 minutes or until a toothpick inserted in the center comes out clean. Cool for 5 minutes before removing from pan to a wire rack. Serve warm.
Freeze option: Wrap muffins in foil and freeze for up to 3 months. To use, thaw at room temperature. Warm if desired.
1 muffin: 230 cal., 9g fat (1g sat. fat), 42mg chol., 165mg sod., 36g carb. (22g sugars, 1g fiber), 3g pro.

"These super flavorful muffins are packed with raisins and are a great use of zucchini. I bake a big batch every summer, individually wrap leftovers in foil and place in a freezer bag for future snacking."
—CHRISTINE RUKAVENA, SENIOR EDITOR

TAHITIAN BREAKFAST TREATS

This is a healthy take on the Tahitian coconut breakfast treat called firi firi, *which is typically fried. My version is baked.*
—Susan Falk, Sterling Heights, MI

Prep: 35 min. + rising • **Bake:** 10 min.
Makes: 8 servings

- 1   pkg. (¼ oz.) active dry yeast
- ¼   cup warm water (110° to 115°)
- ½   cup warm coconut milk (110° to 115°)
- ½   cup sweetened shredded coconut
- ⅓   cup sugar
- ½   tsp. salt
- 2   to 2½ cups all-purpose flour

SPICED SUGAR

- ½   cup sugar
- 1   tsp. ground cinnamon
- ½   tsp. ground ginger
- ½   vanilla bean
- ¼   cup butter, melted

1. Add the yeast to warm water and stir to dissolve; allow to sit until yeast has bubbled, 5-7 minutes. Add yeast mixture to warm coconut milk. In a large bowl, combine the coconut, sugar, salt, yeast mixture and 1 cup flour; beat on medium speed until smooth. Stir in enough of the remaining flour to form stiff dough (dough will be sticky). Turn dough onto a floured surface; knead until smooth and elastic, 6-8 minutes. Place in a greased bowl, turning once to grease the top. Cover and let rise in a warm place until doubled, about 1½ hours.

2. Punch down dough. Turn onto a lightly floured surface; divide into 8 portions. Roll each into a 12-in. rope and form a figure 8 by curling the ends in opposite directions. Tuck each end under where it meets center of roll and pinch lightly to seal. Place 2 in. apart on a parchment-lined baking sheet. Cover with a kitchen towel; let rise in a warm place until almost doubled, about 30 minutes.

3. Preheat oven to 375°. Bake until light brown, 10-12 minutes. Meanwhile, place sugar, cinnamon and ginger in a shallow bowl. Split vanilla bean lengthwise. Using the tip of a sharp knife, scrape seeds from the center; stir into sugar mixture. Brush warm pastries with melted butter; roll in sugar mixture to coat.

1 treat: 251 cal., 8g fat (6g sat. fat), 8mg chol., 191mg sod., 42g carb. (18g sugars, 1g fiber), 4g pro.

TEST KITCHEN TIP
Instead of coating these treats in spiced sugar, try drizzling with a glaze! Combine 1 cup confectioners' sugar, 3 Tbsp. dark rum and 2 Tbsp. melted butter.

TAHITIAN BREAKFAST TREATS

JALAPENO CHEESE BREAD

Cheddar cheese and jalapenos give this savory bread a spicy southwestern flair. It makes a great accompaniment to chili and stew. Top it with sweet cream butter and watch it disappear.
—Julie Delisle, Sainte-Sabine, QC

- -

Prep: 25 min. + rising
Bake: 30 min. + cooling
Makes: 2 loaves (12 pieces each)

1   pkg. (¼ oz.) active dry yeast
1   cup warm water (110° to 115°)
¼   cup sugar
2   Tbsp. canola oil
½   tsp. salt
3   to 3½ cups all-purpose flour
2   cups shredded cheddar cheese
½   cup finely chopped seeded jalapeno peppers

1. Dissolve yeast in warm water. In a large bowl, combine the sugar, oil, salt, yeast mixture and 2 cups flour. Beat on medium speed until smooth. Stir in enough of the remaining flour to form a stiff dough. Stir in cheese and jalapenos.
2. Turn dough onto a floured surface; knead 6-8 minutes or until smooth and elastic. Place in a greased bowl, turning once to grease the top. Cover and let rise in a warm place until doubled, about 1 hour.
3. Punch dough down. Divide in half and shape into loaves. Place in 2 greased 8x4-in. loaf pans. Cover with kitchen towels; let rise in a warm place until almost doubled, about 40 minutes. Preheat oven to 350°.
4. Bake until golden brown, 30-35 minutes. Remove from pans to wire racks to cool.
1 piece: 110 cal., 4g fat (2g sat. fat), 10mg chol., 106mg sod., 15g carb. (2g sugars, 1g fiber), 4g pro.,

TEST KITCHEN TIP
When buying jalapenos, look for bright green, glossy skins. They should be firm and have no signs of soft spots.

**JALAPENO
CHEESE BREAD**

ALMOND BEAR CLAWS

These bear claws are melt-in-your-mouth delicious! It's impossible to resist the delicate pastry, rich almond filling and pretty fanned tops sprinkled with sugar and almonds. I made yummy treats like this when I worked in a bakery years ago.
—Aneta Kish, La Crosse, WI

Prep: 45 min. + chilling • **Bake:** 15 min.
Makes: 1½ dozen

- 1½ cups cold butter, cut into ½-in. pieces
- 5 cups all-purpose flour, divided
- 1 pkg. (¼ oz.) active dry yeast
- 1¼ cups half-and-half cream
- ¼ cup sugar
- ¼ tsp. salt
- 2 large eggs, room temperature, divided use
- 1 large egg white, room temperature
- ¾ cup confectioners' sugar
- ½ cup almond paste, cubed
- 1 Tbsp. water
  Sugar or coarse sugar
  Sliced almonds

1. In a large bowl, toss butter with 3 cups flour until well coated; refrigerate. In a large bowl, combine yeast and remaining 2 cups flour.
2. In a saucepan, heat cream, sugar and salt to 120°-130°. Add to yeast mixture with 1 egg. Beat until smooth. Stir in butter mixture just until moistened.
3. Place dough onto a well-floured surface; roll into a 21x12-in. rectangle. Starting at a short side, fold dough in thirds, forming a 12x7-in. rectangle. Give dough a quarter turn; roll into a 21x12-in. rectangle. Fold into thirds, starting with a short side. Repeat, flouring surface as needed. (Do not chill dough between each rolling and folding.) Cover and chill until firm, 4-24 hours.
4. For filling, in a bowl, beat egg white until foamy. Gradually add confectioners' sugar and almond paste; beat until smooth. Cut dough in half widthwise. Roll each portion into a 12-in. square; cut each square into three 12x4-in. strips. Spread about 2 Tbsp. filling down center of each strip. Fold long edges together over filling; seal edges and ends. Cut into 3 pieces.
5. Place on parchment-lined baking sheets with the folded edge facing away from you. With scissors, cut strips 4 times to within ½ in. of the folded edge; separate slightly. Repeat with remaining dough and filling. Cover and let rise in a warm place until doubled, about 1 hour.
6. Lightly beat water and remaining egg; brush over dough. Sprinkle with sugar and almonds. Bake at 375° until golden brown, about 15 minutes. Remove from pans to wire racks to cool.
1 claw: 352 cal., 19g fat (11g sat. fat), 73mg chol., 207mg sod., 38g carb. (10g sugars, 1g fiber), 6g pro.

HOMEMADE TORTILLAS

I usually have to double this recipe because we go through these so quickly. The tortillas are so tender, chewy and simple, you'll never use store-bought again.
—Kristin Van Dyken, Kennewick, WA

Takes: 30 min. • **Makes:** 8 tortillas

- 2 cups all-purpose flour
- ½ tsp. salt
- ¾ cup water
- 3 Tbsp. olive oil

1. In a large bowl, combine flour and salt. Stir in water and oil. Turn onto a floured surface; knead 10-12 times, adding a little flour or water if needed to achieve smooth dough. Let rest for 10 minutes.
2. Divide the dough into 8 portions. On a lightly floured surface, roll each portion into a 7-in. circle.
3. In a greased cast-iron or other heavy skillet, cook tortillas over medium heat until lightly browned, about 1 minute on each side. Serve warm.
1 tortilla: 159 cal., 5g fat (1g sat. fat), 0 chol., 148mg sod., 24g carb. (1g sugars, 1g fiber), 3g pro. **Diabetic exchanges:** 1½ starch, 1 fat.

**HOMEMADE
TORTILLAS**

BUTTERY CORNBREAD

ROASTED RED PEPPER BREAD

These savory loaves are moist, tender and loaded with flavor from grated Parmesan cheese and roasted sweet red peppers. They're great at dinner or as an appetizer.
—Cheryl Perry, Hertford, NC

- -

Prep: 45 min. + rising • **Bake:** 20 min.
Makes: 2 loaves (12 pieces each)

- 1½ cups roasted sweet red peppers, drained
- 1 pkg. (¼ oz.) active dry yeast
- 2 Tbsp. warm water (110° to 115°)
- 1¼ cups grated Parmesan cheese, divided
- ⅓ cup warm 2% milk (110° to 115°)
- 2 Tbsp. butter, softened
- 1¼ tsp. salt
- 3¼ to 3¾ cups all-purpose flour
- 1 large egg
- 1 Tbsp. water
- 1½ tsp. coarsely ground pepper

1. Place red peppers in a food processor; cover and process until pureed. In a large bowl, dissolve yeast in warm water. Add the red peppers, 1 cup cheese, milk, butter, salt and 1½ cups flour. Beat until smooth. Stir in enough remaining flour to form a firm dough.
2. Turn onto a floured surface; knead until smooth and elastic, 6-8 minutes. Place in a greased bowl, turning once to grease the top. Cover and let rise in a warm place until doubled, about 1 hour.
3. Punch dough down. Turn onto a lightly floured surface; divide dough into 6 pieces. Shape each into an 18-in. rope. Place 3 ropes on a greased baking sheet and braid; pinch ends to seal and tuck under. Repeat with remaining dough. Cover and let rise until doubled, about 1 hour.
4. In a small bowl, combine egg and water; brush over braids. Sprinkle with pepper and remaining cheese. Bake at 350° for 18-22 minutes or until golden brown.
1 piece: 99 cal., 3g fat (1g sat. fat), 15mg chol., 254mg sod., 14g carb. (1g sugars, 1g fiber), 4g pro.

BUTTERY CORNBREAD

A friend gave me this recipe several years ago, and it's my favorite. I love to serve the melt-in-your-mouth cornbread hot from the oven with butter and syrup. It gets rave reviews on holidays and at potluck dinners.
—Nicole Callen, Auburn, CA

- -

Prep: 15 min. • **Bake:** 25 min.
Makes: 15 servings

- ⅔ cup butter, softened
- 1 cup sugar
- 3 large eggs, room temperature
- 1⅔ cups 2% milk
- 2⅓ cups all-purpose flour
- 1 cup cornmeal
- 4½ tsp. baking powder
- 1 tsp. salt

1. Preheat oven to 400°. In a large bowl, cream butter and sugar until light and fluffy, 5-7 minutes. Combine eggs and milk. Combine flour, cornmeal, baking powder and salt; add to the creamed mixture alternately with egg mixture.
2. Pour into a greased 13x9-in. baking pan. Bake for 22-27 minutes or until a toothpick inserted in center comes out clean. Cut into squares; serve warm.
1 piece: 259 cal., 10g fat (6g sat. fat), 68mg chol., 386mg sod., 37g carb. (15g sugars, 1g fiber), 5g pro.
Corny Cornbread: Stir in 1½ cups thawed frozen corn.
Mexican Cheese Cornbread: Stir in 1 cup shredded Mexican cheese blend.
Jalapeno Cheese Cornbread: Stir in 1 cup shredded cheddar cheese and 3 finely chopped seeded jalapeno peppers.

ROASTED
RED PEPPER
BREAD

ZUCCHINI & CHEESE DROP BISCUITS

These colorful little drop biscuits are very easy to put together and yet are packed full of flavor. I serve them warm out of the oven.
—Keith Mesch, Mount Healthy, OH

Prep: 25 min. + standing • **Bake:** 25 min.
Makes: 1 dozen

- ¾ cup shredded zucchini
- 1¼ tsp. salt, divided
- 2½ cups all-purpose flour
- 1 Tbsp. baking powder
- ½ cup cold butter, cubed
- ½ cup shredded cheddar cheese
- ¼ cup shredded part-skim mozzarella cheese
- ¼ cup shredded Parmesan cheese
- 2 Tbsp. finely chopped oil-packed sun-dried tomatoes, patted dry
- 2 Tbsp. minced fresh basil or 2 tsp. dried basil
- 1 cup 2% milk

1. Preheat oven to 425°. Place zucchini in a colander over a plate; sprinkle with ¼ tsp. salt and toss. Let stand 10 minutes. Rinse and drain well. Squeeze the zucchini to remove excess liquid. Pat dry.
2. In a large bowl, whisk the flour, baking powder and remaining salt. Cut in butter until mixture resembles coarse crumbs. Stir in zucchini, cheeses, tomatoes and basil. Add milk; stir just until moistened.
3. Drop by scant ⅓ cupfuls into a greased 13x9-in. baking pan. Bake until golden brown, 22-26 minutes. Serve warm.
1 biscuit: 205 cal., 11g fat (7g sat. fat), 29mg chol., 482mg sod., 22g carb. (2g sugars, 1g fiber), 6g pro.

MOM'S CHOCOLATE BREAD

My mom made this divine chocolaty bread for holidays or at special request. I always think of my family when I smell it baking.
—Rachel Rhodes, Princeton, NC

Prep: 10 min. • **Bake:** 30 min. + cooling
Makes: 1 loaf (12 pieces)

- 4 Tbsp. sugar, divided
- 3 Tbsp. all-purpose flour
- 1 Tbsp. cold butter
- 1 to 3 Tbsp. ground cinnamon
- 1 tube (8 oz.) refrigerated crescent rolls
- ⅔ cup semisweet chocolate chips
- 1 Tbsp. butter, melted

1. Preheat oven to 375°. For streusel, in a small bowl, mix 3 Tbsp. sugar and flour; cut in butter until crumbly. Reserve half the streusel for topping. Stir cinnamon and remaining sugar into remaining streusel.
2. Unroll the crescent dough into a long rectangle; press the perforations to seal. Sprinkle with the chocolate chips and cinnamon mixture. Roll up jelly-roll style, starting with a long side; pinch seam to seal. Fold roll in half lengthwise; transfer to a greased 8x4-in. loaf pan. Brush with butter; sprinkle with reserved streusel.
3. Bake until golden brown, 30-35 minutes. Cool in pan 10 minutes before removing to a wire rack to cool completely.
1 piece: 164 cal., 9g fat (4g sat. fat), 5mg chol., 165mg sod., 21g carb. (11g sugars, 2g fiber), 2g pro.

APPLESAUCE MUFFINS

These are such a popular item at the restaurant I own that I had the recipe printed on a card to share with guests.
—Linda Williams, LaFayette, AL

Prep: 10 min. • **Bake:** 20 min.
Makes: about 2 dozen

- 1 cup butter, softened
- 2 cups sugar
- 2 large eggs, room temperature
- 1 tsp. vanilla extract
- 2 cups applesauce
- 4 cups all-purpose flour
- 1 tsp. baking soda
- 1 tsp. ground cinnamon
- 1 tsp. ground allspice
- ¼ tsp. ground cloves
  Optional: 1 cup chopped walnuts, cinnamon sugar

1. Preheat oven to 350°. In a bowl, cream the butter and sugar until light and fluffy, 5-7 minutes. Beat in eggs and vanilla. Stir in applesauce. Combine flour, baking soda and spices; stir into the creamed mixture. If desired, fold in nuts.
2. Fill greased or paper-lined muffin cups three-fourths full. Bake until a toothpick comes out clean, 20-25 minutes. Cool for 5 minutes before removing from the pans to wire racks. If desired, sprinkle with the cinnamon sugar.
1 muffin: 224 cal., 8g fat (5g sat. fat), 36mg chol., 120mg sod., 35g carb. (19g sugars, 1g fiber), 3g pro. **Diabetic exchanges:** 2 starch, 1½ fat.

SURPRISE MONKEY BREAD

When my neighbor hosts brunch, she always asks that I make this treat. I also make a savory version with garlic and cheese for dinner.
—Lois Rutherford, Elkton, FL

Prep: 25 min. • **Bake:** 40 min.
Makes: 1 loaf (12 servings)

- 1 cup packed brown sugar
- ½ cup butter, cubed
- 2 tubes (12 oz. each) refrigerated flaky buttermilk biscuits
- ½ cup sugar
- 1 Tbsp. ground cinnamon
- 8 oz. cream cheese, cut into 20 cubes
- 1½ cups chopped walnuts

1. In a microwave-safe bowl, heat brown sugar and butter on high for 1 minute or until sugar is dissolved; set aside.
2. Flatten each biscuit into a 3-in. circle. Combine sugar and cinnamon; sprinkle ½ tsp. in the center of each biscuit. Top with a cream cheese cube. Fold dough over filling; pinch edges to seal tightly.
3. Sprinkle ½ cup walnuts into a greased 10-in. fluted tube pan. Layer with half of the biscuits, cinnamon sugar and butter mixture and ½ cup walnuts. Repeat layers.
4. Bake at 350° for 40-45 minutes or until golden brown. Immediately invert onto a serving platter. Serve warm.
1 piece: 467 cal., 24g fat (10g sat. fat), 41mg chol., 625mg sod., 56g carb. (26g sugars, 1g fiber), 10g pro.

BUTTERY CRESCENT ROLLS

I typically double the recipe for these buttery rolls, because they never last very long. You can shape them any way you like.
—Kelly Kirby, Mill Bay, BC

Prep: 35 min. + rising • **Bake:** 10 min.
Makes: 2 dozen

- 1 Tbsp. active dry yeast
- 1 tsp. plus ⅓ cup sugar
- ½ cup warm water (110° to 115°)
- ½ cup butter, softened
- ½ cup warm 2% milk (110° to 115°)
- 1 large egg, room temperature
- ¾ tsp. salt
- 4 cups all-purpose flour

1. In a large bowl, dissolve the yeast and 1 tsp. sugar in warm water. Add the butter, milk, egg, salt, remaining sugar and 2 cups flour. Beat until smooth. Stir in enough remaining flour to form a soft dough.
2. Turn onto a floured surface; knead until smooth and elastic, 6-8 minutes. Place in a greased bowl, turning once to grease the top. Cover and let rise in a warm place until doubled, about 1 hour.
3. Punch dough down. Turn onto a lightly floured surface; divide in half. Roll each portion into a 12-in. circle; cut each circle into 12 wedges. Roll up wedges from wide end and place point side down 2 in. apart on greased baking sheets. Curve ends to form crescents. Cover; let rise in a warm place until doubled, about 30 minutes.
4. Preheat oven to 350°. Bake until golden brown, 10-12 minutes. Remove from pans to wire racks.
1 roll: 128 cal., 4g fat (3g sat. fat), 19mg chol., 107mg sod., 19g carb. (4g sugars, 1g fiber), 3g pro.

ITALIAN-STYLE DROP BISCUITS

My husband and I created this recipe by adding green chiles to our favorite garlicky biscuits. They're even better this way!
—LaDonna Reed, Ponca City, OK

Takes: 20 min. • **Makes:** 6 biscuits

- 1 cup biscuit/baking mix
- ½ cup shredded cheddar cheese
- 2 Tbsp. canned chopped green chiles
- ¼ cup cold water
- 4 tsp. butter, melted
- ½ tsp. dried parsley flakes
- ¼ tsp. garlic powder
- ¼ tsp. Italian seasoning

1. Combine biscuit mix, cheese and chiles. Stir in water until a soft dough forms.
2. Drop dough into 6 mounds in a small ungreased cast-iron or other ovenproof skillet. Bake at 450° until golden brown, 8-10 minutes.
3. In a small bowl, combine butter, parsley, garlic powder and Italian seasoning. Brush over biscuits. Serve warm.
1 biscuit: 138 cal., 8g fat (4g sat. fat), 16mg chol., 301mg sod., 14g carb. (1g sugars, 1g fiber), 4g pro.

MEXICAN CHICKEN CHILI
PAGE 94

Soups & Sandwiches

The combo of soup and sammie is a tried-and-true classic. Here, our staff shares their favorite kettle creations and hand-held goodies that warm the body and soul.

BUFFALO CHICKEN LETTUCE WRAPS

These Buffalo chicken wraps are excellent. Honey and lime juice help tone down the hot wing sauce for a refreshing zing. They're perfect for lunch or a light evening meal. For quicker preparation, use store-bought blue cheese dressing instead of homemade.
—Priscilla Gilbert,
Indian Harbour Beach, FL

Takes: 25 min. • **Makes:** 4 servings

- ⅓ cup crumbled blue cheese
- ¼ cup mayonnaise
- 2 Tbsp. 2% milk
- 4½ tsp. lemon juice
- 1 Tbsp. minced fresh parsley
- 1 tsp. Worcestershire sauce
- 1 lb. boneless skinless chicken breasts, cubed
- 1 tsp. salt
- 1 Tbsp. canola oil
- ¼ cup lime juice
- ¼ cup Louisiana-style hot sauce
- ¼ cup honey
- 1 small cucumber, halved lengthwise, seeded and thinly sliced
- 1 celery rib, thinly sliced
- ¾ cup julienned carrots
- 8 Bibb or Boston lettuce leaves

1. For dressing, in a small bowl, combine first 6 ingredients. Cover and refrigerate until serving.

2. Sprinkle chicken with salt. In a large skillet, cook chicken in oil until no longer pink. Combine the lime juice, hot sauce and honey; pour over chicken. Bring to a boil. Reduce the heat; simmer, uncovered, for 2-3 minutes or until slightly thickened. Remove from heat; stir in the cucumber, celery and carrots.

3. Spoon ½ cup chicken mixture onto each lettuce leaf; fold the sides over filling and secure with a toothpick. Serve with blue cheese dressing.

2 wraps: 378 cal., 20g fat (5g sat. fat), 73mg chol., 1391mg sod., 24g carb. (20g sugars, 2g fiber), 26g pro.

> "These lettuce wraps are healthy, satisfying, authentic, convenient and delicious! I love to freeze any leftover meat for future salads."
> —CHRISTINE RUKAVENA, SENIOR EDITOR

TURKEY SALAD SANDWICHES

Inspired by a turkey salad sandwich at a local deli, I developed my own version to suit my family's tastes. Serve this on croissants for an elegant luncheon or on hearty whole grain bread for a filling meal.
—Merrijane Rice, Kaysville, UT

Takes: 15 min. • **Makes:** 6 servings

- 10 oz. deli turkey, cubed
- 2 cups torn romaine
- 6 bacon strips, cooked and crumbled
- ½ cup shredded Swiss cheese
- ½ cup mayonnaise
- ⅓ cup frozen peas, thawed
- 2 green onions, thinly sliced
- ¼ tsp. pepper
- 12 slices whole wheat bread

In a large bowl, combine first 8 ingredients. Spoon ⅔ cup mixture on each of 6 bread slices. Top with remaining bread slices.
1 sandwich: 398 cal., 22g fat (5g sat. fat), 43mg chol., 1039mg sod., 28g carb. (4g sugars, 5g fiber), 22g pro.

BUFFALO CHICKEN
LETTUCE WRAPS

ONION BEEF AU JUS

Garlic, onions, soy sauce and onion soup mix flavor the tender beef in savory hot sandwiches that are served with a tasty rich broth for dipping. The seasoned beef makes delicious cold sandwiches too.
—Blake Brown, West Union, IA

- -

Prep: 20 min.
Bake: 2½ hours + standing
Makes: 12 servings

- 1 beef rump roast or bottom round roast (4 lbs.)
- 2 Tbsp. canola oil
- 2 large sweet onions, cut into ¼-in. slices
- 6 Tbsp. butter, softened, divided
- 5 cups water
- ½ cup reduced-sodium soy sauce
- 1 envelope onion soup mix
- 1 garlic clove, minced
- 1 tsp. browning sauce, optional
- 1 loaf (1 lb.) French bread
- 1 cup shredded Swiss cheese

1. Preheat oven to 325°. In a Dutch oven over medium-high heat, brown the roast on all sides in oil; drain. In a large skillet, saute the onions in 2 Tbsp. of butter until tender. Add the water, soy sauce, soup mix, garlic and, if desired, browning sauce. Pour over roast.
2. Cover and bake until the meat is tender, 2½ hours.
3. Let meat stand 10 minutes, then thinly slice. Return meat to pan juices. Split bread lengthwise; cut into 3-in. sections. Spread with remaining 4 Tbsp. butter. Place on a baking sheet.
4. Broil bread 4-6 in. from the heat until golden brown, 2-3 minutes. Top with beef and onions; sprinkle with cheese. Broil until cheese is melted, 1-2 minutes. Serve with pan juices.
1 piece: 422 cal., 19g fat (8g sat. fat), 114mg chol., 1179mg sod., 24g carb. (2g sugars, 2g fiber), 38g pro.

ONION BEEF
AU JUS

PRESSURE-COOKER CORN CHOWDER

PRESSURE-COOKER CORN CHOWDER

Corn chowder is a classic staple, with its hearty flavors of creamy sweet corn, bacon crumbles, shredded cheddar cheese and chopped parsley. And now you can make it in record time using a pressure cooker.
—*Taste of Home* Test Kitchen

Takes: 30 min. • **Makes:** 8 servings (2 qt.)

4   medium red potatoes, peeled and cut into ½-in. cubes (about 2½ cups)
2   cans (14½ oz. each) chicken broth
3   cups fresh or frozen corn
1   medium onion, chopped
3   garlic cloves, minced
½   tsp. salt
½   tsp. pepper
2   Tbsp. cornstarch
1   cup half-and-half cream
1   cup shredded cheddar cheese
6   bacon strips, cooked and crumbled
    Chopped fresh parsley

1. Place the first 7 ingredients in a 6-qt. electric pressure cooker. Lock lid; close the pressure-release valve. Adjust to pressure-cook on high for 15 minutes. Quick-release pressure.
2. Select the saute setting and adjust for low heat. Mix cornstarch and cream until smooth; stir into soup. Cook and stir until slightly thickened, 6-8 minutes. Stir in cheese and bacon. Heat through until cheese is melted. Press cancel. Sprinkle servings with parsley and, if desired, additional cheese and bacon.
1 cup: 191 cal., 9g fat (5g sat. fat), 31mg chol., 709mg sod., 21g carb. (5g sugars, 2g fiber), 7g pro. **Diabetic exchanges:** 1½ starch, 1 medium-fat meat, ½ fat.

BURGER SLIDERS WITH SECRET SAUCE

BURGER SLIDERS WITH SECRET SAUCE

These sliders are super easy to put together and are always a hit! I love that they are fast food without having to go to a restaurant. The meat can also be made ahead of time in preparation for your gathering.
—April Lee Wiencek, Chicago, IL

Takes: 30 min. • **Makes:** 12 sliders

2   lbs. ground beef
2   large eggs, beaten
¾   cup minced onion, divided
2   tsp. garlic powder
1   tsp. salt
1   tsp. pepper
1   pkg. (17 oz.) dinner rolls
½   cup Thousand Island salad dressing, divided
10 slices American cheese
12 sliced dill pickles
1½ cups shredded iceberg lettuce
1   Tbsp. butter, melted
1   Tbsp. sesame seeds, toasted

1. Preheat oven to 350°. In a large bowl, mix the beef, eggs, ½ cup minced onion, garlic powder, salt and pepper lightly but thoroughly. Place meat mixture on a large parchment-lined baking sheet; shape into two 6x8-in. rectangles, each about ½ in. thick. Bake until a thermometer reads 160°, 15-20 minutes.
2. Meanwhile, without separating the rolls, cut the bread in half horizontally. Spread ¼ cup of dressing evenly over bottom halves of rolls.
3. Blot meat with paper towels to remove excess fat; top meat with the cheese and return to oven. Bake until cheese has just melted, 2-3 minutes. Place meat on bottom halves of rolls; spread with the remaining ¼ cup dressing. Layer with the pickles, remaining ¼ cup minced onion and shredded lettuce; replace top halves of rolls. Brush butter on top of rolls and sprinkle with sesame seeds; cut into sandwiches. Serve immediately.
1 slider: 397 cal., 21g fat (8g sat. fat), 105mg chol., 785mg sod., 26g carb. (6g sugars, 2g fiber), 22g pro.

"This is a solid slider recipe! It's fun to serve at potlucks and game-day parties."
—RASHANDA COBBINS, FOOD EDITOR

SLOW-COOKED BARBECUED BEEF SANDWICHES

Chuck roast makes delicious shredded beef sandwiches after simmering in a rich homemade sauce all day. The meat really is tender and juicy, and it only takes minutes to prepare before slow cooking.
—Tatina Smith, San Angelo, TX

Prep: 20 min. • **Cook:** 8¼ hours
Makes: 12 servings

- 1 boneless beef chuck roast (3 lbs.)
- 1½ cups ketchup
- ¼ cup packed brown sugar
- ¼ cup barbecue sauce
- 2 Tbsp. Worcestershire sauce
- 2 Tbsp. Dijon mustard
- 1 tsp. liquid smoke, optional
- ½ tsp. salt
- ¼ tsp. garlic powder
- ¼ tsp. pepper
- 12 sandwich buns, split
  Optional: Sliced onions, dill pickles and pickled jalapenos

1. Cut roast in half and place in a 3- or 4-qt. slow cooker. In a small bowl, combine the ketchup, brown sugar, barbecue sauce, Worcestershire sauce, mustard, liquid smoke if desired, and seasonings. Pour over beef.
2. Cover and cook on low for 8-10 hours or until meat is tender. Remove meat; cool slightly. Skim fat from cooking liquid.
3. Shred the beef with 2 forks; return to the slow cooker. Cover and cook for 15 minutes or until heated through. Using a slotted spoon, place ½ cup on each bun. Serve with the onions, pickles and jalapenos if desired.
Freeze option: Place individual portions of cooled meat mixture in freezer containers. To use, partially thaw in the refrigerator overnight. Microwave, covered, on high in a microwave-safe dish until heated through, gently stirring; add broth or water if necessary.
1 sandwich: 458 cal., 15g fat (5g sat. fat), 74mg chol., 1052mg sod., 49g carb. (18g sugars, 1g fiber), 30g pro.
Tex-Mex Beef Sandwiches: Omit the ketchup, brown sugar, barbecue sauce, Worcestershire sauce, mustard, liquid smoke, salt, garlic powder, pepper and optional toppings. Combine 1 envelope burrito seasoning with 2 Tbsp. baking cocoa; rub over beef. Place 1 each coarsely chopped sweet red pepper and green pepper 1 large onion chopped in bottom of slow cooker; top with meat. Combine 1 cup beef broth with ½ cup ketchup pour over meat. Proceed as recipe directs.
Barbecued Venison Sandwiches: Substitute 1 (3-4 pound) boneless venison roast for the beef roast.
Italian Beef Sandwiches: Omit the ketchup, brown sugar, barbecue sauce, Worcestershire sauce, mustard, liquid smoke, salt, garlic powder, pepper and optional toppings. Sprinkle roast with 1 tsp. Italian seasoning, ¼ tsp. cayenne and ¼ tsp. pepper. Place in slow cooker. Combine ¼ cup water, 1 jar (16 oz.) pepperoncini with liquid, 1 each julienned sweet red pepper and green pepper, 1 minced garlic clove, 1 enveloped onion soup mix and 2 Tbsp. Worcestershire sauce. Pour over meat and proceed as recipe directs.

SLOW-COOKED BARBECUED BEEF SANDWICHES

TEST KITCHEN TIP
For easy cleanup, place a liner in your slow cooker before adding the ingredients.

NAVY BEAN VEGETABLE SOUP

My family really likes bean soup, so I came up with this enticing version. The leftovers are, dare I say, even better the next day!
—Eleanor Mielke, Mitchell, SD

- -

Prep: 15 min.
Cook: 9 hours
Makes: 12 servings (3 qt.)

- 4 medium carrots, thinly sliced
- 2 celery ribs, chopped
- 1 medium onion, chopped
- 2 cups cubed fully cooked ham
- 1½ cups dried navy beans
- 1 envelope vegetable recipe mix (Knorr)
- 1 envelope onion soup mix
- 1 bay leaf
- ½ tsp. pepper
- 8 cups water

In a 5-qt. slow cooker, combine the first 9 ingredients. Stir in water. Cover and cook on low until beans are tender, 9-10 hours. Discard bay leaf.

Freeze option: Freeze the cooled soup in freezer containers. To use, partially thaw in refrigerator overnight. Heat through in a saucepan, stirring occasionally; add water or broth if necessary.

1 cup: 157 cal., 2g fat (1g sat. fat), 12mg chol., 763mg sod., 24g carb. (4g sugars, 8g fiber), 11g pro.

Country Cassoulet: Instead of cubed ham, add 1½ pounds smoked ham hocks or pork neck bones or a meaty ham bone to slow cooker. Omit onion soup mix; add ¼ tsp. each dried thyme and rosemary. Remove ham bones at end of cooking; stir 2 cups shredded cooked chicken and ½ pound sliced smoked fully cooked sausage into soup. Heat through. Cut meat from ham bones; add to soup.

SLOW-COOKER PASTA E FAGIOLI

You can make a meal just out of my soup. It's hearty and healthy. Whenever I serve it to guests, I receive many compliments.
—Penny Novy, Buffalo Grove, IL

- -

Prep: 30 min. • **Cook:** 7½ hours
Makes: 8 servings (2½ qt.)

- 1 lb. ground beef
- 1 medium onion, chopped
- 1 carton (32 oz.) chicken broth
- 2 cans (14½ oz. each) diced tomatoes, undrained
- 1 can (15 oz.) cannellini beans, rinsed and drained
- 2 medium carrots, chopped
- 1½ cups finely chopped cabbage
- 1 celery rib, chopped
- 2 Tbsp. minced fresh basil or 2 tsp. dried basil
- 2 garlic cloves, minced
- ½ tsp. salt
- ½ tsp. pepper
- 1 cup ditalini or other small pasta
  Grated Parmesan cheese, optional

1. In a large skillet, cook beef and onion over medium heat until beef is no longer pink and onion is tender; drain.
2. Transfer to a 4- or 5-qt. slow cooker. Stir in broth, tomatoes, beans, carrots, cabbage, celery, basil, garlic, salt and pepper. Cover and cook on low until vegetables are tender, 7-8 hours.
3. Stir in pasta. Cover and cook on high until pasta is tender, about 30 minutes longer. Sprinkle with cheese if desired.

1¼ cups: 258 cal., 8g fat (3g sat. fat), 38mg chol., 885mg sod., 31g carb. (7g sugars, 6g fiber), 17g pro.

NAVY BEAN VEGETABLE SOUP

PEPPERONI PIZZA LOAF

Because this savory stromboli relies on frozen bread dough, it comes together in no time. The golden loaf is stuffed with cheese, pepperoni, mushrooms, peppers and olives. I often add a few thin slices of ham, too.
—Jenny Brown, West Lafayette, IN

Prep: 20 min. • **Bake:** 35 min.
Makes: 12 pieces

- 1 loaf (1 lb.) frozen bread dough, thawed
- 2 large eggs, separated
- 1 Tbsp. grated Parmesan cheese
- 1 Tbsp. olive oil
- 1 tsp. minced fresh parsley
- 1 tsp. dried oregano
- ½ tsp. garlic powder
- ¼ tsp. pepper
- 8 oz. sliced pepperoni
- 2 cups shredded part-skim mozzarella cheese
- 1 can (4 oz.) mushroom stems and pieces, drained
- ¼ to ½ cup pickled pepper rings
- 1 medium green pepper, diced
- 1 can (2¼ oz.) sliced ripe olives
- 1 can (15 oz.) pizza sauce

1. Preheat oven to 350°. On a greased baking sheet, roll out dough into a 15x10-in. rectangle. In a small bowl, combine the egg yolks, Parmesan cheese, oil, parsley, oregano, garlic powder and pepper. Brush over the dough.

2. Sprinkle with the pepperoni, mozzarella cheese, mushrooms, pepper rings, green pepper and olives. Roll up, jelly-roll style, starting with a long side; pinch seam to seal and tuck ends under.

3. Position loaf with the seam side down; brush with egg whites. Do not let rise. Bake until golden brown and dough is cooked through, 35-40 minutes. Warm the pizza sauce; serve with sliced loaf.

Freeze option: Freeze cooled unsliced pizza loaf in heavy-duty foil. To use, remove from freezer 30 minutes before reheating. Remove from foil and reheat on a greased baking sheet in a preheated 325° oven until heated through. Serve as directed.

1 piece: 296 cal., 17g fat (6g sat. fat), 66mg chol., 827mg sod., 24g carb. (4g sugars, 2g fiber), 13g pro.

GROUND BEEF GYROS

If your family likes gyros as much as mine, they'll love this easy version. It's made with ground beef instead of lamb. I found the recipe in a newspaper and adapted it to fit our tastes. A cucumber yogurt sauce adds an authentic finishing touch.
—Ruth Stahl, Shepherd, MT

Takes: 30 min. • **Makes:** 4 servings

- 1 cup plain yogurt
- ⅓ cup chopped seeded cucumber
- 2 Tbsp. finely chopped onion
- 1 garlic clove, minced
- 1 tsp. sugar

GYROS
- 1½ tsp. dried oregano
- 1 tsp. garlic powder
- 1 tsp. onion powder
- 1 tsp. salt, optional
- ¾ tsp. pepper
- 1 lb. ground beef
- 4 pita pocket halves
- 3 cups shredded lettuce
- 1 large tomato, chopped
- 1 small onion, sliced

1. In a bowl, combine first 5 ingredients. Chill. In a large bowl, combine seasonings; crumble beef over mixture and mix lightly but thoroughly. Shape into 4 patties.

2. Grill, covered, over medium heat or broil 4 in. from the heat for 6-7 minutes on each side or until a thermometer reads 160°. Cut the patties into thin slices; stuff into pita halves. Add the lettuce, tomato and onion. Serve with the yogurt sauce.

1 gyro: 357 cal., 16g fat (6g sat. fat), 78mg chol., 257mg sod., 27g carb. (7g sugars, 3g fiber), 26g pro.

PEPPERONI PIZZA LOAF

GROUND BEEF GYROS

CONTEST-WINNING NEW ENGLAND CLAM CHOWDER

This is the best New England clam chowder recipe ever! In the Pacific Northwest, we dig our own razor clams, and I grind them for the chowder. But canned clams are perfectly acceptable.
—Sandy Larson, Port Angeles, WA

Prep: 20 min. • **Cook:** 35 min.
Makes: 5 servings

- 4   center-cut bacon strips
- 2   celery ribs, chopped
- 1   large onion, chopped
- 1   garlic clove, minced
- 3   small potatoes, peeled and cubed
- 1   cup water
- 1   bottle (8 oz.) clam juice
- 3   tsp. reduced-sodium chicken bouillon granules
- ¼   tsp. white pepper
- ¼   tsp. dried thyme
- ⅓   cup all-purpose flour
- 2   cups fat-free half-and-half, divided
- 2   cans (6½ oz. each) chopped clams, undrained

1. In a Dutch oven, cook the bacon over medium heat until crisp. Remove to paper towels to drain; set aside. Saute the celery and onion in the drippings until tender. Add the garlic; cook 1 minute longer. Stir in the potatoes, water, clam juice, bouillon, pepper and thyme. Bring to a boil. Reduce heat; simmer, uncovered, until potatoes are tender, 15-20 minutes.

2. In a small bowl, combine flour and 1 cup half-and-half until smooth. Gradually stir into soup. Bring to a boil; cook and stir until thickened, 1-2 minutes.

3. Stir in clams and remaining half-and-half; heat through (do not boil). Crumble cooked bacon; sprinkle over each serving.

1⅓ cups: 260 cal., 4g fat (1g sat. fat), 22mg chol., 788mg sod., 39g carb. (9g sugars, 3g fiber), 13g pro. **Diabetic exchanges:** 2½ starch, 1 lean meat.

**CONTEST-WINNING
NEW ENGLAND CLAM CHOWDER**

CHICKEN CHORIZO POSOLE

I first tasted posole while visiting a friend in Santa Fe. It was a revelation! I have since been experimenting with many versions, and this one has become a much-loved tradition for my family.
—Jennifer Beckman, Falls Church, VA

Prep: 40 min. • **Cook:** 40 min.
Makes: 9 servings (about 2 qt.)

- 1 lb. tomatillos, husked and cut in half
- 1 large onion, quartered
- 2 jalapeno peppers, halved and seeded
- 4 garlic cloves, peeled
- 4 cups water
- 1 cup reduced-sodium chicken broth
- 1 whole garlic bulb, loose paper removed, cut in half crosswise
- 5 whole cloves
- 2 bay leaves
- 2 boneless skinless chicken breast halves (6 oz. each)
- 1 lb. uncooked chorizo or bulk spicy pork sausage
- 2 cans (15 oz. each) hominy, rinsed and drained
- 3 tsp. lime juice, divided
- 1 tsp. dried oregano
- 1 tsp. ground cumin
- ½ tsp. salt, divided
- 1 cup minced fresh cilantro, divided

SALSA
- 1 medium mango, peeled and cubed
- 1 medium ripe avocado, peeled and cubed
- 5 radishes, chopped

GARNISH
- 6 cups tortilla chips

CHICKEN CHORIZO POSOLE

1. Place the tomatillos, onion, jalapenos and garlic cloves on a greased baking sheet. Bake at 425° for 25-30 minutes or until tomatillos are tender. Cool slightly. Transfer to a food processor; cover and process until blended.

2. In a Dutch oven, bring the water, broth, garlic bulb, cloves and bay leaves to a boil. Reduce heat; add chicken breasts and poach, uncovered, for 15-20 minutes or until no longer pink.

3. Remove chicken from broth and shred. Strain the broth, discarding seasonings. Crumble chorizo into Dutch oven; cook over medium heat for 6-8 minutes or until fully cooked. Drain. Return broth to Dutch oven. Stir in the hominy, 2 tsp. lime juice, oregano, cumin, ¼ tsp. salt, tomatillo mixture and shredded chicken; heat through. Stir in ½ cup cilantro.

4. For salsa, in a small bowl, combine the mango, avocado, radishes and remaining cilantro, lime juice and salt. Serve with soup. Garnish with chips.

Freeze option: Freeze the cooled soup in freezer containers. To use, partially thaw in refrigerator overnight. Heat through in a saucepan, stirring occasionally and adding broth if necessary. Prepare salsa and serve with soup.

1 cup posole with ⅓ cup salsa and ⅔ cup chips: 430 cal., 23g fat (7g sat. fat), 65mg chol., 1292mg sod., 32g carb. (7g sugars, 6g fiber), 22g pro.

"The combination of lime, oregano, cumin and cilantro work so well together in this dish. It's one of my all-time favorites!"
—DAN ROBERTS, PHOTOGRAPHER

CONTEST-WINNING
HEARTY HAMBURGER SOUP

CONTEST-WINNING HEARTY HAMBURGER SOUP

At family get-togethers, our children always request this spirit-warming soup along with a fresh loaf of homemade bread.
—Barbara Brown, Janesville, WI

Prep: 15 min. • **Cook:** 30 min.
Makes: 8 servings (2 qt.)

- 1   lb. ground beef
- 4   cups water
- 1   can (14½ oz.) diced tomatoes, undrained
- 3   medium carrots, sliced
- 2   medium potatoes, peeled and cubed
- 1   medium onion, chopped
- ½   cup chopped celery
- 4   tsp. beef bouillon granules
- 1½ tsp. salt
- ¼   tsp. pepper
- ¼   tsp. dried oregano
- 1   cup cut fresh or frozen green beans

1. In a large saucepan, brown beef; drain. Add the next 10 ingredients; bring to a boil.
2. Reduce the heat; cover and simmer for 15 minutes or until potatoes and carrots are tender. Add green beans. Cover and simmer 15 minutes longer or until the beans are tender.

1 cup: 178 cal., 7g fat (3g sat. fat), 38mg chol., 984mg sod., 15g carb. (5g sugars, 3g fiber), 13g pro.

ASK SARAH

CAN I THICKEN THIS SOUP?
Yes! When the potatoes and carrots are tender, ladle 1 cup of hot broth into a bowl containing 4 Tbsp. of flour; whisk until smooth. Add back to the soup; stir and simmer until green beans are tender and soup is slightly thickened.

PRESSURE-COOKER
SHREDDED CHICKEN GYROS

PRESSURE-COOKER SHREDDED CHICKEN GYROS

Our family has no links of any kind to Greece, but we always have such a marvelous time at the annual Salt Lake City Greek Festival. One of my favorite parts is all the awesome food. This meal is a good way to mix up our menu, and my kids are big fans.
—Camille Beckstrand, Layton, UT

Takes: 30 minutes • **Makes:** 8 servings

- 2   medium onions, chopped
- 6   garlic cloves, minced
- 1   tsp. lemon-pepper seasoning
- 1   tsp. dried oregano
- ½   tsp. ground allspice
- ½   cup lemon juice
- ¼   cup red wine vinegar
- 2   Tbsp. olive oil
- 2   lbs. boneless skinless chicken breasts
- 8   whole pita breads
     Toppings: Tzatziki sauce, torn romaine and sliced tomato, cucumber and onion

1. In a 6-qt. electric pressure cooker, combine the first 8 ingredients; add chicken. Lock lid; close pressure-release valve. Adjust to pressure-cook on high for 6 minutes. Quick-release pressure. A thermometer inserted in the chicken should read at least 165°.
2. Remove chicken; shred with 2 forks. Return to pressure cooker. Using tongs, place chicken mixture on pita breads. Serve with toppings.

Freeze option: Freeze cooled meat mixture and juices in freezer containers. To use, partially thaw in refrigerator overnight. Heat through in a saucepan, stirring occasionally and adding a water or broth if necessary.

1 gyro: 335 cal., 7g fat (1g sat. fat), 63mg chol., 418mg sod., 38g carb. (2g sugars, 2g fiber), 29g pro. **Diabetic exchanges:** 3 lean meat, 2½ starch, ½ fat.

BACON CHEESEBURGER BUNS

Here's a fun way to serve bacon cheeseburgers to a group without all the fuss of assembling sandwiches. Serve ketchup or barbecue sauce on the side for dipping.
—Marjorie Miller, Haven, KS

Prep: 1 hour + rising • **Bake:** 10 min.
Makes: 2 dozen

 2   pkg. (¼ oz. each) active dry yeast
 ⅔   cup warm water (110° to 115°)
 ⅔   cup warm 2% milk (110° to 115°)
 ¼   cup sugar
 ¼   cup shortening
 2   large eggs, room temperature
 2   tsp. salt
4½   to 5 cups all-purpose flour

FILLING
 1   lb. sliced bacon, diced
 2   lbs. ground beef
 1   small onion, chopped
1½   tsp. salt
 ½   tsp. pepper
 1   lb. Velveeta, cubed
 3   to 4 Tbsp. butter, melted
     Optional: Sesame seeds and
     ketchup or barbecue sauce

1. In a large bowl, dissolve the yeast in warm water. Add milk, sugar, shortening, eggs, salt and 3½ cups flour; beat until smooth. Stir in enough remaining flour to form a soft dough.

2. Turn onto a floured surface; knead until smooth and elastic, 6-8 minutes. Place in a greased bowl, turning once to grease top. Cover and let rise in a warm place until doubled, about 1 hour.

3. Meanwhile, in a large skillet, cook the bacon over medium heat until crisp. Using a slotted spoon, remove to paper towels. In a Dutch oven, cook the beef, onion, salt and pepper over medium heat until meat is no longer pink; drain. Add bacon and cheese; cook and stir until the cheese is melted. Remove from the heat.

4. Preheat oven to 400°. Punch dough down. Turn onto a lightly floured surface; divide into fourths. Roll each portion into an 12x8-in. rectangle; cut each into 6 squares. Place ¼ cup meat mixture in the center of each square. Bring corners together in the center and pinch to seal.

5. Place 2 in. apart on greased baking sheets. Bake 9-11 minutes or until lightly browned. Brush with butter. If desired, sprinkle with sesame seeds and serve with ketchup.

1 bun: 310 cal., 17g fat (7g sat. fat), 68mg chol., 720mg sod., 22g carb. (4g sugars, 1g fiber), 16g pro.

DID YOU KNOW?
It's easier to dice bacon when it's very cold, so pop it in the freezer for about 10 minutes before cutting it up.

BACON
CHEESEBURGER
BUNS

CHUNKY CHIPOTLE PORK CHILI

Perfect for using leftover pork roast, this tasty, easy recipe can be made ahead and reheated. It's even better the second day.
—Peter Halferty, Corpus Christi, TX

- -

Prep: 15 min. • **Cook:** 20 min.
Makes: 4 servings

- 1 medium green pepper, chopped
- 1 small onion, chopped
- 1 chipotle pepper in adobo sauce, finely chopped
- 1 Tbsp. canola oil
- 3 garlic cloves, minced
- 1 can (16 oz.) red beans, rinsed and drained
- 1 cup beef broth
- ½ cup salsa
- 2 tsp. ground cumin
- 2 tsp. chili powder
- 2 cups shredded cooked pork
- ¼ cup sour cream
  Sliced jalapeno pepper, optional

1. In a large saucepan, saute the green pepper, onion and chipotle pepper in oil until tender. Add the garlic; cook for 1 minute longer.

2. Add the beans, broth, salsa, cumin and chili powder. Bring to a boil. Reduce heat; simmer, uncovered, until thickened, about 10 minutes. Add pork; heat through. Serve with sour cream and, if desired, jalapenos.

Freeze option: Cool the chili and transfer to freezer containers. Freeze up to 3 months. To use, thaw in the refrigerator. Transfer to a large saucepan to heat through; add water to thin if desired.

1 cup: 340 cal., 14g fat (4g sat. fat), 73mg chol., 834mg sod., 24g carb. (3g sugars, 7g fiber), 27g pro.

CHUNKY CHIPOTLE PORK CHILI

RUSTIC ITALIAN
TORTELLINI SOUP

RUSTIC ITALIAN TORTELLINI SOUP

This is my favorite soup recipe. It's quick to fix on a busy night and full of healthy, tasty ingredients. It originally called for spicy sausage links, but I've found that turkey sausage, or even ground turkey breast, is just as good.
—Tracy Fasnacht, Irwin, PA

Prep: 20 min. • **Cook:** 20 min.
Makes: 6 servings (2 qt.)

- ¾ lb. Italian turkey sausage links, casings removed
- 1 medium onion, chopped
- 6 garlic cloves, minced
- 2 cans (14½ oz. each) reduced-sodium chicken broth
- 1¾ cups water
- 1 can (14½ oz.) diced tomatoes, undrained
- 1 pkg. (9 oz.) refrigerated cheese tortellini
- 1 pkg. (6 oz.) fresh baby spinach, coarsely chopped
- 2¼ tsp. minced fresh basil or ¾ tsp. dried basil
- ¼ tsp. pepper
  Dash crushed red pepper flakes
  Shredded Parmesan cheese, optional

1. Crumble sausage into a Dutch oven; add onion. Cook and stir over medium heat until meat is no longer pink. Add garlic; cook 1 minute longer. Stir in the broth, water and tomatoes. Bring to a boil.
2. Add tortellini; return to a boil. Cook for 5-8 minutes or until almost tender, stirring occasionally. Reduce heat; add spinach, basil, pepper and pepper flakes. Cook 2-3 minutes longer or until spinach is wilted and tortellini are tender. Serve with cheese if desired.
Freeze option: Place individual portions of cooled soup in freezer containers and freeze. To use, partially thaw in refrigerator overnight. Heat through in a saucepan, stirring occasionally; add broth or water if necessary.
1⅓ cups: 203 cal., 8g fat (2g sat. fat), 40mg chol., 878mg sod., 18g carb. (5g sugars, 3g fiber), 16g pro.

ALOHA BURGERS

ALOHA BURGERS

I love hamburgers and pineapple, so it just seemed natural for me to combine them. My family frequently requests these unique sandwiches. It's a nice change of pace from the same old boring burger.
—Joi McKim-Jones, Waikoloa, HI

Takes: 30 min.
Makes: 4 servings

- 1 can (8 oz.) sliced pineapple
- ¾ cup reduced-sodium teriyaki sauce
- 1 lb. ground beef
- 1 large sweet onion, sliced
- 1 Tbsp. butter
- 4 sesame seed or onion buns, split and toasted
- 4 lettuce leaves
- 4 slices Swiss cheese
- 4 bacon strips, cooked

1. Drain pineapple juice into a small bowl; add the teriyaki sauce. Place 3 Tbsp. in a resealable container. Add pineapple slices; toss to coat and set aside.
2. Shape the beef into 4 patties; place in an 8-in. square baking dish. Pour the remaining teriyaki sauce mixture over the beef patties; marinate 5-10 minutes, turning once.
3. Remove burger patties from marinade; discard the marinade. Grill, covered, over medium heat or broil 4 in. from the heat for 6-9 minutes on each side or until a thermometer reads 160°. Meanwhile, in a small skillet, saute onion in butter until tender, about 5 minutes; set aside.
4. Remove the pineapple slices from the marinade; discard marinade. Place the pineapple on grill or under broiler to heat through. Layer bottom buns with lettuce and onion. Top with the burgers, cheese, pineapple and bacon. Replace tops.
1 burger: 513 cal., 25g fat (11g sat. fat), 96mg chol., 716mg sod., 39g carb. (17g sugars, 3g fiber), 33g pro.

CREAMY CHICKEN RICE SOUP

I came up with this flavorful soup while making some adjustments to a favorite stovetop chicken casserole. We like this dish for lunch with a crisp roll and fresh fruit.
—Janice Mitchell, Aurora, CO

Takes: 30 min. • Makes: 4 servings

- 1 Tbsp. canola oil
- 1 medium carrot, chopped
- 1 celery rib, chopped
- ½ cup chopped onion
- ½ tsp. minced garlic
- ⅓ cup uncooked long grain rice
- ¾ tsp. dried basil
- ¼ tsp. pepper
- 2 cans (14½ oz. each) reduced-sodium chicken broth
- 3 Tbsp. all-purpose flour
- 1 can (5 oz.) evaporated milk
- 2 cups cubed cooked chicken breast

1. In a large saucepan, heat the oil over medium-high heat; saute carrot, celery and onion until tender. Add garlic; cook and stir 1 minute. Stir in rice, seasonings and broth; bring to a boil. Reduce heat; simmer, covered, until rice is tender, about 15 minutes.
2. Mix flour and milk until smooth; stir into soup. Bring to a boil; cook and stir until thickened, about 2 minutes. Stir in chicken; heat through.
1¼ cups: 312 cal., 9g fat (3g sat. fat), 71mg chol., 699mg sod., 26g carb. (6g sugars, 1g fiber), 29g pro. **Diabetic exchanges:** 3 lean meat, 2 starch, 1 fat.

SLOPPY JOES SANDWICHES

You'll love this quick, easy and economical recipe. Brown sugar adds a bit of sweetness, both for traditional sandwiches on buns or as a down-home topping for rice, biscuits or baked potatoes.
—Laurie Hauser, Rochester, NY

Takes: 30 min. • Makes: 4 servings

- 1 lb. ground beef
- 1 cup ketchup
- ¼ cup water
- 2 Tbsp. brown sugar
- 2 tsp. Worcestershire sauce
- 2 tsp. prepared mustard
- ½ tsp. garlic powder
- ½ tsp. onion powder
- ½ tsp. salt
- 4 hamburger buns, split

In a skillet, cook beef over medium heat until no longer pink; drain. Stir in ketchup, water, brown sugar, Worcestershire sauce, mustard, garlic powder, onion powder and salt. Bring to a boil. Reduce heat; cover and simmer for 15-20 minutes. Serve on buns.
1 sandwich: 439 cal., 16g fat (6g sat. fat), 75mg chol., 1360mg sod., 46g carb. (17g sugars, 2g fiber), 27g pro.

MEXICAN CHICKEN CHILI

Corn and black beans give this satisfying chili Mexican flair your whole family will love. Adjust the cayenne if you have small children or are looking for a little less zip.
—Stephanie Rabbitt-Schapp, Cincinnati, OH

Prep: 30 min. • Cook: 5 hours
Makes: 6 servings

- 1 lb. boneless skinless chicken breasts, cubed
- 1 Tbsp. canola oil
- 2 cans (14½ oz. each) diced tomatoes, undrained
- 2 cups frozen corn
- 1 can (15 oz.) black beans, rinsed and drained
- 1 can (14½ oz.) reduced-sodium chicken broth
- 1 can (4 oz.) chopped green chiles
- 2 Tbsp. chili powder
- 1 Tbsp. ground cumin
- ½ tsp. salt
- ¼ tsp. cayenne pepper

In a large skillet, brown chicken in oil. Transfer to a 5-qt. slow cooker. Stir in the remaining ingredients. Cover and cook on low until the chicken is no longer pink, 5-6 hours.
1⅓ cups: 254 cal., 5g fat (1g sat. fat), 42mg chol., 843mg sod., 31g carb. (6g sugars, 8g fiber), 23g pro.

TURKEY FOCACCIA CLUB

My family thinks this sandwich is pure heaven thanks to the cranberry-pecan mayo. Not just for the holidays—it's so good that I'm asked to make it all year long.
—Judy Wilson, Sun City West, AZ

Takes: 20 min. • **Makes:** 4 servings

- ½ cup mayonnaise
- ½ cup whole-berry cranberry sauce
- 2 Tbsp. chopped pecans, toasted
- 2 Tbsp. Dijon mustard
- 1 Tbsp. honey
- 1 loaf (8 oz.) focaccia bread
- 3 lettuce leaves
- ½ lb. thinly sliced cooked turkey
- ¼ lb. sliced Gouda cheese
- 8 slices tomato
- 6 bacon strips, cooked

In a small bowl, mix the first 5 ingredients until blended. Using a long serrated knife, cut focaccia horizontally in half. Spread cut sides with mayonnaise mixture. Layer bottom half with lettuce, turkey, cheese, tomato and bacon; replace bread top. Cut into wedges.

1 wedge: 707 cal., 41g fat (10g sat. fat), 96mg chol., 1153mg sod., 53g carb. (17g sugars, 2g fiber), 32g pro.

ONE-POT SPINACH BEEF SOUP

My idea of a winning weeknight meal is a beefy soup that simmers in one big pot. Grate some Parmesan on top and pass the saltines!
—Julie Davis, Jacksonville, FL

Takes: 30 min.
Makes: 8 servings (about 2½ qt.)

- 1 lb. ground beef
- 3 garlic cloves, minced
- 2 cartons (32 oz. each) reduced-sodium beef broth
- 2 cans (14½ oz. each) diced tomatoes with green pepper, celery and onion, undrained
- 1 tsp. dried basil
- ½ tsp. pepper
- ½ tsp. dried oregano
- ¼ tsp. salt
- 3 cups uncooked bow tie pasta
- 4 cups fresh spinach, coarsely chopped
  Grated Parmesan cheese

1. In a 6-qt. stockpot, cook beef and garlic over medium heat until beef is no longer pink, 6-8 minutes; crumble beef; drain. Stir in broth, tomatoes and seasonings; bring to a boil. Stir in pasta; return to a boil. Cook, uncovered, until the pasta is tender, 7-9 minutes.
2. Stir in the spinach until wilted. Sprinkle servings with cheese.

1⅓ cups: 258 cal., 7g fat (3g sat. fat), 40mg chol., 909mg sod., 30g carb. (8g sugars, 3g fiber), 17g pro.

CHICKEN PESTO SANDWICHES

These easy sandwiches are great for game day! They're not only tasty, but so easy to prep ahead and assemble later.
—Colleen Sturma, Milwaukee, WI

Takes: 30 min. • **Makes:** 6 servings

- 6 boneless skinless chicken breast halves (6 oz. each)
- ¾ cup prepared pesto, divided
- ½ tsp. salt
- ¼ tsp. pepper
- 1 jar (12 oz.) roasted sweet red peppers, drained
- 6 Ciabatta buns, split and toasted
- ¼ lb. fresh mozzarella cheese, cut into 6 slices

1. Flatten the chicken to ¼-in. thickness. Spread 1 Tbsp. pesto over each chicken breast; sprinkle with salt and pepper. Grill chicken, covered, over medium heat until no longer pink, 3-5 minutes on each side.
2. Spread 3 Tbsp. pesto over 6 slices of toast; layer with red peppers, chicken and cheese. Spread remaining pesto over remaining toast; place over top.

1 sandwich: 498 cal., 22g fat (6g sat. fat), 111mg chol., 1026mg sod., 27g carb. (6g sugars, 1g fiber), 43g pro.

**AIR-FRYER CHICKEN
PARMESAN PAGE 114**

Meaty Main Dishes

From beef, pork and lamb to chicken and turkey, this chapter is packed with hearty entrees that will fill up family and friends—no matter the occasion!

GRILLED HULI HULI CHICKEN

I got this grilled chicken recipe from a friend while living in Hawaii. It sizzles with the flavors of brown sugar, ginger and soy sauce. The sweet and savory glaze is fantastic on pork chops too.
—Sharon Boling, San Diego, CA

- -

Prep: 15 min. + marinating
Grill: 15 min.
Makes: 12 servings

- 1 cup packed brown sugar
- ¾ cup ketchup
- ¾ cup reduced-sodium soy sauce
- ⅓ cup sherry or chicken broth
- 2½ tsp. minced fresh gingerroot
- 1½ tsp. minced garlic
- 24 boneless skinless chicken thighs (about 6 lbs.)

1. In a small bowl, mix first 6 ingredients. Reserve 1⅓ cups for basting; cover and refrigerate. Divide remaining marinade between 2 large shallow dishes. Add 12 chicken thighs to each dish; turn to coat. Refrigerate, covered, for 8 hours or overnight.

2. Drain chicken, discarding marinade. Grill chicken, covered, on an oiled rack over medium heat for 6-8 minutes on each side or until a thermometer inserted into chicken reads 170°; baste occasionally with the reserved marinade during the last 5 minutes.

2 chicken thighs: 391 cal., 16g fat (5g sat. fat), 151mg chol., 651mg sod., 15g carb. (14g sugars, 0 fiber), 43g pro.

> "This never fails to impress, yet it's so simple to make. I've grilled, smoked, sauteed, deep-fried and air-fried the chicken, and it is amazing each and every way!"
> —JAMES SCHEND, DEPUTY CULINARY EDITOR

BALSAMIC CHICKEN WITH BROCCOLI COUSCOUS

This quick-fix recipe uses an ingenious shortcut: The broccoli cooks right along with the couscous. The result is pure satisfaction on a plate.
—*Taste of Home* Test Kitchen

- -

Takes: 30 min. • **Makes:** 4 servings

- 4 boneless skinless chicken breast halves (4 oz. each)
- ½ tsp. salt
- ¼ tsp. pepper
- 1 Tbsp. olive oil
- 2 Tbsp. balsamic vinegar
- 1 Tbsp. honey
- ¼ tsp. Italian seasoning

COUSCOUS

- 1 can (14½ oz.) chicken broth
- ¼ tsp. garlic powder
- ¼ tsp. pepper
- 3 cups frozen chopped broccoli, thawed and drained
- 1 cup uncooked couscous
- ¼ cup grated Parmesan cheese

1. Sprinkle chicken with salt and pepper. In a large skillet, heat oil over medium heat. Add chicken; cook 4-6 minutes on each side or until a thermometer reads 165°. Stir in the vinegar, honey and Italian seasoning; heat through.

2. Meanwhile, in a small saucepan, bring broth, garlic powder and pepper to a boil. Stir in broccoli and couscous. Remove from heat; let stand, covered, 5-10 minutes or until broth is absorbed. Stir in cheese. Serve chicken with couscous.

1 chicken breast half with 1 cup couscous: 397 cal., 9g fat (2g sat. fat), 69mg chol., 905mg sod., 47g carb. (9g sugars, 5g fiber), 35g pro. **Diabetic exchanges:** 3 lean meat, 2½ starch, 1 vegetable, ½ fat.

GRILLED HULI HULI CHICKEN

BLUE-RIBBON BEEF NACHOS

Chili powder and salsa season this zesty mixture of ground beef and refried beans.
—Diane Hixon, Niceville, FL

Takes: 20 min. • **Makes:** 6 servings

- 1   lb. ground beef
- 1   small onion, chopped
- 1   can (16 oz.) refried beans
- 1   jar (16 oz.) salsa
- 1   can (6 oz.) pitted ripe olives, chopped
- ½   cup shredded cheddar cheese
- 1   green onion, chopped
- 2   Tbsp. chili powder
- 1   tsp. salt
-     Tortilla chips
-     Optional: Sliced ripe olives, chopped green onions and diced tomatoes

In a large skillet, cook the beef and onion over medium heat until meat is no longer pink, breaking the beef into crumbles; drain. Stir in the next 7 ingredients; heat through. Serve over tortilla chips. Top with olives, onions and tomatoes if desired.

1 serving: 294 cal., 14g fat (6g sat. fat), 53mg chol., 1353mg sod., 19g carb. (5g sugars, 9g fiber), 20g pro.

ASK SARAH

DO I NEED TO COOK GROUND BEEF IN OIL?

If you're using lean ground beef or a stainless steel skillet prone to sticking, you may want to add 1 Tbsp. oil to the pan before adding the beef and onion.

BLUE-RIBBON
BEEF NACHOS

SESAME GINGER
BEEF SKEWERS

SESAME GINGER BEEF SKEWERS

My family loves the flavors of these zippy kabobs. They're perfect for a laid-back cookout in the backyard.
—Jasey McBurnett, Rock Springs, WY

- -

Prep: 20 min. + marinating • **Grill:** 5 min.
Makes: 6 servings

- 1 beef flank steak (1½ lbs.)
- 1 cup rice vinegar
- 1 cup soy sauce
- ¼ cup packed brown sugar
- 2 Tbsp. minced fresh gingerroot
- 6 garlic cloves, minced
- 3 tsp. sesame oil
- 2 tsp. Sriracha chili sauce or 1 tsp. hot pepper sauce
- ½ tsp. cornstarch
  Optional: Sesame seeds and thinly sliced green onions

1. Cut the beef into ¼-in.-thick strips. In a large bowl, whisk the next 7 ingredients until blended. Pour 1 cup marinade into a shallow dish. Add the beef; turn to coat. Refrigerate, covered, 2-8 hours. Cover and refrigerate remaining marinade.
2. Drain the beef, discarding marinade in dish. Thread beef onto 12 metal or soaked wooden skewers. Grill kabobs, covered, over medium-high heat or broil 4 in. from heat until meat reaches desired doneness (for medium-rare, a thermometer should read 135°; medium, 140°; medium-well, 145°), 4-5 minutes, turning occasionally and basting frequently using ½ cup reserved marinade.
3. To make the glaze, bring the remaining marinade (about ¾ cup) to a boil; whisk in ½ tsp. cornstarch. Cook, whisking constantly until thickened, 1-2 minutes. Brush the kabobs with glaze just before serving. If desired, top with sesame seeds and sliced green onions.

2 kabobs: 264 cal., 10g fat (4g sat. fat), 54mg chol., 1480mg sod., 18g carb. (15g sugars, 0 fiber), 24g pro.

"This recipe is so delicious and easy. The marinade is a real winner!"
— SARAH TRAMONTE, CULINARY PRODUCER

CRESCENT TURKEY CASSEROLE

CRESCENT TURKEY CASSEROLE

How do you make a dinner of turkey and vegetables appealing to kids? You turn it into a pie, of course! My version tastes classic but doesn't take any time at all.
—Daniela Essman, Perham, MN

- -

Takes: 30 min.
Makes: 4 servings

- ½ cup mayonnaise
- 2 Tbsp. all-purpose flour
- 1 tsp. chicken bouillon granules
- ⅛ tsp. pepper
- ¾ cup 2% milk
- 2 cups frozen mixed vegetables (about 10 oz.), thawed
- 1½ cups cubed cooked turkey breast
- 1 tube (4 oz.) refrigerated crescent rolls

1. Preheat oven to 375°. In a saucepan, mix the first 4 ingredients until smooth; gradually stir in milk. Bring to a boil over medium heat; cook and stir until thickened, about 2 minutes. Add the vegetables and turkey; cook and stir until heated through.

Transfer mixture to a greased 8-in. square baking pan.
2. Unroll crescent dough and separate into 8 triangles; arrange over turkey mixture. Bake until casserole is heated through and topping is golden brown, 15-20 minutes.

1 piece: 453 cal., 28g fat (6g sat. fat), 48mg chol., 671mg sod., 26g carb. (7g sugars, 3g fiber), 22g pro.

Turkey Biscuit Potpie: In a bowl, combine turkey breast, thawed mixed vegetables, one 10¾-oz. can condensed cream of chicken soup and ¼ tsp. dried thyme. Place in a greased 9-in. deep-dish pie plate. Mix 1 cup biscuit/baking mix, ½ cup milk and 1 lightly beaten large egg; spoon over top. Bake at 400° for 25-30 minutes.

Turkey Asparagus Casserole: In a bowl, combine turkey breast, one thawed 10-oz. package frozen cut asparagus, one 10¾-oz. can condensed cream of chicken soup and ¼ cup water. Bake at 350° for 30 minutes, topping with one 2.8-oz. can french-fried onions during the last 5 minutes.

GREEN CHILE ADOBADO POUTINE

This Canadian comfort-food classic is even better when served southwestern style as either an appetizer or an entree. Although these ribs are done without fuss in a slow cooker, you can also bake them at 325°, covered with foil, for about 45 minutes. Then uncover and bake them for another 20 minutes.
—Johnna Johnson, Scottsdale, AZ

- -

Prep: 50 min. • **Cook:** 3 hours
Makes: 8 servings

- 3 garlic cloves, unpeeled
- 4 dried guajillo or ancho chiles, stemmed and seeded
- 1 can (10 oz.) enchilada sauce, divided
- 3 cans (4 oz. each) chopped green chiles, divided
- 1 Tbsp. cider vinegar
- 2 tsp. dried oregano
- ½ tsp. ground cumin
- ½ tsp. salt
- ½ tsp. pepper
- ⅛ tsp. ground cinnamon
- 2 lbs. boneless country-style pork ribs, cut into 2-in. pieces
- 1 pkg. (32 oz.) frozen french-fried potatoes
- 1 cup queso fresco
   Pico de gallo, optional

1. Lightly smash the garlic cloves with the bottom of a heavy skillet to flatten. Cook in a large skillet over medium-low heat until softened and browned, about 10 minutes. Cool and peel.

2. In same skillet at the same time, cook dried chiles, pressing them against the bottom with a spatula or tongs until lightly toasted and fragrant, 1-2 minutes. Transfer to a bowl. Pour boiling water over chiles to cover; let stand 15 minutes. Drain.

3. Place the chiles and garlic in a food processor. Add ½ cup enchilada sauce, 2 cans green chiles, vinegar, oregano, cumin, salt, pepper and cinnamon; process until blended. Stir in remaining enchilada sauce and green chiles. Transfer to a 5- or 6-qt. slow cooker. Add ribs; turn to coat. Cover and cook on high until meat is tender, 3-4 hours. During the final 30 minutes, cook the fries according to package directions.

4. Remove pork; shred with 2 forks. Top fries with meat, queso fresco, enchilada gravy and, if desired, pico de gallo.

1 serving: 434 cal., 19g fat (7g sat. fat), 75mg chol., 1065mg sod., 31g carb. (2g sugars, 5g fiber), 28g pro.

TEST KITCHEN TIP
Cutting carbs? Swap some steamed or roasted cauliflower for the french fries.

GARLIC CHICKEN WITH MAPLE-CHIPOTLE GLAZE

This herby one-dish garlic chicken dinner is a updated version of an old standby recipe. The smoky flavors pair well with the savory chicken and the hint of sweetness from the maple syrup.
—*Taste of Home* Test Kitchen

Prep: 35 min. • **Bake:** 45 min.
Makes: 4 servings

- 4 chicken leg quarters
- 1¼ tsp. kosher salt, divided
- ½ tsp. coarsely ground pepper
- 1 cup all-purpose flour
- ½ tsp. dried rosemary, crushed
- ½ tsp. dried thyme
- ½ tsp. rubbed sage
- ½ tsp. dried marjoram
- ¼ tsp. dried parsley flakes
- 1 large egg, lightly beaten
- ½ cup 2% milk
- 1 Tbsp. lemon juice
- ½ cup plus 1 Tbsp. canola oil, divided
- ½ lb. red potatoes, halved
- 1 medium onion, halved and sliced
- 20 garlic cloves, peeled

GLAZE
- ⅓ cup maple syrup
- 2 tsp. finely chopped chipotle peppers in adobo sauce
- 1 tsp. Dijon mustard
- ¾ tsp. kosher salt
- ½ tsp. chili powder

1. With a sharp knife, cut leg quarters at the joints. Sprinkle chicken with ¾ tsp. salt and the pepper.

2. In a large bowl, combine the flour, rosemary, thyme, sage, marjoram and parsley. In a shallow bowl, combine the egg, milk and lemon juice. Add chicken pieces, 1 at a time, to flour mixture. Toss to coat. Dip chicken in egg mixture and coat again with flour mixture.

3. In a 12-in. cast-iron or other ovenproof skillet, heat ½ cup oil. Fry the chicken, a few pieces at a time, until golden brown, 5-6 minutes. Remove chicken and keep warm; drain drippings.

4. In the same skillet, cook the potatoes in the remaining oil until slightly tender, 8-10 minutes. Add onion and remaining salt; cook until onion is tender, 5-6 minutes longer. Stir in garlic; top with chicken.

5. Bake, uncovered, at 375° 45-50 minutes or until a thermometer reads 170°-175° and potatoes are tender.

6. In a bowl, combine the glaze ingredients. Brush over chicken just before serving.

1 chicken quarter with about ½ cup potato mixture: 834 cal., 55g fat (8g sat. fat), 142mg chol., 1112mg sod., 49g carb. (20g sugars, 3g fiber), 36g pro.

GARLIC CHICKEN WITH
MAPLE-CHIPOTLE GLAZE

BEEF BRACIOLE

CREOLE PASTA WITH SAUSAGE & SHRIMP

A creamy white sauce pairs well with the andouille sausage and slightly spicy seasonings in this pleasing pasta dish.
—*Taste of Home* Test Kitchen

- -

Prep: 20 min. • **Cook:** 15 min.
Makes: 6 servings

6	oz. uncooked fettuccine
1	large onion, chopped
2	celery ribs, chopped
½	cup each julienned sweet red, yellow and green peppers
¼	cup chopped green onions
6	garlic cloves, minced
4	Tbsp. butter, divided
1½	cups heavy whipping cream
¼	cup white wine or chicken broth
¼ to ½	tsp. Creole seasoning
¼	tsp. salt
⅛ to ¼	tsp. crushed red pepper flakes
⅛	tsp. pepper
½	lb. fully cooked andouille sausage, sliced
½	lb. uncooked shrimp (31-40 per lb.), peeled and deveined
2	cups chopped tomatoes

1. Cook fettuccine according to package directions. Meanwhile, in a large skillet, saute the onion, celery, peppers, green onions and garlic in 2 Tbsp. butter until tender. Stir in the cream, wine, Creole seasoning, salt, pepper flakes and pepper. Bring to a boil. Reduce the heat; simmer, uncovered, until thickened, 5-6 minutes.
2. In another large skillet, saute sausage and shrimp in remaining butter over medium heat until shrimp turn pink, 5-6 minutes. Drain the fettuccine; toss with vegetable mixture, tomatoes and sausage mixture.
1⅓ cups: 538 cal., 38g fat (21g sat. fat), 207mg chol., 653mg sod., 31g carb. (7g sugars, 3g fiber), 20g pro.

BEEF BRACIOLE

My great aunt used to make the most amazing braciole, but it was a laborious and time-consuming effort. I took her basic recipe and transformed it into a slow-cooker version, making it easier for today's hurried cook. Delicioso!
—Lisa Renshaw, Kansas City, MO

- -

Prep: 30 min. • **Cook:** 6 hours
Makes: 6 servings

2	jars (24 oz. each) tomato basil pasta sauce
1	tsp. crushed red pepper flakes
1	beef flank steak (1½ lbs.)
½	tsp. salt
½	tsp. pepper
2	large eggs, beaten
½	cup seasoned bread crumbs
8	thin slices prosciutto or deli ham
1	cup shredded Italian cheese blend
2	Tbsp. olive oil

1. In a 5- or 6-qt. oval slow cooker, combine the pasta sauce and pepper flakes. Pound the steak with a meat mallet to ½-in. thickness; sprinkle with salt and pepper.
2. In a small bowl, combine the eggs and bread crumbs. Spoon over beef to within 1 in. of edges; press onto meat. Layer with prosciutto and cheese. Roll up jelly-roll style, starting with a long side; tie at 2-in. intervals with kitchen string.
3. In a Dutch oven, brown meat in oil on all sides. Transfer to slow cooker; spoon sauce over meat. Cover and cook on low until beef is tender, 6-8 hours.
4. Remove meat from sauce and discard string. Cut into slices; serve with sauce.
1 serving: 515 cal., 25g fat (8g sat. fat), 155mg chol., 1881mg sod., 31g carb. (17g sugars, 6g fiber), 38g pro.

> "I first made this recipe for a work video and fell madly in love! Friends and family give it rave reviews."
> —SARAH FARMER, EXECUTIVE CULINARY DIRECTOR

CREOLE PASTA WITH
SAUSAGE & SHRIMP

CHEESEBURGER CUPS

A terrific recipe for moms with young kids and busy lives, this inexpensive, simple dish is made with handy ingredients and takes just a short time. Best of all, kids will go absolutely crazy for these darling dinner bites!
—Jeri Millhouse, Ashland, OH

- -

Takes: 30 min. • **Makes:** 5 servings

1	lb. ground beef
½	cup ketchup
2	Tbsp. brown sugar
1	Tbsp. prepared mustard
1½	tsp. Worcestershire sauce
1	tube (12 oz.) refrigerated buttermilk biscuits
½	cup cubed Velveeta

1. In a large skillet, cook beef over medium heat until no longer pink, breaking it into crumbles; drain. Stir in the ketchup, brown sugar, mustard and Worcestershire sauce. Remove from the heat; set aside.

2. Press each biscuit onto bottom and up sides of a greased muffin cup. Spoon beef mixture into cups; top with cheese cubes. Bake at 400° for 14-16 minutes or until cups are golden brown.

Freeze option: Freeze the cooled pastries in a freezer container, separating layers with waxed paper. To use, thaw pastries in the refrigerator for 8 hours. Reheat on a baking sheet in a preheated 375° oven until heated through.

2 cheeseburger cups: 440 cal., 16g fat (7g sat. fat), 78mg chol., 1142mg sod., 45g carb. (13g sugars, 0 fiber), 27g pro.

TEST KITCHEN TIP
Buy ground beef when it's on sale, brown it and freeze it for a head start on this recipe.

CHEESEBURGER CUPS

MEXICAN-STYLE STUFFED PEPPERS

We've always liked stuffed peppers, but everyone is pleasantly surprised at this mildly spicy version. For convenience, you can assemble these pretty peppers ahead of time and bake them later.
—LaDonna Reed, Ponca City, OK

- -

Prep: 20 min. • **Bake:** 50 min.
Makes: 6 servings

- 1 lb. lean ground beef (90% lean)
- ⅓ cup chopped onion
- ⅓ cup chopped celery
- 2 tsp. chili powder
- ¼ tsp. salt
- 1 Tbsp. canned chopped green chiles
- 1¼ cups salsa, divided
- 3 cups cooked rice
- 6 medium sweet red or green peppers
- ¼ cup water
- 1 cup shredded reduced-fat Mexican cheese blend

1. Preheat oven to 350°. In a large skillet, cook and crumble beef with onion and celery over medium-high heat until no longer pink, 5-7 minutes. Stir in the seasonings, green chiles, 1 cup salsa and rice.
2. Cut off and discard the tops from the peppers; remove seeds. Fill peppers with beef mixture. Place in a 13x9-in. baking dish coated with cooking spray. Add water to dish.
3. Bake, covered, 45-50 minutes or until peppers are tender and filling is heated through. Top peppers with the remaining salsa and the cheese. Bake, uncovered, until cheese is melted, 2-3 minutes.
1 stuffed pepper: 322 cal., 11g fat (5g sat. fat), 57mg chol., 506mg sod., 33g carb. (5g sugars, 3g fiber), 23g pro. **Diabetic exchanges:** 3 lean meat, 2 starch.

ZIPPY TURKEY ZOODLES

Eating healthy doesn't mean sacrificing flavor—and these spiced-up zoodles prove it. If you don't have a spiralizer, simply slice the zucchini julienne-style.
—Elizabeth Bramkamp, Gig Harbor, WA

- -

Prep: 25 min. • **Cook:** 20 min.
Makes: 4 servings

- 4 tsp. olive oil, divided
- 1 lb. ground turkey
- 1 small onion, finely chopped
- 1 jalapeno pepper, seeded and chopped
- 2 garlic cloves, minced
- ¾ tsp. ground cumin
- ½ tsp. salt
- ¼ tsp. chili powder
- ¼ tsp. crushed red pepper flakes
- ¼ tsp. pepper
- 3 medium zucchini, spiralized
- 4 plum tomatoes, chopped
- 1 cup frozen corn, thawed
- 1 cup black beans, rinsed and drained
- Optional: Chopped fresh cilantro and shredded cheddar cheese

1. In a large nonstick skillet, heat 2 tsp. olive oil over medium heat. Add turkey, onion, jalapeno and garlic; cook until turkey is no longer pink and vegetables are tender, 8-10 minutes, breaking turkey into crumbles; drain. Stir in seasonings; remove and keep warm. Wipe out pan.
2. In same pan, heat remaining olive oil; cook zucchini over medium heat until crisp-tender, 3-5 minutes. Stir in tomatoes, corn, beans and reserved turkey mixture; heat through. If desired, serve with cilantro and cheese.
1¾ cups: 332 cal., 14g fat (3g sat. fat), 75mg chol., 500mg sod., 26g carb. (7g sugars, 6g fiber), 29g pro. **Diabetic exchanges:** 3 medium-fat meat, 2 vegetable, 1 starch, 1 fat.

ZIPPY TURKEY ZOODLES

AIR-FRYER SMOKED PORK CHOPS

Air-fryer pork chops are so delicious and so easy to make. My husband loves them.
—Lynn Moretti, Oconomowoc, WI

Takes: 30 min. • **Makes:** 2 servings

- 1 **large egg**
- 2 **Tbsp. 2% milk**
- ½ **cup panko bread crumbs**
- ½ **cup finely chopped pecans**
- 2 **smoked bone-in pork chops (7½ oz. each)**
- 2 **Tbsp. all-purpose flour**
  Cooking spray
- 3 **Tbsp. balsamic vinegar**
- 1 **Tbsp. brown sugar**
- 1 **Tbsp. seedless raspberry jam**
- 1½ **tsp. thawed frozen orange juice concentrate**

1. Preheat air fryer to 400°. In a shallow bowl, whisk together the egg and milk. In another shallow bowl, toss bread crumbs with pecans.
2. Coat pork chops with flour; shake off excess. Dip in egg mixture, then in crumb mixture, patting to help adhere. Place chops in single layer on greased tray in air-fryer basket; spritz with cooking spray.
3. Cook until golden brown, 12-15 minutes, turning halfway through cooking and spritzing with additional cooking spray. Meanwhile, place remaining ingredients in a small saucepan; bring to a boil. Cook and stir for 6-8 minutes or until slightly thickened. Serve with chops.
1 pork chop with 1 Tbsp. glaze: 560 cal., 34g fat (10g sat. fat), 103mg chol., 1369mg sod., 35g carb. (22g sugars, 2g fiber), 32g pro.

SPICY FLANK STEAK

The cool and creamy sour cream sauce in this recipe is a wonderful accompaniment to the spicy steak. If you prefer, you can grill the steak over medium-high heat instead of broiling it.
—*Taste of Home* Test Kitchen

Takes: 25 min. • **Makes:** 6 servings

- ⅓ **cup sour cream**
- 2 **Tbsp. mayonnaise**
- ½ **tsp. garlic powder**
- ¼ **tsp. celery salt**
- 2 **Tbsp. chili sauce**
- 1 **Tbsp. lime juice**
- ½ **to 1 tsp. crushed red pepper flakes**
- ¼ **tsp. salt**
- 1 **beef flank steak (1½ lbs.)**

1. In a small bowl, combine the sour cream, mayonnaise, garlic powder and celery salt; cover and refrigerate until serving. Combine the chili sauce, lime juice, pepper flakes and salt; brush on each side of steak.
2. Broil 2-3 in. from the heat until meat reaches desired doneness (for medium-rare, a thermometer should read 135°; medium, 140°; medium-well, 145°), 4-6 minutes on each side. Let stand for 5 minutes. To serve, thinly slice across the grain. Serve with sour cream sauce.
3 oz. cooked beef with about 1 Tbsp. sauce: 230 cal., 14g fat (6g sat. fat), 57mg chol., 318mg sod., 2g carb. (2g sugars, 0 fiber), 22g pro.

DID YOU KNOW?

Flank steak is one of many cuts of lean beef. It packs in 10 essential nutrients, including more than 20 grams of protein per serving. Other lean cuts include top sirloin steak, strip steak and tenderloin.

SPICY FLANK STEAK

CHICKEN TIKKA MEATBALLS WITH GINGER RICE

Tikka is an Indian dish made of small pieces of meat or veggies marinated in spices. Our version features chicken meatballs served over flavored rice.
—*Taste of Home* Test Kitchen

Prep: 1 hour • **Cook:** 25 min.
Makes: 8 servings

```
 5   in. fresh gingerroot, peeled
 6   garlic cloves, halved
 4   tsp. canola oil, divided
1½   cups uncooked long grain rice
 3   cups water
 6   green onions, sliced
4½   tsp. garam masala, divided
 1   can (28 oz.) crushed tomatoes
 ½   cup heavy whipping cream
1½   tsp. salt, divided
 ⅔   cup chopped fresh
     cilantro leaves, divided
 ¼   tsp. pepper
 2   lbs. ground chicken
```
TOPPING
```
 ½   cup sour cream
 1   Tbsp. lime juice
 ¼   tsp. ground cumin
     Dash salt
```

1. Place the ginger in a food processor; process until it forms a paste. Remove and set aside. Repeat with garlic; remove and set aside.
2. In a small saucepan, heat 1 tsp. oil over medium heat. Add rice and 1 tsp. ginger paste; cook and stir until rice is lightly browned, 3-4 minutes. Stir in water; bring to a boil. Reduce heat; simmer, covered, until rice is tender, 15-20 minutes.
3. Meanwhile, for sauce, in a Dutch oven, heat remaining 1 Tbsp. oil over medium heat. Add half the garlic paste and half the remaining ginger paste. Cook and stir until fragrant, about 1 minute. Add half the green onions and 1 Tbsp. garam masala; cook and stir 1 minute longer. Stir in tomatoes, cream and ½ tsp. salt; heat through (do not allow to boil).
4. For meatballs, preheat oven to 375°. In a large bowl, combine half cilantro, the pepper and the remaining green onions, ginger and garlic pastes, 1½ tsp. garam masala and 1 tsp. salt. Add the chicken; mix lightly but thoroughly. Shape mixture into 1½-in. balls. Place the meatballs on

CHICKEN TIKKA MEATBALLS WITH GINGER RICE

a greased rack in a 15x10x1-in. baking pan. Bake until browned, 15-20 minutes. Transfer meatballs to sauce; cook until heated through. Stir in remaining cilantro.
5. For topping, combine sour cream, lime juice, cumin and salt. Fluff rice with a fork; serve with meatballs and sauce. Drizzle with topping; top with additional cilantro and green onions if desired.
1 serving: 441 cal., 21g fat (8g sat. fat), 95mg chol., 731mg sod., 42g carb. (6g sugars, 3g fiber), 24g pro.

> "This entree is a wonderful mashup of cuisines and flavors. The sauce is bright and is sure to become a family favorite."
> —MARGARET KNOEBEL, ASSOCIATE RECIPE EDITOR/TEST COOK

HERB-STUFFED
ROASTED CORNISH HENS

HERB-STUFFED ROASTED CORNISH HENS

If you're looking for an elegant dinner for two, we suggest these delightful Cornish game hens. As a bonus, crisp, tasty potatoes cook right alongside the meat.
—*Taste of Home* Test Kitchen

Prep: 20 min. • **Bake:** 70 min.
Makes: 2 servings

- 2 Cornish game hens (20 to 24 oz. each)
- 12 fresh sage leaves
- 4 lemon wedges
- 6 green onions, cut into 2-in. lengths, divided
- 2 Tbsp. butter, melted
- 1 Tbsp. olive oil
- 1 Tbsp. lemon juice
- 2 garlic cloves, minced
- 1 tsp. kosher salt or sea salt
- ¼ tsp. coarsely ground pepper
- 6 small red potatoes, halved

1. Preheat oven to 375°. Gently lift skin from hen breasts and place sage leaves under skin. Place lemon wedges and a third of the onions in the cavities. Tuck wings under hens; tie the legs together. Place in a small greased roasting pan.
2. Combine butter, oil, lemon juice and garlic; spoon half the mixture over hens. Sprinkle with salt and pepper.
3. Bake 30 minutes. Add potatoes and remaining onions to pan. Brush hens with remaining butter mixture. Bake until a thermometer inserted in the thickest part of thigh reads 170°-175° and potatoes are tender, 40-45 minutes longer.
4. Remove hens to a serving platter. Stir the potatoes and onions to coat with pan drippings. Serve with hens.
1 serving: 984 cal., 68g fat (22g sat. fat), 381mg chol., 1239mg sod., 29g carb. (3g sugars, 4g fiber), 64g pro.

CAST-IRON FAVORITE PIZZA

CAST-IRON FAVORITE PIZZA

Cast-iron skillets are the perfect vessel for a crisp, deep-dish pizza without needing any extra cookware. Our team developed this meaty pizza that is fabulous for any time of year.
—*Taste of Home* Test Kitchen

Prep: 30 min. + rising • **Bake:** 30 min.
Makes: 8 slices

- 1 pkg. (¼ oz.) active dry yeast
- ½ cup warm water (110° to 115°)
- ½ cup butter, melted and cooled
- 3 large eggs, room temperature
- ¼ cup grated Parmesan cheese
- 1 tsp. salt
- 3 to 3½ cups bread flour
- 2 Tbsp. yellow cornmeal
- ½ lb. ground beef
- ½ lb. bulk Italian sausage
- 1 small onion, chopped
- 1 can (8 oz.) pizza sauce
- 1 jar (4½ oz.) sliced mushrooms, drained
- 1 pkg. (3 oz.) sliced pepperoni
- ½ lb. deli ham, cubed
- ½ cup chopped pitted green olives
- 1 can (4¼ oz.) chopped ripe olives, drained
- 1½ cups shredded part-skim mozzarella cheese
- ½ cup shredded Parmesan cheese
  Additional pizza sauce

1. In a small bowl, dissolve yeast in warm water. In a large bowl, combine the butter, eggs, grated Parmesan, salt, yeast mixture and 2 cups flour; beat on medium speed until smooth. Stir in enough remaining flour to form a soft dough.
2. Turn dough onto a floured surface; knead dough until smooth and elastic, 6-8 minutes. Place in a greased bowl, turning once to grease the top. Cover; let rise in a warm place until doubled, about 1 hour.
3. Punch dough down; let rest 5 minutes. Grease a 12-in. deep-dish cast-iron skillet or other ovenproof skillet; sprinkle with cornmeal. Press dough into pan; build up edges slightly.
4. Preheat oven to 400°. In a large skillet, cook the beef, sausage and onion over medium heat until meat is no longer pink and onion is tender, 8-10 minutes, breaking meat into crumbles; drain. Spread pizza sauce over dough to within 1 in. of edges; sprinkle with the meat mixture. Top with the mushrooms, pepperoni, ham, olives, mozzarella and shredded Parmesan.
5. Bake until crust is golden brown and cheese is melted, 30-35 minutes. Serve with additional pizza sauce.
1 piece: 712 cal., 42g fat (19g sat. fat), 184mg chol., 1865mg sod., 48g carb. (3g sugars, 3g fiber), 36g pro.

MOM'S MEAT LOAF

Mom made the best meat loaf, and now I do too. When I first met my husband, he wasn't a meat loaf guy, but this recipe won him over.
—Michelle Beran, Claflin, KS

Prep: 15 min. • **Bake:** 1 hour + standing
Makes: 6 servings

- 2 large eggs, lightly beaten
- ¾ cup 2% milk
- ⅔ cup finely crushed saltines
- ½ cup chopped onion
- 1 tsp. salt
- ½ tsp. rubbed sage
- Dash pepper
- 1½ lbs. lean ground beef (90% lean)
- 1 cup ketchup
- ½ cup packed brown sugar
- 1 tsp. Worcestershire sauce

1. Preheat oven to 350°. In a large bowl, combine the first 7 ingredients. Add beef; mix lightly but thoroughly. Shape into an 8x4-in. loaf in an ungreased 15x10x1-in. baking pan.

2. In a small bowl, combine remaining ingredients, stirring to dissolve sugar; remove ½ cup for sauce. Spread the remaining mixture over meat loaf.

3. Bake for 60-65 minutes or until a thermometer reads 160°. Let stand for 10 minutes before slicing. Serve with reserved sauce.

1 piece: 366 cal., 12g fat (5g sat. fat), 135mg chol., 1092mg sod., 38g carb. (31g sugars, 0 fiber), 26g pro.

CHICKEN FRANCESE

CHICKEN FRANCESE

I grew up on this tender, lemony chicken Francese dish that's a classic in Italian cooking. It's delicious as is, but we often add sauteed mushrooms. Serve it with pasta or crusty bread to mop up all that delicious pan sauce.
—Joe Losardo, New York, NY

Prep: 20 min. • **Cook:** 20 min.
Makes: 4 servings

- 1 lb. boneless skinless chicken breasts
- 1 large egg, beaten
- ¾ cup dry bread crumbs
- 3 Tbsp. grated Parmesan cheese
- 1 tsp. dried parsley flakes
- ½ tsp. garlic powder
- ½ tsp. salt
- ½ tsp. pepper
- ¼ cup olive oil

LEMON SAUCE

- 1 cup water
- ⅓ cup lemon juice
- 2 chicken bouillon cubes
- Lemon slices

1. Pound chicken breasts with a meat mallet to ¼-in. thickness; slice into cutlets 1½ in. wide. Place beaten egg in a shallow bowl; in a separate shallow bowl, combine the next 6 ingredients. Dip chicken in egg, then in the crumb mixture, patting to help coating adhere.

2. In a large skillet, heat 2 Tbsp. oil over medium heat. Brown chicken in batches, adding oil as needed, until golden brown, 2-3 minutes per side. Remove; drain on paper towels.

3. For lemon sauce, add water, lemon juice and bouillon to skillet, stirring to loosen browned bits from pan. Bring to a boil over medium-high heat. Reduce heat; simmer, uncovered, until liquid is reduced by half, 8-10 minutes. Return chicken to the pan; toss to coat. Cook until heated through, 4-6 minutes. Serve with lemon slices.

1 serving: 318 cal., 19g fat (3g sat. fat), 111mg chol., 806mg sod., 10g carb. (2g sugars, 1g fiber), 27g pro.

MOUSSAKA

Moussaka is traditionally made with lamb, but I sometimes use ground beef instead. The recipe looks a bit daunting, but if you prepare one step while working on another, it will save time.

—Kim Powell, Knoxville, TN

- -

Prep: 45 min. • **Cook:** 30 min. + standing
Makes: 8 servings

- 3 medium potatoes, peeled and cut lengthwise into ¼-in. slices
- 1 medium eggplant, cut lengthwise into ½-in. slices
- 1½ lbs. ground lamb or ground beef
- 1 small onion, chopped
- 2 garlic cloves, minced
- 2 plum tomatoes, chopped
- 1¼ cups hot water
- 1 can (6 oz.) tomato paste, divided
- 1¼ tsp. salt, divided
- ½ tsp. dried oregano
- ½ tsp. paprika
- ½ tsp. ground cinnamon
- ½ tsp. ground nutmeg, divided
- 3 Tbsp. butter
- ¼ cup all-purpose flour
- 4 cups 2% milk
- 2 cups shredded mozzarella cheese

1. Preheat oven to 450°. Arrange potato and eggplant slices in 2 greased 15x10x1-in. baking pans, overlapping as needed. Bake until cooked through, 20 minutes. Set aside; reduce oven setting to 400°.

2. In a large skillet, cook lamb, onion and garlic over medium heat until meat is no longer pink, 7-9 minutes, breaking into crumbles; drain. Stir in tomatoes, water, tomato paste, ¼ tsp. salt, oregano, paprika, cinnamon and ¼ tsp. nutmeg. Bring to a boil. Reduce the heat; simmer, uncovered, 5 minutes.

3. In a large saucepan, melt butter over medium heat. Stir in flour until smooth; gradually whisk in milk. Bring to a boil, stirring constantly; cook and stir until thickened, 2-3 minutes. Stir in remaining 1 tsp. salt and ¼ tsp. nutmeg.

4. Arrange the parcooked potatoes in a greased 13x9-in. baking dish, overlapping as needed. Top with the lamb mixture. Arrange eggplant over top, overlapping as needed.

5. Top with the bechamel sauce. Sprinkle with mozzarella cheese. Bake, uncovered, for 30 minutes or until bubbly and golden brown. Let casserole stand 20 minutes before serving.

1 serving: 453 cal., 25g fat (13g sat. fat), 99mg chol., 700mg sod., 30g carb. (12g sugars, 4g fiber), 28g pro.

TEST KITCHEN TIP
Eggplant will stay fresh in your refrigerator crisper drawer for 7 to 10 days.

MOUSSAKA

BEEFY SWISS BUNDLES

AIR-FRYER CHICKEN PARMESAN

Quick, simple and oh-so-tasty, this air-fryer chicken Parmesan recipe is the perfect weeknight dish to have on hand. It's just as crispy as the classic, if not crispier!
—*Taste of Home* Test Kitchen

Takes: 20 min. • **Makes:** 4 servings

2	large eggs
½	cup seasoned bread crumbs
⅓	cup grated Parmesan cheese
¼	tsp. pepper
4	boneless skinless chicken breast halves (6 oz. each)
1	cup pasta sauce
1	cup shredded mozzarella cheese **Optional: Chopped fresh basil and hot cooked pasta**

1. Preheat air fryer to 375°. In a shallow bowl, lightly beat eggs. In another shallow bowl, combine bread crumbs, Parmesan cheese and pepper. Dip chicken in egg, then coat with crumb mixture.
2. Place the chicken in a single layer on greased tray in air-fryer basket. Cook until a thermometer reads 165°, 10-12 minutes, turning halfway through. Top chicken with sauce and cheese. Cook until cheese is melted, 3-4 minutes longer. If desired, sprinkle with chopped basil and additional Parmesan cheese and serve with pasta.
1 chicken breast half: 416 cal., 16g fat (7g sat. fat), 215mg chol., 863mg sod., 18g carb. (6g sugars, 2g fiber), 49g pro.

TEST KITCHEN TIP
When cooking in an air fryer, it's important not to overcrowd your basket because that will prevent the food from crisping and browning. Either cook your food in batches or invest in a larger air fryer.

BEEFY SWISS BUNDLES

Kids and adults alike are sure to devour these comforting meaty pockets. Boasting creamy mashed potatoes, gooey cheese and flavorful seasonings, they offer a lot to love.
—*Taste of Home* Test Kitchen

Prep: 20 min.
Bake: 20 min.
Makes: 4 servings

1	lb. ground beef
1½	cups sliced fresh mushrooms
½	cup chopped onion
1½	tsp. minced garlic
4	tsp. Worcestershire sauce
¾	tsp. dried rosemary, crushed
¾	tsp. paprika
½	tsp. salt
¼	tsp. pepper
1	sheet frozen puff pastry, thawed
⅔	cup refrigerated mashed potatoes
1	cup shredded Swiss cheese
1	large egg
2	Tbsp. water

1. In a large skillet, cook beef, mushrooms and onion over medium heat until meat is no longer pink, breaking the meat into crumbles. Add garlic; cook 1 minute longer. Drain. Stir in Worcestershire sauce and seasonings. Remove from heat; set aside.
2. On a lightly floured surface, roll puff pastry into a 15x13-in. rectangle. Cut into four 7½x6½-in. rectangles. Place about 2 Tbsp. potatoes over each rectangle; spread to within 1 in. of edges. Top each with ¾ cup beef mixture; sprinkle with ¼ cup cheese.
3. Beat egg and water; brush some over pastry edges. Bring opposite corners of pastry over each bundle; pinch seams to seal. Transfer to a greased baking sheet; brush with remaining egg mixture. Bake at 400° for 17-20 minutes or until golden brown.
Freeze option: Freeze unbaked pastries on a waxed paper-lined baking sheet until firm. Transfer to an airtight container; return to freezer. To use, bake on a parchment-lined baking sheet in a preheated 400° oven for 20-25 minutes or until golden brown and heated through.
1 bundle: 679 cal., 38g fat (16g sat. fat), 138mg chol., 865mg sod., 48g carb. (3g sugars, 6g fiber), 36g pro.

AIR-FRYER
CHICKEN PARMESAN

TACORITOS

This mild and meaty southwestern dish combines the delicious flavor of tacos with the heartiness of burritos. Your family is going to love 'em!
—Monica Flatford, Knoxville, TN

Prep: 40 min. • **Bake:** 20 min.
Makes: 8 servings

¼ cup butter, cubed
¼ cup all-purpose flour
4 cups water
3 Tbsp. chili powder
1 tsp. garlic salt
1 lb. ground beef
1 lb. bulk pork sausage
¼ cup chopped onion
1 cup refried beans
8 flour tortillas (8 in.), warmed
3 cups shredded
   Monterey Jack cheese
   Optional toppings: Shredded
   lettuce, chopped tomatoes,
   sliced ripe olives and sour cream

1. In a large saucepan, melt butter. Stir in flour until smooth; gradually add water. Bring to a boil; cook and stir for 1 minute or until thickened. Stir in chili powder and garlic salt. Bring to a boil. Reduce heat; simmer, uncovered, for 10 minutes.
2. In a large skillet over medium heat, cook the beef, sausage and onion until meat is no longer pink, breaking it into crumbles; drain. Stir in refried beans; heat through.
3. Spread ¼ cup sauce in a greased 13x9-in. baking dish. Spread 1 Tbsp. sauce over each tortilla; place ⅔ cup meat mixture down center of each tortilla. Top each with ¼ cup cheese. Roll up and place seam side down in baking dish. Pour remaining sauce over top; sprinkle with remaining cheese.
4. Bake, uncovered, at 350° 18-22 minutes or until bubbly and cheese is melted. Serve with optional toppings as desired.
1 tacorito: 627 cal., 40g fat (19g sat. fat), 111mg chol., 1131mg sod., 36g carb. (2g sugars, 3g fiber), 31g pro.

TACORITOS

PELOPONNESIAN CHICKEN PASTA

We love a homemade meal at the end of the day. But the prep involved? Not so much. My Greek-inspired pasta is lemony, herby and, thankfully, easy.
—Roxanne Chan, Albany, CA

Prep: 30 min. • **Cook:** 10 min.
Makes: 4 servings

- 1 can (14½ oz.) reduced-sodium chicken broth
- 1 can (14½ oz.) no-salt-added diced tomatoes, undrained
- ¾ lb. boneless skinless chicken breasts, cut into 1-in. pieces
- ½ cup white wine or water
- 1 garlic clove, minced
- ½ tsp. dried oregano
- 4 oz. multigrain thin spaghetti
- 1 jar (7½ oz.) marinated quartered artichoke hearts, drained and coarsely chopped
- 2 cups fresh baby spinach
- ¼ cup roasted sweet red pepper strips
- ¼ cup sliced ripe olives
- 1 green onion, finely chopped
- 2 Tbsp. minced fresh parsley
- ½ tsp. grated lemon zest
- 2 Tbsp. lemon juice
- 1 Tbsp. olive oil
- ½ tsp. pepper
  Crumbled reduced-fat feta cheese, optional

1. In a large skillet, combine the first 6 ingredients; add spaghetti. Bring to a boil. Cook until chicken is no longer pink and spaghetti is tender, 5-7 minutes.
2. Stir in artichoke hearts, spinach, red pepper, olives, green onion, parsley, lemon zest, lemon juice, oil and pepper. Cook and stir until spinach is wilted, 2-3 minutes. If desired, sprinkle with cheese.
1½ cups: 373 cal., 15g fat (3g sat. fat), 47mg chol., 658mg sod., 30g carb. (8g sugars, 4g fiber), 25g pro. **Diabetic exchanges:** 2 starch, 2 lean meat, 2 fat, 1 vegetable.

CORN DOG CASSEROLE

Reminiscent of traditional corn dogs, this fun main dish really hits the spot. It tastes especially good right from the oven.
—Marcy Suzanne Olipane, Belleville, IL

Prep: 25 min. • **Bake:** 30 min.
Makes: 10 servings

- 2 cups thinly sliced celery
- 2 Tbsp. butter
- 1½ cups sliced green onions
- 1½ lbs. hot dogs
- 2 large eggs
- 1½ cups 2% milk
- 2 tsp. rubbed sage
- ¼ tsp. pepper
- 2 pkg. (8½ oz. each) cornbread/muffin mix
- 2 cups shredded sharp cheddar cheese, divided

1. In a small skillet, saute the celery in butter 5 minutes. Add onions; saute until vegetables are tender, 5 minutes longer. Place in a large bowl; set aside.
2. Preheat oven to 400°. Cut the hot dogs into ½-in. slices. In the same skillet, saute the hot dogs until lightly browned, about 5 minutes; add to the vegetables. Reserve 1 cup mixture.
3. In a large bowl, whisk the eggs, milk, sage and pepper. Add remaining hot dog mixture. Stir in cornbread mixes. Add 1½ cups cheese. Spread into a shallow 3-qt. baking dish. Top with reserved hot dog mixture and remaining cheese.
4. Bake, uncovered, until golden brown, about 30 minutes.
1 cup: 578 cal., 38g fat (16g sat. fat), 108mg chol., 1307mg sod., 40g carb. (13g sugars, 4g fiber), 19g pro.

"I love corn dogs, and I love casseroles, so trying this was a no-brainer for me. Sage, green onions and sharp cheddar kick things up a notch. I crave this dish several times a year."
—MARK HAGEN, CONTENT DIRECTOR

CORN DOG CASSEROLE

SLOW-COOKED SIRLOIN

My family of five likes to eat beef, so this is a favorite. I usually serve it with homemade bread or rolls to soak up the tasty gravy.
—Vicki Tormaschy, Dickinson, ND

Prep: 20 min. • **Cook:** 3½ hours
Makes: 6 servings

- 1 beef top sirloin steak (1½ lbs.)
- 1 medium onion, cut into 1-in. chunks
- 1 medium green pepper, cut into 1-in. chunks
- 1 can (14½ oz.) reduced-sodium beef broth
- ¼ cup Worcestershire sauce
- ¼ tsp. dill weed
- ¼ tsp. dried thyme
- ¼ tsp. pepper
  Dash crushed red pepper flakes
- 2 Tbsp. cornstarch
- 2 Tbsp. cold water

1. In a large nonstick skillet, brown beef on both sides. Place onion and green pepper in a 3-qt. slow cooker. Top with the beef. Combine broth, Worcestershire sauce, dill, thyme, pepper and pepper flakes; pour over beef. Cover and cook on high until meat reaches desired doneness and vegetables are crisp-tender, 3-4 hours.

2. Remove beef and keep warm. Combine the cornstarch and water until smooth; gradually stir into cooking juices. Cover and cook on high until slightly thickened, about 30 minutes. Return beef to slow cooker; heat through.

3 oz. cooked beef with ¼ cup vegetables and ½ cup gravy: 199 cal., 6g fat (2g sat. fat), 68mg chol., 305mg sod., 8g carb. (2g sugars, 1g fiber), 26g pro. **Diabetic exchanges:** 3 lean meat, 1 vegetable.

SPICY SAUSAGE RIGATONI

My inspiration for this recipe came from a Cajun pasta dish I make with blackened chicken, but here I substitute Italian sausage. I love this dish. It makes a hearty meal that warms you up all over.
—Toni Dishman, Mooresville, NC

Prep: 10 min. • **Cook:** 25 min.
Makes: 6 servings

- 12 oz. uncooked rigatoni or large tube pasta
- 3 pork and chicken Italian sausage links (3½ oz. each), casings removed
- 1½ cups sliced fresh mushrooms
- 1 medium onion, chopped
- 2 garlic cloves, minced
- ¼ tsp. crushed red pepper flakes
- 1 can (10 oz.) diced tomatoes and green chiles, drained
- 1 carton (8 oz.) mascarpone cheese
- ¼ cup half-and-half cream
- ⅛ tsp. ground nutmeg
- 1 cup shredded fontina cheese
- ¼ cup grated Parmesan cheese
- 1 Tbsp. minced fresh parsley

1. Cook rigatoni or tube pasta according to package directions.

2. Meanwhile, in a large skillet, cook the sausage, mushrooms, onion, garlic and pepper flakes over medium heat for 8-10 minutes or until sausage is no longer pink and vegetables are tender, breaking up sausage into crumbles; drain. Add tomatoes, mascarpone cheese, cream and nutmeg; cook and stir over medium-low heat until sauce is blended. Stir in fontina cheese until melted.

3. Drain rigatoni; add to sausage mixture and toss to combine. Sprinkle with the Parmesan cheese and parsley.

1½ cups: 544 cal., 30g fat (16g sat. fat), 104mg chol., 627mg sod., 48g carb. (5g sugars, 3g fiber), 22g pro.

SPICY SAUSAGE
RIGATONI

SAUCY GARLIC CHICKEN

Roasted garlic lends a rich flavor to this chicken entree and complements the spinach nicely. Ideal for entertaining, the recipe can be assembled in advance and popped in the oven when guests arrive.
—Joanna Johnson, Flower Mound, TX

Prep: 40 min. + cooling • **Bake:** 35 min.
Makes: 6 servings

- 4 whole garlic bulbs
- 2 Tbsp. olive oil, divided
- 1 pkg. (9 oz.) fresh baby spinach
- ¾ tsp. salt, divided
- ½ tsp. coarsely ground pepper, divided
- 6 boneless skinless chicken breast halves (6 oz. each)
- 6 Tbsp. butter, cubed
- 6 Tbsp. all-purpose flour
- 3 cups 2% milk
- 2½ cups grated Parmesan cheese, divided
- ⅛ tsp. nutmeg
  Hot cooked pasta
  Optional: Chopped tomato and minced fresh parsley

1. Remove papery outer skin from garlic (do not peel or separate cloves). Cut tops off garlic bulbs; brush bulbs with 1 Tbsp. oil. Wrap each bulb in heavy-duty foil. Bake at 425° for 30-35 minutes or until softened. Cool for 10-15 minutes.

2. Meanwhile, place spinach in a greased 13x9-in. baking dish; sprinkle with ¼ tsp. each salt and pepper. In a large skillet, brown chicken in remaining oil on both sides; place over spinach.

3. In a large saucepan, melt butter. Stir in flour until smooth; gradually add milk. Bring to a boil; cook and stir 1-2 minutes or until thickened. Stir in 2 cups cheese, nutmeg, and remaining salt and pepper.

4. Transfer to a blender; squeeze softened garlic into blender. Cover and process until smooth. Pour mixture over chicken.

5. Cover; bake at 425° for 30-35 minutes or until a thermometer reads 170° and sauce is bubbly. Uncover; sprinkle with remaining cheese. Bake 5 minutes longer. Serve with pasta. Sprinkle with chopped tomato and minced parsley if desired.

Freeze option: Replace fresh spinach with 5 oz. frozen chopped spinach that has been thawed and squeezed dry. Cool unbaked casserole and sprinkle with remaining cheese; cover and freeze. To use, partially thaw in refrigerator overnight. Remove from refrigerator 30 minutes before baking. Preheat oven to 425°. Bake casserole as directed, increasing time as necessary to heat through and for a thermometer inserted in chicken to read 170°.

1 chicken breast half: 601 cal., 32g fat (16g sat. fat), 163mg chol., 1066mg sod., 23g carb. (7g sugars, 2g fiber), 55g pro.

SAUCY GARLIC CHICKEN

TEST KITCHEN TIP
You can save time when making this recipe by roasting the garlic bulb in advance. Then squeeze the softened garlic into a small container. Cover tightly and refrigerate for up to 2 weeks or freeze for up to 1 month.

WHITE WINE GARLIC CHICKEN

This garlic chicken is fantastic over cooked brown rice or your favorite pasta. Don't forget a sprinkle of Parmesan cheese too.
—Heather Esposito, Rome, NY

- -

Takes: 30 min. • **Makes:** 4 servings

  4 **boneless skinless chicken breast halves (6 oz. each)**
  ½ **tsp. salt**
  ¼ **tsp. pepper**
  1 **Tbsp. olive oil**
  2 **cups sliced baby portobello mushrooms (about 6 oz.)**
  1 **medium onion, chopped**
  2 **garlic cloves, minced**
  ½ **cup dry white wine or reduced-sodium chicken broth**

1. Pound chicken breasts with a meat mallet to ½-in. thickness; sprinkle with salt and pepper. In a large skillet, heat oil over medium heat; cook chicken until no longer pink, 5-6 minutes per side. Remove from pan; keep warm.
2. Add the mushrooms and onion to pan; cook and stir over medium-high heat until tender and lightly browned, 2-3 minutes. Add garlic; cook and stir 30 seconds. Add the wine; bring to a boil, stirring to loosen browned bits from the pan. Cook until the liquid is slightly reduced, 1-2 minutes; serve over chicken.
1 chicken breast half with ¼ cup mushroom mixture: 243 cal., 7g fat (2g sat. fat), 94mg chol., 381mg sod., 5g carb. (2g sugars, 1g fiber), 36g pro. **Diabetic exchanges:** 5 lean meat, 1 fat.

SAVORY ROASTED CHICKEN

When you want an impressive centerpiece for Sunday dinner or a special-occasion meal, you can't go wrong with this golden chicken. The moist, tender meat is enhanced with hints of orange, savory and thyme.
—*Taste of Home* Test Kitchen

- -

Prep: 10 min. • **Bake:** 1½ hours + standing
Makes: 10 servings

  1 **roasting chicken (6 to 7 lbs.)**
  1 **tsp. onion salt**
  ½ **tsp. dried thyme**
  ½ **tsp. dried savory**
  ¼ **tsp. grated orange zest**
  ¼ **tsp. pepper**
  1 **tsp. canola oil**

1. Place chicken on a rack in a shallow roasting pan. Carefully loosen the skin above the breast meat. Combine onion salt, thyme, savory, orange zest and pepper; rub half the herb mixture under the loosened skin. Rub chicken skin with oil; sprinkle with remaining herb mixture.
2. Bake at 375° for 1½-2 hours or until a thermometer inserted in the thickest part of thigh reads 170°-175°. Let stand for 10-15 minutes. Remove skin before carving. Skim fat and thicken pan juices for gravy if desired.
4 oz. cooked chicken: 197 cal., 8g fat (2g sat. fat), 86mg chol., 267mg sod., 0 carb. (0 sugars, 0 fiber), 29g pro. **Diabetic exchanges:** 4 lean meat.

ROAST BEEF WITH CHIVE ROASTED POTATOES

It's hard to believe that last night's beef roast could get any better, but it shines in this heartwarming dish.
—*Taste of Home* Test Kitchen

- -

Prep: 20 min. • **Bake:** 25 min.
Makes: 6 servings

  2 **lbs. red potatoes, cut into 1-in. cubes**
  2 **Tbsp. olive oil**
  2 **tsp. minced chives**
  ¾ **tsp. salt, divided**
  2 **medium onions, halved and thinly sliced**
  1 **lb. sliced fresh mushrooms**
  ¼ **cup butter, cubed**
  1 **garlic clove, minced**
  1 **tsp. dried rosemary, crushed**
  ¼ **tsp. pepper**
  ⅓ **cup dry red wine or beef broth**
  2 **cups cubed cooked roast beef**
  1 **cup beef gravy**

1. Place potatoes in a greased 15x10x1-in. baking pan. Drizzle with oil; sprinkle with chives and ¼ tsp. salt. Toss to coat. Bake, uncovered, at 425° until tender, 25-30 minutes, stirring occasionally.
2. Meanwhile, in a large skillet, saute onions and mushrooms in butter until tender. Add the garlic, rosemary, pepper and remaining ½ tsp. salt; cook 1 minute longer. Stir in wine. Add beef and gravy; heat through. Serve with potatoes.
1 serving: 379 cal., 15g fat (6g sat. fat), 66mg chol., 591mg sod., 35g carb. (6g sugars, 5g fiber), 24g pro.

UPSIDE-DOWN FRITO PIE

Using ground turkey is a smart way to lighten this hearty family pleaser!
—Mary Berg, Lake Elmo, MN

- -

Prep: 15 min. • **Cook:** 2 hours 5 min.
Makes: 6 servings

- 2 lbs. ground turkey or beef
- 1 medium onion, chopped
- 2 envelopes chili seasoning mix
- 1 can (10 oz.) diced tomatoes and green chiles, undrained
- 1 can (8 oz.) tomato sauce
- 1 can (15 oz.) pinto beans, rinsed and drained
- 1 cup shredded cheddar cheese
- 3 cups corn chips
  Optional: Sour cream, minced fresh cilantro and additional chopped onion

1. In a large skillet, cook turkey and onion over medium heat until meat is no longer pink, 8-10 minutes, breaking meat into crumbles; stir in chili seasoning. Transfer to a 3- or 4-qt. slow cooker. Pour tomatoes and tomato sauce over turkey.
2. Cook, covered, on low for 2-3 hours or until heated through. Stir turkey mixture to combine. Top with the beans. Sprinkle with cheese. Cook, covered, 5-10 minutes or until cheese is melted. Top with chips. If desired, serve with sour cream, minced cilantro and additional onion.
1⅓ cups: 524 cal., 26g fat (8g sat. fat), 118mg chol., 1662mg sod., 33g carb. (5g sugars, 6g fiber), 41g pro.

GRILLED CAESAR CHICKEN BREASTS

Marinated overnight in creamy Caesar dressing, this chicken grills up juicy and tender. It is a real hit with foodie friends and couldn't be easier.
—Marcia Wallenfeldt, Kent, OH

- -

Prep: 10 min. + marinating • **Grill:** 15 min.
Makes: 4 servings

- ½ cup creamy Caesar salad dressing
- 3 Tbsp. olive oil
- 3 Tbsp. Dijon mustard
- 6 garlic cloves, minced
- 4 boneless skinless chicken breast halves (6 oz. each)

1. In a shallow dish, combine dressing, oil, mustard and garlic. Add chicken; turn to coat. Cover and refrigerate for 8 hours or overnight.
2. Drain chicken, discarding marinade. Grill the chicken, covered, over medium heat or broil 4 in. from heat 7-8 minutes on each side or until a thermometer reads 165°.
1 chicken breast half: 318 cal., 18g fat (3g sat. fat), 100mg chol., 395mg sod., 2g carb. (0 sugars, 0 fiber), 35g pro.

TEST KITCHEN TIP
For more even cooking, use the flat side of a meat mallet to pound the chicken breasts to ¼-in. thickness.

SUMMER TURKEY KABOBS

These kabobs let you enjoy Thanksgiving flavors at any time of the year! We enjoy grilling them in the summer.
—Angela Mathews, Fayetteville, NY

- -

Takes: 30 min. • **Makes:** 6 kabobs

- 2 small yellow summer squash
- 2 small zucchini
- 1 can (about 15 oz.) whole potatoes, drained
- 2 Tbsp. olive oil
- 1 pkg. (20 oz.) turkey breast tenderloins
- ½ tsp. pepper
- ¼ tsp. salt
- 1 pkg. (5 oz.) torn mixed salad greens
- 1 cup salad croutons
- ½ cup red wine vinaigrette

1. Trim ends of yellow squash and zucchini; cut crosswise into 1-in. slices. Place slices in a large bowl; add potatoes. Pour oil over mixture, tossing to coat.
2. Cut the turkey into 24 cubes; add to the vegetables. Sprinkle with pepper and salt; toss again.
3. On 6 metal or soaked wooden skewers, alternately thread turkey cubes, squash, zucchini and potatoes. Grill, covered, over medium heat, turning occasionally, until the turkey is no longer pink and vegetables are crisp-tender, 12-15 minutes. Serve on salad greens with croutons. Drizzle with red wine vinaigrette.
1 kabob: 274 cal., 13g fat (1g sat. fat), 38mg chol., 720mg sod., 15g carb. (3g sugars, 2g fiber), 26g pro. **Diabetic exchanges:** 2 lean meat, 1 vegetable, 1 fat, ½ starch.

PORTOBELLO &
CHICKPEA SHEET-PAN
SUPPER PAGE 131

Taste of Home

Fish, Seafood & Meatless

Even the most die-hard landlubbers (and meat lovers!) will fall hook, line and sinker for the flavorful from-the-sea fare (and vegetarian options!) featured here.

SALMON GRILLED IN FOIL

This tender salmon steams up in foil packets, meaning easy cleanup later.
—Merideth Berkovich, The Dalles, OR

Takes: 20 min. • **Makes:** 4 servings

- 4 salmon fillets (4 oz. each)
- 1 tsp. garlic powder
- 1 tsp. lemon-pepper seasoning
- 1 tsp. curry powder
- ½ tsp. salt
- 1 small onion, cut into rings
- 2 medium tomatoes, seeded and chopped

1. Place the salmon, skin side down, on a double thickness of heavy-duty foil (about 18x12 in.). Combine garlic powder, lemon pepper, curry and salt; sprinkle over the salmon. Top with onion and tomatoes. Fold foil over fish and seal tightly.

2. Grill, covered, over medium heat until fish flakes easily with a fork, 10-15 minutes. Open the foil carefully to allow the steam to escape.

1 packet: 232 cal., 13g fat (3g sat. fat), 67mg chol., 482mg sod., 5g carb. (3g sugars, 1g fiber), 24g pro. **Diabetic exchanges:** 3 lean meat.

HONEY GRILLED SHRIMP

My husband was given this super simple recipe by a man who sold shrimp at the fish market. It's now become our family's absolute favorite shrimp recipe. We've often served it to company with terrific success. Enjoy!
—Lisa Blackwell, Henderson, NC

Prep: 20 min. + marinating • **Grill:** 10 min.
Makes: 8 servings

- ¾ cup Italian salad dressing
- ¾ cup honey
- ¼ tsp. minced garlic
- 2 lbs. uncooked shrimp (31-40 per lb.), peeled and deveined

1. In a bowl or shallow dish, combine the salad dressing, honey and garlic; remove and set aside ½ cup. Add the shrimp to the remaining marinade in the bowl. Turn to coat; cover and refrigerate for 30 minutes. Cover and refrigerate reserved marinade for basting.

2. Drain the shrimp, discarding marinade. Thread shrimp onto 8 metal or soaked wooden skewers. On a greased grill rack, grill, uncovered, over medium heat for 1½-2 minutes on each side. Baste with the reserved marinade. Grill 2-3 minutes longer or until shrimp are pink and firm, turning and basting frequently.

1 skewer: 175 cal., 5g fat (1g sat. fat), 168mg chol., 383mg sod., 14g carb. (13g sugars, 0 fiber), 18g pro.

SALMON GRILLED IN FOIL

MEDITERRANEAN BULGUR BOWL

You can transform this tasty bowl into an Italian version with mozzarella, pesto, tomatoes, spinach and basil.
—Renata Smith, Brookline, MA

Takes: 30 min. • **Makes:** 4 servings

- 1 cup bulgur
- ½ tsp. ground cumin
- ¼ tsp. salt
- 2 cups water
- 1 can (15 oz.) garbanzo beans or chickpeas, rinsed and drained
- 6 oz. fresh baby spinach (about 8 cups)
- 2 cups cherry tomatoes, halved
- 1 small red onion, halved and thinly sliced
- ½ cup crumbled feta cheese
- ¼ cup hummus
- 2 Tbsp. chopped fresh mint
- 2 Tbsp. lemon juice

1. In a 6-qt. stockpot, combine the first 4 ingredients; bring to a boil. Reduce the heat; simmer, covered, until tender, 10-12 minutes. Stir in garbanzo beans; heat through.

2. Remove from heat; stir in spinach. Let stand, covered, until the spinach is wilted, about 5 minutes. Stir in the remaining ingredients. Serve warm, or refrigerate and serve cold.

2 cups: 311 cal., 7g fat (2g sat. fat), 8mg chol., 521mg sod., 52g carb. (6g sugars, 12g fiber), 14g pro.

MEDITERRANEAN BULGUR BOWL

CHEESE
ENCHILADAS

CHEESE ENCHILADAS

You won't bring home leftovers when you take these easy enchiladas to a potluck. With a homemade tomato sauce and cheesy filling, they always go fast. You can substitute any type of cheese you wish.
—Ashley Schackow, Defiance, OH

- -

Prep: 25 min. • **Bake:** 25 min.
Makes: 8 servings

- 2 cans (15 oz. each) tomato sauce
- 1⅓ cups water
- 2 Tbsp. chili powder
- 2 garlic cloves, minced
- 1 tsp. dried oregano
- ½ tsp. ground cumin
- 1 cup sour cream
- ¼ cup minced fresh parsley
- ½ tsp. salt
- ½ tsp. pepper
- 4 cups shredded Monterey Jack cheese
- 2½ cups shredded cheddar cheese, divided
- 2 medium onions, finely chopped
- 16 flour tortillas (8 in.), warmed
  Optional toppings: Shredded lettuce, sliced ripe olives, chopped tomatoes and additional sour cream

1. Preheat oven to 350°. In a small saucepan, combine first 6 ingredients; bring to a boil. Reduce heat; simmer, uncovered, until thickened, 4-5 minutes, stirring occasionally.
2. In a large bowl, mix the sour cream, parsley, salt and pepper; stir in Monterey Jack cheese, 2 cups cheddar cheese and onions. Spread 2 Tbsp. sauce over each tortilla; top each with about ⅓ cup cheese mixture and roll up. Place in 2 greased 13x9-in. baking dishes, seam side down. Pour remaining sauce over top.
3. Bake, uncovered, 20 minutes. Sprinkle with remaining cheddar cheese. Bake until cheese is melted, 4-5 minutes. If desired, serve with toppings.
Freeze option: Cover and freeze enchiladas before baking. To use, partially thaw in the refrigerator overnight. Remove from the refrigerator 30 minutes before baking. Preheat oven to 350°. Bake as directed, increasing time as necessary to heat through and for a thermometer inserted in center to read 165°.

LEMON-GARLIC CREAM FETTUCCINE

2 enchiladas: 778 cal., 42g fat (23g sat. fat), 106mg chol., 1741mg sod., 66g carb. (4g sugars, 6g fiber), 34g pro.

LEMON-GARLIC CREAM FETTUCCINE

I've been making this for my family for years. It's both simple and indulgent enough to make it a go-to recipe.
—Anne Miller, Glenfield, NY

- -

Prep: 25 min. • **Cook:** 15 min.
Makes: 4 servings

- 3 tsp. grated lemon zest
- 2 tsp. minced fresh parsley
- 2 garlic cloves, minced
- 8 oz. uncooked fettuccine
SAUCE
- ¼ cup butter
- 1 small onion, chopped
- 2 garlic cloves, minced
- 1 tsp. grated lemon zest
- ½ cup heavy whipping cream
- ¼ tsp. salt
- ⅛ tsp. pepper
- 4 oz. cream cheese, cubed
- 2 Tbsp. lemon juice
- 2 plum tomatoes, chopped
- 2 tsp. minced fresh parsley
  Grated Parmesan cheese, optional

1. In a small bowl, mix lemon zest, parsley and garlic. Cook fettuccine according to package directions; drain.
2. For sauce, in a large skillet, heat butter over medium-high heat. Add onion; cook and stir 2-3 minutes or until tender. Add the garlic and lemon zest; cook 1 minute longer. Stir in the cream, salt and pepper. Whisk in the cream cheese until melted. Remove from the heat; cool slightly. Stir in lemon juice.
3. Add the pasta, tomatoes and parsley to skillet; toss to combine. Serve immediately with lemon zest mixture and, if desired, Parmesan cheese.

1 cup: 518 cal., 34g fat (21g sat. fat), 102mg chol., 346mg sod., 46g carb. (4g sugars, 3g fiber), 11g pro.

TILAPIA FLORENTINE

Get a little more heart-healthy fish into your weekly diet with this quick and easy entree. It's sure to become a favorite!
—Melanie Bachman, Ulysses, PA

Takes: 30 min. • **Makes:** 4 servings

- 1 pkg. (6 oz.) fresh baby spinach
- 6 tsp. canola oil, divided
- 4 tilapia fillets (4 oz. each)
- 2 Tbsp. lemon juice
- 2 tsp. garlic-herb seasoning blend
- 1 large egg, lightly beaten
- ½ cup part-skim ricotta cheese
- ¼ cup grated Parmesan cheese
  Optional: Lemon wedges and additional grated Parmesan cheese

1. Preheat oven to 375°. In a large nonstick skillet, cook the spinach in 4 tsp. oil until wilted; drain. Meanwhile, place tilapia in a greased 13x9-in. baking dish. Drizzle with lemon juice and remaining 2 tsp. oil. Sprinkle with seasoning blend.
2. In a small bowl, combine egg, ricotta cheese and spinach; spoon over fillets. Sprinkle with Parmesan cheese.
3. Bake until fish just begins to flake easily with a fork, 15-20 minutes. If desired, serve with lemon and additional Parmesan.
1 fillet with ⅓ cup spinach mixture:
249 cal., 13g fat (4g sat. fat), 122mg chol., 307mg sod., 4g carb. (1g sugars, 1g fiber), 29g pro.

RAGIN' CAJUN EGGPLANT & SHRIMP SKILLET

RAGIN' CAJUN EGGPLANT & SHRIMP SKILLET

We always have a large summer garden where lots of produce lingers into fall. That's when we harvest our onions, peppers, tomatoes and eggplant—key ingredients of this dish. This recipe turns Cajun with the holy trinity (onion, celery and bell pepper), shrimp and red pepper flakes.
—Barbara Hahn, Park Hills, MO

Prep: 30 min. • **Bake:** 35 min.
Makes: 4 servings

- 1 medium eggplant, peeled and cut into ½-in. cubes
- 3 Tbsp. olive oil
- 2 celery ribs, diced
- 1 medium onion, diced
- 1 small green pepper, seeded and diced
- 3 plum tomatoes, diced
- 1 tsp. crushed red pepper flakes
- ½ tsp. pepper
- 12 oz. uncooked shell-on shrimp (31-40 per lb.), peeled and deveined
- ½ cup seasoned bread crumbs
- 1½ cups shredded part-skim mozzarella cheese

1. Place the eggplant in a large saucepan; add water to cover. Bring to a boil. Reduce the heat; simmer, covered, until tender, 3-4 minutes. Drain.
2. Preheat oven to 350°. In an ovenproof skillet, heat oil over medium-high heat. Add celery, onion and green pepper; saute until tender, about 5 minutes. Reduce heat to medium; stir in tomatoes and eggplant. Saute 5 minutes. Stir in the seasonings. Add the shrimp and bread crumbs; saute 5 minutes longer, stirring well.
3. Bake for 30 minutes. Remove the skillet from the oven; top with the cheese. Bake 5 minutes more.
1 serving: 399 cal., 21g fat (7g sat. fat), 131mg chol., 641mg sod., 26g carb. (9g sugars, 5g fiber), 28g pro.

VEGGIE NICOISE SALAD

More and more people in my workplace are becoming vegetarians. When we cook or eat together, the focus is on fresh produce. This salad combines some of our favorite ingredients in one dish—and with the hard-boiled eggs and kidney beans, it delivers enough protein to satisfy those who are skeptical of vegetarian fare.
—Elizabeth Kelley, Chicago, IL

Prep: 40 min. • **Cook:** 25 min.
Makes: 8 servings

⅓ cup olive oil
¼ cup lemon juice
2 tsp. minced fresh oregano
2 tsp. minced fresh thyme
1 tsp. Dijon mustard
1 garlic clove, minced
¼ tsp. coarsely ground pepper
⅛ tsp. salt
1 can (16 oz.) kidney beans, rinsed and drained
1 small red onion, halved and thinly sliced
1 lb. small red potatoes (about 9), halved
1 lb. fresh asparagus, trimmed
½ lb. fresh green beans, trimmed
12 cups torn romaine (about 2 small bunches)
6 hard-boiled large eggs, quartered
1 jar (6½ oz.) marinated quartered artichoke hearts, drained
½ cup Nicoise or kalamata olives

1. For the vinaigrette, whisk together the first 8 ingredients. In another bowl, toss the kidney beans and onion with 1 Tbsp. vinaigrette. Set aside bean mixture and remaining vinaigrette.

2. Place potatoes in a saucepan and cover with water. Bring to a boil. Reduce heat; simmer, covered, 10-15 minutes or until tender. Drain. While potatoes are warm, toss with 1 Tbsp. vinaigrette; set aside.

3. In a pot of boiling water, cook asparagus for 2-4 minutes or just until crisp-tender. Remove with tongs and immediately drop into ice water. Drain and pat dry. In same pot of boiling water, cook green beans until crisp-tender, 3-4 minutes. Remove beans; place in ice water. Drain and pat dry.

4. To serve, toss asparagus with 1 Tbsp. vinaigrette; toss green beans with 2 tsp. vinaigrette. Toss romaine with remaining vinaigrette; place on a platter. Arrange vegetables, kidney bean mixture, eggs, artichoke hearts and olives over top.

1 serving: 329 cal., 19g fat (4g sat. fat), 140mg chol., 422mg sod., 28g carb. (6g sugars, 7g fiber), 12g pro. **Diabetic exchanges:** 3 fat, 2 vegetable, 2 medium-fat meat, 1½ starch.

ASK SARAH

HOW LONG DO HARD-BOILED EGGS STAY FRESH?
Hard-boiled eggs will last for 3-4 days in the fridge. Cook some for this salad and for quick breakfasts!

VEGGIE NICOISE SALAD

PINEAPPLE PORK STIR-FRY

There's no need for takeout when you've got this recipe in your collection. Omit the cayenne pepper if serving young kids.
—*Taste of Home* Test Kitchen

Takes: 30 min. • **Makes:** 6 servings

- 1 can (8 oz.) unsweetened pineapple chunks, undrained
- 3 Tbsp. cornstarch, divided
- 1 Tbsp. plus ½ cup cold water, divided
- ¾ tsp. garlic powder
- 1 pork tenderloin (1 lb.), cut into thin strips
- ½ cup soy sauce
- 3 Tbsp. brown sugar
- ½ tsp. ground ginger
- ¼ tsp. cayenne pepper
- 2 Tbsp. canola oil, divided
- 4 cups fresh broccoli florets
- 1 cup fresh baby carrots, cut in half lengthwise
- 1 small onion, cut into wedges
  Hot cooked rice

1. Drain the pineapple, reserving ¼ cup juice; set aside. In a bowl or shallow dish, combine 2 Tbsp. cornstarch, 1 Tbsp. water, the garlic powder and 1 Tbsp. reserved pineapple juice; add pork and turn to coat.
2. In a small bowl, combine soy sauce, brown sugar, ginger, cayenne and the remaining water, cornstarch and reserved pineapple juice until smooth; set aside.
3. In a large skillet or wok over medium-high heat, stir-fry pork in 1 Tbsp. oil until no longer pink; remove and keep warm.
4. Stir-fry the broccoli, carrots and onion in remaining oil until tender. Stir soy sauce mixture and add to the pan. Bring to a boil; cook and stir 2 minutes or until thickened. Add pork and pineapple; heat through. Serve with rice.
1 cup: 230 cal., 7g fat (1g sat. fat), 42mg chol., 1295mg sod., 21g carb. (13g sugars, 2g fiber), 19g pro.

**PINEAPPLE
PORK STIR-FRY**

SHRIMP MONTEREY

For a special occasion or any weeknight dinner, this cheesy seafood dish makes a lasting impression. We love it served over rice or pasta.
—Jane Birch, Edison, NJ

- -

Takes: 25 min. • **Makes:** 6 servings

- 2 Tbsp. butter
- 2 lbs. uncooked shrimp
  (31-40 per lb.),
  peeled and deveined
- 2 garlic cloves, minced
- ½ cup white wine or chicken broth
- 2 cups shredded
  Monterey Jack cheese
- 2 Tbsp. minced fresh parsley
  Hot cooked linguine, optional

1. Preheat oven to 350°. In a large skillet, heat butter over medium-high heat; saute shrimp and garlic just until shrimp turn pink, 3-5 minutes. Using a slotted spoon, transfer to a greased 11x7-in. baking dish.
2. Add wine to the skillet; bring to a boil. Cook until liquid is reduced by half; pour over shrimp.
3. Sprinkle with the cheese and parsley. Bake, uncovered, until the cheese is melted, 8-10 minutes. If desired, serve over linguine.
1 cup shrimp mixture: 321 cal., 17g fat (10g sat. fat), 228mg chol., 437mg sod., 2g carb. (0 sugars, 0 fiber), 34g pro.

PORTOBELLO & CHICKPEA SHEET-PAN SUPPER

This is a fantastic meatless dinner or an amazing side dish. It works well with a variety of sheet-pan-roasted vegetables. We enjoy using zucchini or summer squash in the summer, and you can also change up the herbs in the dressing.
—Elisabeth Larsen, Pleasant Grove, UT

- -

Prep: 15 min. • **Bake:** 35 min.
Makes: 4 servings

- ¼ cup olive oil
- 2 Tbsp. balsamic vinegar
- 1 Tbsp. minced fresh oregano
- ¾ tsp. garlic powder
- ½ tsp. salt
- ¼ tsp. pepper
- 1 can (15 oz.) chickpeas or garbanzo
  beans, rinsed and drained
- 4 large portobello mushrooms
  (4 to 4½ in.), stems removed
- 1 lb. fresh asparagus, trimmed
  and cut into 2-in. pieces
- 8 oz. cherry tomatoes

1. Preheat oven to 400°. In a bowl, combine the first 6 ingredients. Toss chickpeas with 2 Tbsp. oil mixture. Transfer to a 15x10x1-in. baking pan. Bake 20 minutes.
2. Brush the mushrooms with 1 Tbsp. oil mixture; add to pan. Toss the asparagus and tomatoes with remaining oil mixture; arrange around the mushrooms. Bake 15-20 minutes longer or until vegetables are tender.
1 mushroom with 1 cup vegetables: 279 cal., 16g fat (2g sat. fat), 0 chol., 448mg sod., 28g carb. (8g sugars, 7g fiber), 8g pro.
Diabetic exchanges: 3 fat, 2 starch.

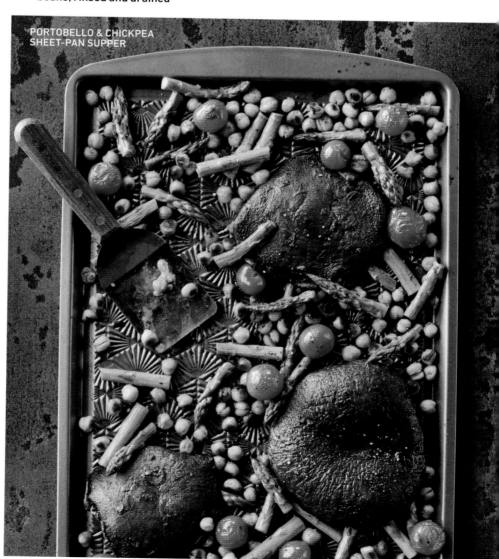

PORTOBELLO & CHICKPEA
SHEET-PAN SUPPER

EASY CRAB CAKES

ONE-POT BLACK BEAN ENCHILADA PASTA

I love this cozy pasta dish because it is ready in less than 30 minutes and is full of healthy ingredients—just what a busy weeknight meal calls for.
—Nora Rushev, Reitnau, Switzerland

Takes: 30 min. • **Makes:** 6 servings

- 4 cups uncooked mini penne or other small pasta
- 4 cups vegetable broth or water
- 1 can (15 oz.) black beans, rinsed and drained
- 1 can (14½ oz.) diced tomatoes, undrained
- 1 medium sweet yellow pepper, chopped
- 1 medium sweet red pepper, chopped
- 1 cup fresh or frozen corn, thawed
- 1 can (10 oz.) enchilada sauce
- 2 Tbsp. taco seasoning
- ½ cup shredded cheddar cheese
  Optional: Fresh cilantro leaves, cherry tomatoes and lime wedges

In a Dutch oven or large skillet, combine the first 9 ingredients. Bring to a boil; reduce heat. Simmer, uncovered, until pasta is al dente and sauce has thickened slightly, 12-15 minutes. Add cheese; stir until melted. Serve with desired toppings.

1¾ cups: 444 cal., 5g fat (2g sat. fat), 9mg chol., 1289mg sod., 84g carb. (8g sugars, 8g fiber), 18g pro.

TEST KITCHEN TIP
Serve this pasta with your favorite taco toppings, including avocado, sour cream and olives.

EASY CRAB CAKES

Ready-to-go crabmeat makes these delicate patties ideal for dinner when you are pressed for time. You can also form the crab mixture into four thick patties instead of eight cakes.
—Charlene Spelock, Apollo, PA

Takes: 25 min. • **Makes:** 4 servings

- 1 cup seasoned bread crumbs, divided
- 2 green onions, finely chopped
- ¼ cup finely chopped sweet red pepper
- 1 large egg, lightly beaten
- ¼ cup reduced-fat mayonnaise
- 1 Tbsp. lemon juice
- ½ tsp. garlic powder
- ⅛ tsp. cayenne pepper
- 2 cans (6 oz. each) crabmeat, drained, flaked and cartilage removed
- 1 Tbsp. butter

1. In a large bowl, combine ⅓ cup bread crumbs, green onions, red pepper, egg, mayonnaise, lemon juice, garlic powder and cayenne; fold in crab.
2. Place the remaining bread crumbs in a shallow bowl. Divide the crab mixture into 8 portions; shape into 2-in. balls. Gently coat with the bread crumbs and shape into ½-in.-thick patties.
3. In a large nonstick skillet, heat butter over medium-high heat. Add crab cakes; cook until golden brown, 3-4 minutes on each side.

2 crab cakes: 239 cal., 11g fat (3g sat. fat), 141mg chol., 657mg sod., 13g carb. (2g sugars, 1g fiber), 21g pro. **Diabetic exchanges:** 3 lean meat, 2 fat, 1 starch.

ONE-POT BLACK BEAN
ENCHILADA PASTA

SEASONED TILAPIA FILLETS

If you need a healthy and keep-it-simple solution to dinner tonight, you just found it. This restaurant-quality dish relies on everyday spices to deliver big flavor.
—Dana Alexander, Lebanon, MO

- -

Takes: 25 min. • **Makes:** 2 servings

- 2 tilapia fillets (6 oz. each)
- 1 Tbsp. butter, melted
- 1 tsp. Montreal steak seasoning
- ½ tsp. dried parsley flakes
- ¼ tsp. paprika
- ¼ tsp. dried thyme
- ⅛ tsp. onion powder
- ⅛ tsp. salt
- ⅛ tsp. pepper
  Dash garlic powder

1. Preheat oven to 425°. Place the tilapia in a greased 11x7-in. baking dish; drizzle with butter. In a small bowl, mix remaining ingredients; sprinkle over fillets.
2. Bake, covered, 10 minutes. Uncover; bake until fish just begins to flake easily with a fork, 5-8 minutes.
1 fillet: 193 cal., 7g fat (4g sat. fat), 98mg chol., 589mg sod., 1g carb. (0 sugars, 0 fiber), 32g pro. **Diabetic exchanges:** 5 lean meat, 1½ fat.

TEST KITCHEN TIP
Tilapia is a freshwater, farmed fish with a mild flavor and medium-firm texture. Sole, catfish and roughy can be substituted for tilapia.

CREAMY TOMATO SHRIMP WITH PENNE

People love this creamy pasta and think it's complicated, but jarred sauces make it so quick to prepare. It feels special enough for festive dinners.
—Cassandra Gourley, Williams, AZ

- -

Takes: 20 min. • **Makes:** 4 servings

- 2 cups uncooked penne pasta
- 2 Tbsp. olive oil
- 1 lb. uncooked shrimp (31-40 per lb.), peeled and deveined
- 1 tsp. minced garlic
- ½ tsp. crushed red pepper flakes
- 1½ cups pasta sauce
- 1 carton (10 oz.) refrigerated Alfredo sauce
- 2 Tbsp. butter
- ¼ tsp. salt
- ⅛ tsp. pepper
- 2 Tbsp. minced fresh parsley

1. Cook the pasta according to package directions. Meanwhile, in a large skillet, heat oil over medium heat. Add shrimp, garlic and pepper flakes; cook and stir until shrimp turn pink, 3-5 minutes. Stir in pasta sauce, Alfredo sauce, butter, salt and pepper; heat through.
2. Drain pasta; serve with shrimp mixture. Sprinkle with parsley.
1 serving: 554 cal., 30g fat (13g sat. fat), 188mg chol., 1097mg sod., 42g carb. (11g sugars, 4g fiber), 30g pro.

SEASONED TILAPIA FILLETS

BUTTERNUT & PORTOBELLO LASAGNA

Lasagna gets fresh flavor and color when you make it with roasted butternut squash, portobello mushrooms, basil and spinach.
—Edward and Danielle Walker, Traverse City, MI

Prep: 1 hour • Bake: 45 min. + standing
Makes: 12 servings

- 1 pkg. (10 oz.) frozen cubed butternut squash, thawed
- 2 tsp. olive oil
- 1 tsp. brown sugar
- ¼ tsp. salt
- ⅛ tsp. pepper

MUSHROOMS
- 4 large portobello mushrooms, coarsely chopped
- 2 tsp. balsamic vinegar
- 2 tsp. olive oil
- ¼ tsp. salt
- ⅛ tsp. pepper

SAUCE
- 2 cans (28 oz. each) whole tomatoes, undrained
- 2 tsp. olive oil
- 2 garlic cloves, minced
- 1 tsp. crushed red pepper flakes
- ½ cup fresh basil leaves, thinly sliced
- ¼ tsp. salt
- ⅛ tsp. pepper

LASAGNA
- 9 no-cook lasagna noodles
- 4 oz. fresh baby spinach (about 5 cups)
- 3 cups part-skim ricotta cheese
- 1½ cups shredded part-skim mozzarella cheese

BUTTERNUT & PORTOBELLO LASAGNA

1. Preheat oven to 350°. In a large bowl, combine the first 5 ingredients. In another bowl, combine the ingredients for the mushrooms. Transfer the vegetables to 2 separate foil-lined 15x10x1-in. baking pans. Roast 14-16 minutes or until tender, stirring occasionally.
2. Meanwhile, for sauce, drain tomatoes, reserving juices; coarsely chop tomatoes. In a large saucepan, heat oil over medium heat. Add garlic and pepper flakes; cook 1 minute longer. Stir in chopped tomatoes, reserved tomato juices, basil, salt and pepper; bring to a boil. Reduce the heat; simmer, uncovered, 35-45 minutes or until thickened, stirring occasionally.
3. Spread 1 cup sauce into a greased 13x9-in. baking dish. Layer with 3 lasagna noodles, 1 cup sauce, the spinach and the mushrooms. Continue layering with 3 noodles, 1 cup sauce, ricotta cheese and roasted squash. Top with remaining noodles and sauce. Sprinkle with the mozzarella cheese.
4. Bake, covered, 30 minutes. Bake, uncovered, 15-20 minutes longer or until bubbly. Let stand for 15 minutes before serving.
1 piece: 252 cal., 10g fat (5g sat. fat), 27mg chol., 508mg sod., 25g carb. (5g sugars, 4g fiber), 15g pro. **Diabetic exchanges:** 2 starch, 1 medium-fat meat, ½ fat.

RUSTIC SUMMER VEGETABLE PASTA

My veggie pasta proves you can't have too much of a good thing. Feel free to change it up with whatever fresh veggies are in the garden or at the farmers market.
—Bryn Namavari, Chicago, IL

Prep: 15 min. • **Cook:** 30 min.
Makes: 8 servings

- 3 Tbsp. olive oil, divided
- 1 medium zucchini, cut into ¾-in. pieces
- 1 medium yellow summer squash, cut into ¾-in. pieces
- 1 medium onion, chopped
- 1 medium eggplant, peeled and cut into ¾-in. pieces
- 2 cups sliced fresh mushrooms
- 2 garlic cloves, minced
- ¾ tsp. crushed red pepper flakes
- 1 can (28 oz.) crushed tomatoes
- ½ tsp. salt
- ½ tsp. pepper
- 1 Tbsp. minced fresh oregano or 1 tsp. dried oregano
- 1 Tbsp. minced fresh parsley
- 3 Tbsp. minced fresh basil or 1 Tbsp. dried basil, divided
- 1 pkg. (14½ oz.) uncooked multigrain spaghetti
- ½ cup shredded Parmesan cheese

1. In a 6-qt. stockpot, heat 1 Tbsp. oil over medium-high heat. Add the zucchini and yellow squash; cook and stir until tender. Remove from pan.
2. In the same pot, heat 1 Tbsp. oil over medium-high heat. Add onion, eggplant and mushrooms; cook and stir until tender. Add the garlic and pepper flakes; cook 1 minute longer. Add the tomatoes, salt and pepper. Stir in the oregano, parsley and half the basil; bring to a boil. Reduce heat; simmer, uncovered, 15 minutes, stirring occasionally.
3. Meanwhile, cook spaghetti according to package directions. Drain; add spaghetti and squash to vegetable mixture. Drizzle with remaining oil; toss to combine. Top with cheese and remaining basil.
2 cups: 315 cal., 8g fat (2g sat. fat), 4mg chol., 445mg sod., 50g carb. (9g sugars, 8g fiber), 15g pro.

BAKED FISH & RICE

The first time I tried this meal-in-one dish, it was an instant hit at our house. Fish and rice are a tasty change of pace from traditional meat-and-potato fare.
—Jo Groth, Plainfield, IA

Prep: 5 min. • **Bake:** 35 min.
Makes: 4 servings

- 1½ cups chicken broth
- ½ cup uncooked long grain rice
- ¼ tsp. Italian seasoning
- ¼ tsp. garlic powder
- 3 cups frozen chopped broccoli, thawed and drained
- 1 Tbsp. grated Parmesan cheese
- 1 can (2.8 oz.) french-fried onions, divided
- 1 lb. cod
  Dash paprika
- ½ cup shredded cheddar cheese

1. In a large saucepan, combine broth, rice, Italian seasoning and garlic powder; bring to a boil. Transfer to a greased 11x7-in. baking dish. Cover and bake at 375° for 10 minutes. Add the broccoli, Parmesan cheese and half the onions. Top with fish fillets; sprinkle with paprika.
2. Cover and bake 20-25 minutes longer or until the fish flakes easily with a fork. Uncover; sprinkle with cheddar cheese and remaining onions. Return to the oven for 3 minutes or until cheese is melted.
1 cup: 392 cal., 16g fat (6g sat. fat), 81mg chol., 722mg sod., 31g carb. (2g sugars, 2g fiber), 29g pro.

RUSTIC SUMMER VEGETABLE PASTA

SOUTHERN SHRIMP & GRITS

A southern specialty, sometimes called breakfast shrimp, this dish tastes wonderful for brunch or dinner, or anytime company's coming. It's down-home comfort food at its very finest.

—Mandy Rivers, Lexington, SC

- -

Prep: 15 min. • **Cook:** 20 min.
Makes: 4 servings

- 2 cups reduced-sodium chicken broth
- 2 cups 2% milk
- ⅓ cup butter, cubed
- ¾ tsp. salt
- ½ tsp. pepper
- ¾ cup uncooked old-fashioned grits
- 1 cup shredded cheddar cheese

SHRIMP

- 8 thick-sliced bacon strips, chopped
- 1 lb. uncooked shrimp (31-40 per lb.), peeled and deveined
- 3 garlic cloves, minced
- 1 tsp. Cajun or blackened seasoning
- 4 green onions, chopped

1. In a large saucepan, bring the broth, milk, butter, salt and pepper to a boil. Slowly stir in grits. Reduce heat. Cover and cook 15-20 minutes or until thickened, stirring occasionally. Stir in cheese until melted. Set aside and keep warm.

2. In a large skillet, cook the bacon over medium heat until crisp. Remove to paper towels with a slotted spoon and drain, reserving 4 tsp. drippings. Saute the shrimp, garlic and seasoning in drippings until shrimp turn pink. Stir in reserved bacon; heat through. Serve with grits and sprinkle with onions.

1 cup grits with ½ cup shrimp mixture:
674 cal., 42g fat (22g sat. fat), 241mg chol., 1845mg sod., 33g carb. (7g sugars, 1g fiber), 41g pro.

SOUTHERN SHRIMP & GRITS

MARTHA'S
FISH TACOS

MARTHA'S FISH TACOS

We can't get enough barbecued fish at our house. This recipe can be made ahead and served cold, or you can eat it hot off the grill. It's fantastic either way!
—Martha Benoit, Proctorsville, VT

Prep: 25 min. • **Grill:** 10 min.
Makes: 6 servings

2	**large ears sweet corn, husked**
1	**tsp. butter, softened**
⅛	**tsp. salt**
⅛	**tsp. pepper**
1	**haddock fillet (8 oz.)**
2	**tsp. chili powder, divided**
2	**cups shredded lettuce**
2	**medium tomatoes, seeded and chopped**
1	**medium sweet red pepper, chopped**
1	**medium ripe avocado, peeled and chopped**
3	**Tbsp. taco sauce**
2	**Tbsp. lime juice, divided**
1	**Tbsp. minced fresh cilantro**
1½	**tsp. grated lime zest**
12	**flour tortillas (8 in.)**

1. Spread corn with butter and sprinkle with salt and pepper. Grill, covered, over medium heat until tender, 10-12 minutes, turning occasionally.

2. Meanwhile, sprinkle fish with 1 tsp. chili powder. On a lightly oiled grill rack, grill fish, covered, over medium heat until fish flakes easily with a fork, 7-9 minutes.

3. Cool corn slightly; remove kernels from cobs. Place in a large bowl. Add the lettuce, tomatoes, red pepper, avocado, taco sauce, 1 Tbsp. lime juice, cilantro, lime zest and the remaining chili powder.

4. Drizzle remaining lime juice over fish; cut into ½-in. cubes.

5. Add fish to corn mixture. Spoon ½ cup mixture over each tortilla.

2 tacos: 446 cal., 12g fat (2g sat. fat), 23mg chol., 650mg sod., 68g carb. (5g sugars, 5g fiber), 19g pro.

SOUTHWEST VEGETARIAN BAKE

SOUTHWEST VEGETARIAN BAKE

This veggie-packed casserole hits the spot on chilly nights. But it's equally good anytime I have a taste for Mexican food with all the fixings.
—Patricia Gale, Monticello, IL

Prep: 40 min. • **Bake:** 35 min. + standing
Makes: 8 servings

¾	**cup uncooked brown rice**
1½	**cups water**
1	**can (15 oz.) black beans, rinsed and drained**
1	**can (11 oz.) Mexicorn, drained**
1	**can (10 oz.) diced tomatoes and green chiles**
1	**cup shredded reduced-fat cheddar cheese**
1	**cup salsa**
1	**cup reduced-fat sour cream**
¼	**tsp. pepper**
½	**cup chopped red onion**
1	**can (2¼ oz.) sliced ripe olives, drained**
1	**cup shredded reduced-fat Mexican cheese blend**

1. In a small saucepan, bring the rice and water to a boil. Reduce the heat; simmer, covered, until rice is tender, 35-40 minutes.

2. Preheat oven to 350°. Place beans, corn, tomatoes, cheddar cheese and rice in a large bowl; stir in salsa, sour cream and pepper. Transfer to a shallow 2½-qt. baking dish coated with cooking spray. Sprinkle with onion and olives.

3. Bake, uncovered, 30 minutes. Sprinkle with Mexican cheese; bake, uncovered, until heated through and the cheese is melted, 5-10 minutes longer. Let stand for 10 minutes before serving.

1 cup: 285 cal., 10g fat (5g sat. fat), 21mg chol., 759mg sod., 36g carb. (6g sugars, 4g fiber), 15g pro. **Diabetic exchanges:** 2 starch, 2 vegetable, 1 lean meat, 1 fat.

SALSA SPAGHETTI SQUASH

If you want spaghetti but are eating gluten free or trying to keep a lid on carbs, there's always spaghetti squash as a flavorful alternative. Subtly sweet, tender and satisfying, this is one colorful dish.
—Clara Coulson Minney, Washington Court House, OH

- -

Takes: 30 min. • **Makes:** 4 servings

- 1   medium spaghetti squash
- 1   medium onion, chopped
- 2   cups salsa
- 1   can (15 oz.) black beans, rinsed and drained
- 3   Tbsp. minced fresh cilantro
- 1   medium ripe avocado, peeled and cubed

1. Cut squash lengthwise in half; discard seeds. Place the squash on a microwave-safe plate, cut side down. Microwave, uncovered, on high for 15-18 minutes or until tender.

2. Meanwhile, in a lightly oiled nonstick skillet, cook and stir onion over medium heat until tender. Stir in salsa, beans and cilantro; heat through. Gently stir in the avocado; cook 1 minute longer.

3. When squash is cool enough to handle, use a fork to separate strands. Serve squash topped with salsa mixture.

1 cup: 308 cal., 9g fat (2g sat. fat), 0 chol., 822mg sod., 46g carb. (6g sugars, 16g fiber), 8g pro.

VEGETABLE PAD THAI

VEGETABLE PAD THAI

Classic flavors of Thailand abound in this fragrant, delicious dish featuring peanuts, tofu and noodles. Tofu gives the entree its satisfying protein.
—Sara Landry, Brookline, MA

- -

Prep: 25 min. • **Cook:** 15 min.
Makes: 6 servings

- 1   pkg. (12 oz.) whole wheat fettuccine
- ¼   cup rice vinegar
- 3   Tbsp. reduced-sodium soy sauce
- 2   Tbsp. brown sugar
- 2   Tbsp. fish sauce or additional reduced-sodium soy sauce
- 1   Tbsp. lime juice
     Dash Louisiana-style hot sauce
- 3   tsp. canola oil, divided
- 1   pkg. (12 oz.) extra-firm tofu, drained and cut into ½-in. cubes
- 2   medium carrots, grated
- 2   cups fresh snow peas
- 3   garlic cloves, minced
- 2   large eggs, lightly beaten
- 2   cups bean sprouts
- 3   green onions, chopped
- ½   cup minced fresh cilantro
- ¼   cup unsalted peanuts, chopped

1. Cook fettuccine according to package directions. Meanwhile, in a small bowl, combine vinegar, soy sauce, brown sugar, fish sauce, lime juice and hot sauce until smooth; set aside.

2. In a large skillet or wok, heat 2 tsp. oil over medium-high heat. Add tofu; cook and stir until golden brown, 4-6 minutes. Remove and keep warm. Cook and stir carrots and snow peas in remaining 1 tsp. oil until crisp-tender, 3-5 minutes. Add garlic; cook 1 minute longer. Add eggs; cook and stir until set.

3. Drain pasta; add to vegetable mixture. Stir vinegar mixture and add to the skillet. Bring to a boil. Add tofu, bean sprouts and onions; heat through. Sprinkle with cilantro and peanuts.

1⅓ cups: 404 cal., 11g fat (2g sat. fat), 62mg chol., 951mg sod., 59g carb. (13g sugars, 9g fiber), 20g pro.

MAD ABOUT "MEAT" LOAF

*Give meat loaf some new accessories—
spinach, carrots, zucchini and whole grains.
Grind the nuts in a food processor, but be
sure to add a little flour so you don't end
up with nut butter.*
—Susan Preston, Eagle Creek, OR

- -

Prep: 30 min. • **Bake:** 50 min.
Makes: 6 servings

- 1 pkg. (6 oz.) fresh baby spinach
- 1 cup shredded cheddar cheese, divided
- ⅔ cup mashed cooked carrots
- 1 slice whole wheat bread, torn into pieces
- 2 large eggs, lightly beaten
- ½ cup grated zucchini
- ½ cup tomato sauce, divided
- ⅓ cup grated Parmesan cheese
- ¼ cup finely chopped onion
- 3 Tbsp. ground flaxseed
- 3 Tbsp. ground walnuts
- 1 Tbsp. olive oil
- 1 garlic clove, minced
- 1 tsp. Italian seasoning
- ½ tsp. dried sage leaves
- ¼ tsp. salt
- ⅛ tsp. pepper

1. In a large saucepan, bring ½ in. water to a boil. Add spinach; cover and boil for 3-4 minutes or until wilted. Drain and squeeze dry.
2. Combine ¾ cup cheddar cheese, carrots, bread, eggs, zucchini, ¼ cup tomato sauce, Parmesan cheese, onion, flaxseed, walnuts, oil, garlic, seasonings and spinach. Pat into a greased 8x4-in. loaf pan; top with remaining tomato sauce.
3. Bake, uncovered, at 325° for 45 minutes. Sprinkle with remaining cheddar cheese. Bake 4-7 minutes longer or until heated through and cheese is melted. Let stand for 5 minutes before slicing.
1 piece: 198 cal., 14g fat (6g sat. fat), 94mg chol., 451mg sod., 9g carb. (2g sugars, 3g fiber), 11g pro.

FALAFEL

FALAFEL

*Falafel are a common street food in
the Middle East. They are gluten free,
crunchy on the outside, tender on the inside,
and full of flavor from the cilantro, mint,
coriander and nutty sesame seeds. Serve
in or alongside pita bread with red onion,
tomato, pickled cucumber and tahini sauce.*
—Nithya Narasimhan, Chennai, India

- -

Prep: 10 min. + chilling
Cook: 15 min. • **Makes:** 16 pieces

- 1 cup dried garbanzo beans or chickpeas
- ½ tsp. baking soda
- 1 cup fresh cilantro leaves
- ½ cup fresh mint leaves
- 5 garlic cloves
- 1 tsp. salt
- ½ tsp. pepper, optional
- 1 tsp. ground coriander
- 1 tsp. chili powder
- 1 tsp. sesame seeds
- 1 tsp. baking powder
  Oil for deep-fat frying

1. In a large bowl, cover beans with water. Stir in baking soda. Cover and let stand overnight. Drain beans; rinse and pat dry.
2. In a food processor, pulse cilantro and mint until finely chopped. Add beans, garlic, salt, pepper if desired, coriander and chili powder. Pulse until blended and texture of coarse meal. Transfer to a large bowl. Cover and refrigerate at least 1 hour.
3. Stir in the sesame seeds and baking powder. Shape into sixteen 2-in. balls. In an electric skillet or a deep-fat fryer, heat oil to 375°. Fry falafel balls, a few at a time, until golden brown, about 2 minutes, turning occasionally. Drain on paper towels.
4 pieces: 224 cal., 13g fat (1g sat. fat), 0 chol., 760mg sod., 32g carb. (1g sugars, 16g fiber), 9g pro.

*"I love falafel at restaurants,
but I've never found a recipe
that I've enjoyed as much. This
authentic version starts with
dried garbanzo beans—the key
to great falafel. Falafel is perfect
to make ahead and freeze too."*
—PEGGY WOODWARD, SENIOR FOOD EDITOR

ASIAN TOFU

This tasty tofu was the first meatless recipe my fiance made for me. Tofu is a wonderful light protein and is so easy to pair with broiled or grilled veggies, such as eggplant and asparagus, or even tomatoes.
—Emily Steers, Los Angeles, CA

- -

Prep: 10 min. + marinating • **Broil:** 10 min.
Makes: 4 servings

¼	cup olive oil
3	Tbsp. reduced-sodium soy sauce
2	green onions, chopped
2	garlic cloves, minced
¼	tsp. ground cumin
¼	tsp. crushed red pepper flakes
1	pkg. (14 oz.) extra-firm tofu

1. Whisk together the first 6 ingredients. Cut tofu lengthwise into ⅜-in. thick slices; cut each slice in half diagonally to make triangles. Place tofu and marinade in a large shallow bowl; turn to coat. Cover and refrigerate 3-5 hours, turning occasionally.
2. Preheat broiler. Reserving marinade, place the tofu in a 15x10x1-in. pan. Drizzle remaining marinade over tops. Broil 5-6 in. from heat until lightly browned and heated through, about 10 minutes.
2 pieces: 208 cal., 18g fat (3g sat. fat), 0 chol., 440mg sod., 4g carb. (1g sugars, 1g fiber), 9g pro. **Diabetic exchanges:** 3 fat, 1 lean meat.

"People who don't usually love tofu tend to be huge fans of this recipe. The marinade packs a ton of flavor, and the cook time is short because you use the broiler."
—SARAH TRAMONTE, CULINARY PRODUCER

ASIAN TOFU

ORZO SHRIMP STEW

My husband and I really enjoy seafood, so I don't skimp on shrimp in this mildly seasoned stew. We also adore the broccoli, tomatoes and pasta.
—Lisa Stinger, Hamilton, NJ

- -

Takes: 20 min. • **Makes:** 4 servings

2½ cups reduced-sodium
  chicken broth
5 cups fresh broccoli florets
1 can (14½ oz.) diced tomatoes,
  undrained
1 cup uncooked orzo
1 lb. uncooked shrimp (31-40 per lb.),
  peeled and deveined
¼ tsp. salt
¼ tsp. pepper
2 tsp. dried basil
2 Tbsp. butter

1. Bring broth to a boil in a Dutch oven. Add the broccoli, tomatoes and orzo. Reduce heat; simmer, uncovered, for 5 minutes, stirring occasionally.
2. Add shrimp, salt and pepper. Cover and cook 4-5 minutes or until shrimp turn pink and orzo is tender. Stir in basil and butter.
1¾ cups: 387 cal., 8g fat (4g sat. fat), 153mg chol., 875mg sod., 48g carb. (7g sugars, 5g fiber), 30g pro.

LOADED MEXICAN PIZZA

My husband is a picky eater, but this healthful pizza has such amazing flavor that he actually looks forward to it. Leftovers taste even better the next day.
—Mary Barker, Knoxville, TN

- -

Takes: 30 min. • **Makes:** 6 servings

1 can (15 oz.) black beans,
  rinsed and drained
1 medium red onion, chopped
1 small sweet yellow pepper,
  chopped
3 tsp. chili powder
¾ tsp. ground cumin
3 medium tomatoes, chopped
1 jalapeno pepper, seeded
  and finely chopped
1 garlic clove, minced
1 prebaked 12-in. thin pizza crust
2 cups chopped fresh spinach
2 Tbsp. minced fresh cilantro
  Hot pepper sauce to taste
½ cup shredded reduced-fat
  cheddar cheese
½ cup shredded pepper jack cheese

1. In a small bowl, mash black beans. Stir in the onion, yellow pepper, chili powder and cumin. In another bowl, combine the tomatoes, jalapeno and garlic.
2. Place crust on an ungreased 12-in. pizza pan; spread with bean mixture. Top with tomato mixture and spinach. Sprinkle with cilantro, pepper sauce and cheeses.
3. Bake at 400° for 12-15 minutes or until cheese is melted.
1 piece: 295 cal., 8g fat (3g sat. fat), 17mg chol., 581mg sod., 40g carb. (5g sugars, 6g fiber), 15g pro. **Diabetic exchanges:** 2½ starch, 1 lean meat, 1 vegetable.

TEST KITCHEN TIP
Have leftover cilantro? Wash and pat it dry with a paper towel. Place the sprigs in a resealable container and toss it in the freezer.

LOADED
MEXICAN PIZZA

LINGUINE WITH HERBED CLAM SAUCE

GRILLED LOBSTER TAILS

I'd never made lobster at home until I tried this convenient and deliciously different grilled recipe. It turned out amazing and has left me with little reason to ever order lobster at a restaurant again.
—Katie Rush, Kansas City, MO

- -

Prep: 15 min. + marinating • **Grill:** 10 min.
Makes: 6 servings

- 6 frozen lobster tails (8 to 10 oz. each), thawed
- ¾ cup olive oil
- 3 Tbsp. minced fresh chives
- 3 garlic cloves, minced
- ½ tsp. salt
- ½ tsp. pepper

1. Using scissors, cut 3 to 4 lengthwise slits in underside of tail to loosen shell slightly. Cut top of lobster shell lengthwise down the center with scissors, leaving tail fin intact. Cut shell at an angle away from the center of the tail at base of tail fin. Loosen meat from shell, keeping fin end attached; lift meat and lay over shell.
2. In a small bowl, combine the remaining ingredients; spoon over the lobster meat. Cover and refrigerate for 20 minutes.
3. Place lobster tails, meat side up, on grill rack. Grill, covered, over medium heat until meat is opaque, 10-12 minutes.

1 lobster tail: 446 cal., 29g fat (4g sat. fat), 215mg chol., 869mg sod., 2g carb. (0 sugars, 0 fiber), 43g pro.
Baked Lobster Tails: Preheat oven to 375°. Place prepared lobster tails on a baking sheet. Bake, uncovered, 15-20 minutes or until meat is firm and opaque.

TEST KITCHEN TIP
Look for cold water lobster tails. They may be more expensive than warm water lobster tails, but the flavor is superior.

LINGUINE WITH HERBED CLAM SAUCE

This impressive pasta looks and tastes so much like fancy restaurant fare that you'll want to serve it to guests. But the recipe is easy enough to prepare just about anytime.
—Carolee Snyder, Hartford City, IN

- -

Prep: 20 min. • **Cook:** 15 min.
Makes: 4 servings

- 1 can (10 oz.) whole baby clams
- 1 can (6½ oz.) minced clams
- ½ cup finely chopped onion
- ¼ cup olive oil
- ¼ cup butter
- ⅓ cup minced fresh parsley
- 4 garlic cloves, minced
- 2 Tbsp. cornstarch
- ½ cup white wine or chicken broth
- ¼ cup minced fresh basil or 4 tsp. dried basil
  Dash pepper
  Dash cayenne pepper
  Hot cooked linguine
  Shredded Parmesan cheese

1. Drain baby and minced clams, reserving juice; set clams and juice aside. In a large skillet, saute the onion in oil and butter until tender. Add the parsley and garlic; saute for 2 minutes. Add the clams; saute 2 minutes longer.
2. Combine cornstarch and clam juice until smooth; stir into skillet with wine or broth. Bring to a boil; cook and stir 1-2 minutes or until thickened. Stir in the basil, pepper and cayenne. Serve sauce over linguine; sprinkle with Parmesan cheese.

1⅔ cups: 328 cal., 26g fat (9g sat. fat), 73mg chol., 521mg sod., 10g carb. (1g sugars, 1g fiber), 10g pro.

GRILLED
LOBSTER TAILS

MEATLESS TACO SALAD

This colorful entree combines popular taco ingredients—minus the ground beef. And you won't miss the meat at all! I top each serving with a creamy guacamole dressing, crunchy corn chips and cheese.
—Kimberly Dray, Pflugerville, TX

Takes: 20 min. • **Makes:** 2 servings

- ⅓ cup guacamole
- ¼ cup sour cream
- 1 Tbsp. prepared Italian salad dressing
- 1 Tbsp. chopped green onions
- 2 Tbsp. chopped green pepper
- ¼ tsp. pepper
- ¼ tsp. chili powder
- 3 cups shredded lettuce
- 8 cherry tomatoes, halved
- ½ cup canned kidney beans, rinsed and drained
- ¼ cup sliced ripe olives
- ½ cup crushed corn chips
- ½ cup shredded cheddar cheese

In a small bowl, combine the first 7 ingredients; set aside. In a large bowl, combine the lettuce, tomatoes, beans and olives. Arrange lettuce mixture on 2 serving plates; top with guacamole mixture. Sprinkle with corn chips and cheese.

1 serving: 486 cal., 33g fat (12g sat. fat), 35mg chol., 849mg sod., 34g carb. (7g sugars, 9g fiber), 16g pro.

ROSEMARY SALMON & VEGGIES

My husband and I eat a lot of salmon. One night while in a rush to get dinner on the table, I created this meal. It's a keeper! You can also include sliced zucchini, small cauliflower florets or fresh green beans.
—Elizabeth Bramkamp, Gig Harbor, WA

Takes: 30 min. • **Makes:** 4 servings

- 1½ lbs. salmon fillets, cut into 4 portions
- 2 Tbsp. melted coconut oil or olive oil
- 2 Tbsp. balsamic vinegar
- 2 tsp. minced fresh rosemary or ¾ tsp. dried rosemary, crushed
- 1 garlic clove, minced
- ½ tsp. salt
- 1 lb. fresh asparagus, trimmed
- 1 medium sweet red pepper, cut into 1-in. pieces
- ¼ tsp. pepper
  Lemon wedges

1. Preheat oven to 400°. Place salmon in a greased 15x10x1-in. baking pan. Combine the oil, vinegar, rosemary, garlic and salt. Pour half over salmon. Place asparagus and red pepper in a large bowl; drizzle with remaining oil mixture and toss to coat. Arrange around salmon in pan; sprinkle with pepper.
2. Bake 12-15 minutes or until salmon flakes easily with a fork and vegetables are tender. Serve with lemon wedges.
1 serving: 357 cal., 23g fat (9g sat. fat), 85mg chol., 388mg sod., 7g carb. (4g sugars, 2g fiber), 31g pro. **Diabetic exchanges:** 4 lean meat, 1½ fat, 1 vegetable.

POTATO-LENTIL STEW

Jampacked with veggies, this main-dish soup equals a meal the whole family will love. Serve with a loaf of your favorite bread and dinner's done!
—Krista Goodwin, Ypsilanti, MI

Prep: 20 min. • **Cook:** 40 min.
Makes: 6 servings (2½ qt.)

- 1 large onion, chopped
- 2 medium carrots, chopped
- 2 tsp. olive oil
- 4 tsp. chili powder
- 3 garlic cloves, minced
- 3 tsp. ground cumin
- 1 tsp. dried oregano
- 1 carton (32 oz.) vegetable broth
- ¾ cup dried lentils, rinsed
- 2 cans (10 oz. each) diced tomatoes and green chiles
- 3½ cups frozen cubed hash brown potatoes
- 1 can (16 oz.) kidney beans, rinsed and drained
- ½ tsp. salt
- ¼ tsp. pepper
  Minced fresh oregano, optional

1. In a Dutch oven, saute onion and carrots in oil 3 minutes. Add chili powder, garlic, cumin and oregano; cook 1 minute longer.
2. Stir in broth and lentils. Bring to a boil. Reduce the heat; cover and simmer for 20-22 minutes or until lentils are tender. Stir in the tomatoes, potatoes, beans, salt and pepper. Return to a boil. Reduce heat; cover and simmer 10-15 minutes longer or until the potatoes are tender. If desired, garnish with oregano.
1⅔ cups: 295 cal., 2g fat (0 sat. fat), 0 chol., 1478mg sod., 56g carb. (6g sugars, 16g fiber), 15g pro.

VEGAN QUINOA SALAD

Toasting the quinoa before it simmers isn't essential, but it does add a nice nuttiness to the flavor of this dish. You can mix and match whatever fresh herbs and veggies you have on hand.
—*Taste of Home* Test Kitchen

Takes: 30 min. • **Makes:** 6 cups

- 1½ **cups quinoa, rinsed and well drained**
- 3 **cups water**
- ¼ **cup plus 2 Tbsp. olive oil**
- 1 **Tbsp. grated lemon zest**
- ¼ **cup lemon juice**
- 4 **garlic cloves, minced**
- 6 **Tbsp. minced fresh parsley**
- 6 **Tbsp. minced fresh mint**
- 1½ **tsp. salt**
- 1 **cup cherry tomatoes, halved**
- 2 **mini cucumbers, sliced**
- 1 **medium sweet red pepper, chopped**
- ½ **cup chopped red onion**

1. In a large saucepan, cook and stir quinoa over medium-high heat for 3-5 minutes or until toasted. Add water; bring to a boil. Reduce heat; simmer, covered, until liquid is absorbed, 12-15 minutes. Transfer to a large bowl. Cool slightly.

2. In a small bowl, whisk oil, lemon zest, lemon juice, garlic, parsley, mint and salt. Add vegetables to quinoa; drizzle with the dressing and toss to combine. Cover and refrigerate until ready to serve.

¾ cup: 227 cal., 12g fat (2g sat. fat), 0 chol., 449mg sod., 25g carb. (3g sugars, 3g fiber), 5g pro. **Diabetic exchanges:** 2 fat, 1½ starch.

SIMPLE HERBED SCALLOPS

Living in Kansas, fresh seafood can be hard to come by. Luckily, frozen scallops aren't. This dish offers coastal flavor to those of us in landlocked areas.
—Sarah Befort, Hays, KS

Takes: 30 min. • **Makes:** 2 servings

- ½ **to ¾ lb. sea scallops**
- 3 **Tbsp. butter, divided**
- ¾ **tsp. lemon juice**
- 1 **tsp. minced fresh parsley or ¼ tsp. dried parsley**
- 1½ **tsp. minced fresh chives or ½ tsp. dried chives**
- ¼ **tsp. minced fresh tarragon or ⅛ tsp. dried tarragon**
- ⅛ **tsp. garlic salt**
  Dash pepper
- 2 **Tbsp. dry bread crumbs**

1. Preheat oven to 350°. Place scallops in a greased 1-qt. baking dish. Mix 2 Tbsp. melted butter, lemon juice, herbs, garlic salt and pepper; drizzle over scallops.

2. Mix bread crumbs with remaining melted butter; sprinkle over top. Bake, uncovered, until scallops are firm and opaque, 20-25 minutes.

1 serving: 260 cal., 18g fat (11g sat. fat), 73mg chol., 754mg sod., 9g carb. (1g sugars, 1g fiber), 15g pro.

CRUMB-COATED RED SNAPPER

I reel in compliments with this moist and crispy red snapper recipe. Heart-healthy omega-3 oils are an added bonus with my simple but delicious entree that's done in minutes. It's one of the best red snapper recipes I've found.
—Charlotte Elliott, Neenah, WI

Takes: 30 min. • **Makes:** 4 servings

- ½ **cup dry bread crumbs**
- 2 **Tbsp. grated Parmesan cheese**
- 1 **tsp. lemon-pepper seasoning**
- ¼ **tsp. salt**
- 4 **red snapper fillets (6 oz. each)**
- 2 **Tbsp. olive oil**

1. In a shallow bowl, combine the bread crumbs, cheese, lemon pepper and salt; add fillets, 1 at a time, and turn to coat.

2. In a heavy skillet over medium heat, cook fillets in oil, in batches, until the fish just begins to flake easily with a fork, 4-5 minutes on each side.

1 fillet: 288 cal., 10g fat (2g sat. fat), 62mg chol., 498mg sod., 10g carb. (0 sugars, 0 fiber), 36g pro. **Diabetic exchanges:** 5 lean meat, 1½ fat, ½ starch.

MASHED RED POTATOES
PAGE 168

Side Dishes & Salads

From comforting potatoes and pastas to crunchy salads and farm-fresh veggies, these sides rank among our most requested when we cook for our families.

SPINACH SALAD WITH HOT BACON DRESSING

After having a salad like this at a restaurant years ago, I came up with this recipe. It is especially good when the spinach comes right from the garden to the table.
—Wanda Cover, Mediapolis, IA

Takes: 25 min. • **Makes:** 2 servings

- 2 cups fresh baby spinach, torn
- 2 hard-boiled large eggs, sliced
- 4 cherry tomatoes, halved
- 3 medium fresh mushrooms, sliced
- ¼ cup salad croutons
- 6 pitted ripe olives, halved
- 3 slices red onion, halved

DRESSING

- 4 bacon strips, diced
- 1 Tbsp. chopped onion
- 2 Tbsp. sugar
- 2 Tbsp. ketchup
- 1 Tbsp. red wine vinegar
- 1 Tbsp. Worcestershire sauce

1. Divide the spinach between 2 plates. Arrange the eggs, tomatoes, mushrooms, croutons, olives and red onion over top.
2. In a small skillet, cook the bacon over medium heat until crisp. Using a slotted spoon, remove to paper towels; drain, reserving 2 Tbsp. drippings. Saute onion in drippings until tender.
3. Stir in the sugar, ketchup, vinegar and Worcestershire sauce. Bring to a boil. Reduce heat; simmer, uncovered, until thickened, 1-2 minutes. Sprinkle bacon over salads; drizzle with dressing.
1⅓ cups: 367 cal., 21g fat (6g sat. fat), 238mg chol., 1178mg sod., 29g carb. (21g sugars, 2g fiber), 17g pro.

ZUCCHINI ONION PIE

We have a lot of zucchini on hand when it's in season. This is a good and different way to use large amounts.
—Lucia Johnson, Massena, NY

Takes: 30 min. • **Makes:** 6 servings

- 3 large eggs
- 1 cup grated Parmesan cheese
- ½ cup canola oil
- 1 Tbsp. minced fresh parsley
- 1 garlic clove, minced
- ¼ tsp. salt
- ⅛ tsp. pepper
- 3 cups sliced zucchini
- 1 cup biscuit/baking mix
- 1 small onion, chopped

In a large bowl, whisk first 7 ingredients. Stir in the zucchini, baking mix and onion. Pour into a greased 9-in. deep-dish pie plate. Bake at 350° for 25-35 minutes or until lightly browned.
1 piece: 353 cal., 27g fat (5g sat. fat), 104mg chol., 627mg sod., 18g carb. (2g sugars, 1g fiber), 9g pro.

TEST KITCHEN TIP

If you don't have a deep-dish pie plate, feel free to use a small baking dish (8-in. square) or a souffle dish (1½-2 qt.). Reduce oven time as needed, baking pie until lightly browned and eggs have reached an internal temperature of 160°.

SPINACH SALAD WITH HOT BACON DRESSING

AIR-FRYER GARLIC-ROSEMARY BRUSSELS SPROUTS

This is my go-to Thanksgiving side dish. It's healthy and easy, and it doesn't take very much time or effort to make. I usually use rosemary for my turkey, so this lets me use up some of the leftover herbs!
—Elisabeth Larsen, Pleasant Grove, UT

Takes: 30 min. • **Makes:** 4 servings

- 3 Tbsp. olive oil
- 2 garlic cloves, minced
- ½ tsp. salt
- ¼ tsp. pepper
- 1 lb. Brussels sprouts, trimmed and halved
- ½ cup panko bread crumbs
- 1½ tsp. minced fresh rosemary

1. Preheat air fryer to 350°. Place first 4 ingredients in a small microwave-safe bowl; microwave on high 30 seconds.
2. Toss Brussels sprouts with 2 Tbsp. oil mixture. Place Brussels sprouts on tray in air-fryer basket; cook 4-5 minutes. Stir sprouts. Cook until the sprouts are lightly browned and near desired tenderness, about 8 minutes longer, stirring halfway through cooking time.
3. Toss the bread crumbs with rosemary and remaining oil mixture; sprinkle over sprouts. Continue cooking until crumbs are browned and sprouts are tender, 3-5 minutes. Serve immediately.
¾ cup: 164 cal., 11g fat (1g sat. fat), 0 chol., 342mg sod., 15g carb. (3g sugars, 4g fiber), 5g pro. **Diabetic exchanges:** 2 fat, 1 vegetable, ½ starch.

AIR-FRYER GARLIC-ROSEMARY BRUSSELS SPROUTS

GRILLED VEGETABLE
PLATTER

GRILLED VEGETABLE PLATTER

This is the best of summer in one dish! These pretty veggies are perfect for entertaining. Grilling brings out their natural sweetness, and the marinade really perks up the flavor.
—Heidi Hall, North St. Paul, MN

- -

Prep: 20 min. + marinating • **Grill:** 10 min.
Makes: 6 servings

¼ cup olive oil
2 Tbsp. honey
4 tsp. balsamic vinegar
1 tsp. dried oregano
½ tsp. garlic powder
⅛ tsp. pepper
   Dash salt
1 lb. fresh asparagus, trimmed
3 small carrots,
   cut in half lengthwise
1 large sweet red pepper,
   cut into 1-in. strips
1 medium yellow summer squash,
   cut into ½-in. slices
1 medium red onion, cut into wedges

1. In a bowl, whisk the first 7 ingredients. Place 3 Tbsp. marinade in a large bowl. Add the vegetables; turn to coat. Cover; marinate 1½ hours at room temperature.
2. Transfer vegetables to a grilling grid; place grid on grill rack. Grill vegetables, covered, over medium heat until crisp-tender, 8-12 minutes, turning occasionally.
3. Place the vegetables on a large serving plate. Drizzle with remaining marinade.
Note: If you do not have a grilling grid, use a disposable foil pan. Poke holes in the bottom of pan with a meat fork to allow liquid to drain.
1 serving: 144 cal., 9g fat (1g sat. fat), 0 chol., 50mg sod., 15g carb. (11g sugars, 3g fiber), 2g pro. **Diabetic exchanges:** 2 vegetable, 2 fat.

TEST KITCHEN TIP

Common olive oil works better for cooking at high heat than virgin or extra virgin oil. These higher grades have ideal flavor for cold foods, but they smoke at lower temperatures.

SPRINGTIME POTATO SALAD

SPRINGTIME POTATO SALAD

Traditional potato salad gets fun flavor from sweet pickles and a hearty crunch from celery and radishes in this recipe. I'm especially fond of the creamy dressing.
—Ellen Benninger, Greenville, PA

- -

Prep: 20 min. + chilling
Makes: 10 servings

6 cups cubed peeled potatoes
4 hard-boiled large eggs, chopped
1 celery rib, chopped
½ cup chopped sweet pickles
⅓ cup chopped onion
⅓ cup chopped radishes
½ cup mayonnaise
3 Tbsp. sugar
1 Tbsp. white vinegar
1 Tbsp. 2% milk
1½ tsp. prepared mustard
½ tsp. salt
   Optional: Sliced green onions
   and paprika

1. Place potatoes in a saucepan and cover with water; bring to a boil. Reduce heat. Cook until tender, 10-15 minutes; drain. Place in a large bowl; add eggs, celery, pickles, onion and radishes.
2. In a small bowl, combine mayonnaise, sugar, vinegar, milk, mustard and salt; stir into potato mixture. Cover and refrigerate at least 1 hour before serving. If desired, garnish with green onions and paprika.
¾ cup: 221 cal., 11g fat (2g sat. fat), 89mg chol., 297mg sod., 26g carb. (8g sugars, 2g fiber), 5g pro.

OVEN FRIES

I jazz up my fries with paprika and garlic powder. Something about the combination of spices packs a punch. The leftovers are even good cold!
—Heather Byers, Pittsburgh, PA

Prep: 10 min. • **Bake:** 40 min.
Makes: 4 servings

4	medium potatoes
1	Tbsp. olive oil
2½	tsp. paprika
¾	tsp. salt
¾	tsp. garlic powder

1. Preheat oven to 400°. Cut each potato into 12 wedges. In a large bowl, combine oil, paprika, salt and garlic powder. Add potatoes; toss to coat.
2. Transfer to a greased 15x10x1-in. baking pan. Bake until tender, 40-45 minutes, turning once.

12 pieces: 200 cal., 4g fat (1g sat. fat), 0 chol., 457mg sod., 38g carb. (2g sugars, 5g fiber), 5g pro.

SPECIAL CREAMED CORN

SPECIAL CREAMED CORN

This corn has earned a permanent place on our special-occasion menus. While my whole family loves it, my son would be especially disappointed if I forgot to include our corn dish.
—Deb Hauptmann, Mohnton, PA

Takes: 20 min. • **Makes:** 8 servings

⅓	cup butter
⅓	cup all-purpose flour
1	cup heavy whipping cream
1	cup whole milk
¼	cup sugar
1	tsp. salt
	Dash white pepper
5	cups frozen corn, thawed
¼	cup grated Parmesan cheese

1. In a saucepan, melt butter over medium heat. Stir in flour until smooth. Gradually add cream, milk, sugar, salt and pepper. Bring to a boil; boil and stir for 2 minutes. Add corn; heat through.
2. Transfer mixture to an ungreased 1½-qt. broiler-proof dish. Sprinkle with Parmesan. Broil 5 in. from the heat for 3-5 minutes or until lightly browned and bubbly.

⅔ cup: 317 cal., 21g fat (13g sat. fat), 59mg chol., 425mg sod., 31g carb. (11g sugars, 2g fiber), 6g pro.

ASPARAGUS & EGG SALAD WITH WALNUTS & MINT

I found this asparagus egg salad recipe while I was hiding from a pot of brisket, which is the kind of thing that happens three days after Passover. That brisket was instantly relegated to a side dish.
—Deb Perelman, New York, NY

Takes: 30 min.
Makes: 4 servings

- 4 large eggs, cold
- ½ cup grated Parmesan cheese
- ½ cup finely chopped walnuts, toasted
- 1 tsp. grated lemon zest
- 1 tsp. kosher salt
- ½ tsp. coarsely ground pepper
- ½ tsp. crushed red pepper flakes
- 1 lb. fresh asparagus, trimmed
- ¼ cup fresh lemon juice
- ¼ cup lightly packed fresh mint leaves, chopped
- ¼ cup olive oil, preferably extra virgin Toasted bread

1. In a saucepan, bring to a boil enough water to cover eggs by an inch. Gently lower in eggs and reduce heat to a simmer. Boil for 8½ minutes, then quickly transfer eggs to an ice-cold water bath. Leave them there while you prepare the other ingredients, but ideally at least 10 minutes.
2. Place Parmesan, walnuts and lemon zest in the bottom of a large bowl, along with salt, coarsely ground pepper and red pepper flakes. Stir to combine.
3. Cut the asparagus on a sharp angle into very thin slices and add to the Parmesan mixture. Add ¼ cup lemon juice and toss mixture some more. Taste and adjust the flavors to your preference by adding more salt, pepper, red pepper flakes or lemon juice. Add the mint and olive oil; toss, adjusting seasoning again.
4. Peel the eggs. Cut in half, then each half into 6-8 chunks. Add to bowl with the asparagus and gently stir just to combine. Serve over toasted bread.
1 serving: 349 cal., 31g fat (6g sat. fat), 195mg chol., 740mg sod., 8g carb. (2g sugars, 2g fiber), 13g pro.

> "This is one of the most creative recipes I've ever come across. I like eating this salad over slices of toasted sourdough bread. It's the perfect light meal."
> —ANNAMARIE HIGLEY, ASSOCIATE EDITOR

ASPARAGUS & EGG SALAD WITH WALNUTS & MINT

CLASSIC MACARONI SALAD

This classic recipe is a refreshingly light take on an all-time favorite. It's perfect for a fast weeknight dinner or a festive weekend barbecue.
—Dorothy Bayes, Sardis, OH

- -

Takes: 30 min. • **Makes:** 8 servings

2 cups uncooked elbow macaroni
1 cup fat-free mayonnaise
2 Tbsp. sweet pickle relish
2 tsp. sugar
¾ tsp. ground mustard
¼ tsp. salt
⅛ tsp. pepper
½ cup chopped celery
⅓ cup chopped carrot
¼ cup chopped onion
1 hard-boiled large egg, chopped
Dash paprika

1. Cook macaroni according to package directions; drain and rinse with cold water. Cool completely.
2. For dressing, in a small bowl, combine mayonnaise, pickle relish, sugar, mustard, salt and pepper. In a large bowl, combine the macaroni, celery, carrot and onion. Add dressing and toss gently to coat.
3. Refrigerate until serving. Garnish with egg and paprika.
¾ cup: 115 cal., 2g fat (0 sat. fat), 27mg chol., 362mg sod., 21g carb. (6g sugars, 2g fiber), 4g pro. **Diabetic exchanges:** 1½ starch.

CLASSIC MACARONI SALAD

TACO PASTA SALAD

I blend the best of two popular salads into one satisfying dish to share. Serve tortilla or corn chips on the side, and you have a complete meal.
—Gert Rosenau, Pewaukee, WI

- -

Takes: 30 min. • **Makes:** 4 servings

- 2 cups uncooked spiral pasta
- 1 lb. ground beef
- 1 envelope taco seasoning
- 3 cups shredded lettuce
- 2 cups halved cherry tomatoes
- 1 cup shredded cheddar cheese
- ½ cup chopped onion
- ½ cup chopped green pepper
- ½ cup Catalina salad dressing
  Tortilla chips

1. Cook pasta according to package directions. Meanwhile, in a large skillet, cook beef over medium heat until no longer pink, breaking it into crumbles; drain. Stir in the taco seasoning; cool.
2. Drain pasta and rinse in cold water; stir into meat mixture. Add the lettuce, tomatoes, cheese, onion, green pepper and dressing; toss to coat. Serve with tortilla chips.
1 serving: 624 cal., 30g fat (12g sat. fat), 98mg chol., 1454mg sod., 55g carb. (13g sugars, 3g fiber), 33g pro.

DID YOU KNOW?
Sharp cheddar cheese has been aged longer than regular cheddar. As the cheese ages, its flavor becomes more pronounced. Using aged cheese in a recipe can add complexity and rich flavor.

CREAMY TWICE-BAKED POTATOES

With a yummy cream cheese filling, these rich, delicious potatoes are sure winners. They look fancy but are not tricky to make.
—Linda Wheeler, Harrisburg, PA

- -

Prep: 1¼ hours • **Bake:** 20 min.
Makes: 2 servings

- 2 medium baking potatoes
- 2 Tbsp. butter, softened
- 1 Tbsp. 2% milk
- ¼ tsp. salt
- 3 oz. cream cheese, cubed
- 2 Tbsp. sour cream
  Paprika
  Optional: Minced fresh parsley and green onion slices

1. Preheat oven to 350°. Pierce potatoes and bake on a baking sheet until tender, about 1 hour. When cool enough to handle, cut a thin slice off the top of each potato and discard. Scoop out the pulp, leaving a thin shell.
2. In a small bowl, mash pulp with butter, milk and salt. Stir in cream cheese and sour cream. Spoon into potato shells. Sprinkle with paprika.
3. Place potatoes on a baking sheet. Bake, uncovered, until heated through and the tops are golden brown, 20-25 minutes. If desired, sprinkle with parsley and onions.
1 potato: 448 cal., 30g fat (18g sat. fat), 78mg chol., 541mg sod., 40g carb. (4g sugars, 4g fiber), 8g pro.

CREAMY TWICE-BAKED POTATOES

FIESTA CORN & BEANS

MANDARIN ORANGE CHICKEN SALAD

My sister-in-law introduced me to this colorful salad with a delicious homemade dressing. I reduced the oil and salt and switched to light soy sauce. Sometimes I use toasted sesame seeds for the nuts.
—Renee Heimerl, Oakfield, WI

Prep: 25 min. + chilling
Makes: 4 servings

- ¾ lb. boneless skinless chicken breast, cubed
- ¼ cup reduced-sodium teriyaki sauce
- 2 tsp. canola oil
- 8 cups torn mixed salad greens
- 1 can (11 oz.) mandarin oranges, drained
- 1 medium carrot, shredded
- ¼ cup slivered almonds, toasted
- 3 Tbsp. thinly sliced green onions

DRESSING

- 2 Tbsp. white vinegar
- 2 Tbsp. olive oil
- 1 Tbsp. reduced-sodium soy sauce
- 2 tsp. sugar
- ½ tsp. ground ginger
- ¼ tsp. salt
- ¼ tsp. pepper

1. In a shallow dish, combine the chicken and teriyaki sauce. Cover and refrigerate for 1-2 hours.
2. Drain chicken, discarding marinade. In a large nonstick skillet, heat oil over medium-high heat. Add the chicken; cook and stir for 5-7 minutes or until no longer pink. Refrigerate until chilled.
3. In a large bowl, combine salad greens, chicken, oranges, carrot, almonds and onions. In a jar with a tight-fitting lid, combine dressing ingredients; shake well. Drizzle over salad; toss to coat.
2 cups: 308 cal., 15g fat (2g sat. fat), 47mg chol., 738mg sod., 25g carb. (18g sugars, 4g fiber), 22g pro. **Diabetic exchanges:** 3 lean meat, 2 vegetable, 2 fat, 1 starch.

FIESTA CORN & BEANS

Bursting with southwestern flavors, the zesty veggie medley here can be served as a side dish or a meatless meal-in-one. The dollop of yogurt is a cool, creamy finishing touch.
—Gerald Hetrick, Erie, PA

Prep: 25 min. • **Cook:** 3 hours
Makes: 10 servings

- 1 large onion, chopped
- 1 medium green pepper, cut into 1-in. pieces
- 1 to 2 jalapeno peppers, seeded and sliced
- 1 Tbsp. olive oil
- 1 garlic clove, minced
- 2 cans (16 oz. each) kidney beans, rinsed and drained
- 1 pkg. (16 oz.) frozen corn
- 1 can (14½ oz.) diced tomatoes, undrained
- 1 tsp. chili powder
- ¾ tsp. salt
- ½ tsp. ground cumin
- ½ tsp. pepper
- Optional: Plain yogurt and sliced ripe olives

1. In a large skillet, saute the onion and peppers in oil until tender. Add garlic; cook 1 minute longer. Transfer to a 4-qt. slow cooker. Stir in beans, corn, tomatoes and seasonings.
2. Cover and cook on low for 3-4 hours or until heated through. Serve with yogurt and olives if desired.
¾ cup: 149 cal., 2g fat (0 sat. fat), 0 chol., 380mg sod., 28g carb. (5g sugars, 7g fiber), 8g pro. **Diabetic exchanges:** 1 starch, 1 vegetable, 1 lean meat.

> "Not only is this an amazing side dish, but I like to stuff it in flour tortillas with cheese and greens for a terrific meatless lunch."
> —MARK HAGEN, CONTENT DIRECTOR

MANDARIN ORANGE
CHICKEN SALAD

BLUE CHEESE KALE SALAD

Instead of the standard spinach, romaine or iceberg, try kale in your salad! I didn't even like the leafy green until I made the recipe, and now I'm a total convert.
—Kathryn Egly, Colorado Springs, CO

Takes: 20 min. • **Makes:** 12 servings

- ½ cup olive oil
- 3 Tbsp. lime juice
- 2 Tbsp. honey
- ¼ tsp. salt
- ⅛ tsp. pepper
- 1 bunch kale (about 12 oz.), trimmed and chopped (about 14 cups)
- ½ cup sliced almonds, toasted
- ½ cup dried cranberries
- ½ cup shredded Parmesan cheese
- ½ cup crumbled blue cheese

In a small bowl, whisk first 5 ingredients. Place the kale in a large bowl. Drizzle with the dressing; toss to coat. Top with remaining ingredients.

1¼ cups: 181 cal., 14g fat (3g sat. fat), 7mg chol., 183mg sod., 13g carb. (8g sugars, 1g fiber), 4g pro. **Diabetic exchanges:** 3 fat, 1 vegetable, ½ starch.

TEST KITCHEN TIP

To trim kale, fold the leaf in half and use a knife to slice away the stem from the leaf.

CREAMED PEAS

I can still taste these wonderful peas in Mama's delicious white sauce. Our food was pretty plain during the week, so I thought this white sauce made the peas extra fancy and fitting for a Sunday meal.
—Imogene Hutton, Brownwood, TX

Takes: 15 min. • **Makes:** 4 servings

- 1 pkg. (10 oz.) frozen peas
- 1 Tbsp. butter
- 1 Tbsp. all-purpose flour
- ¼ tsp. salt
- ⅛ tsp. pepper
- ½ cup whole milk
- 1 tsp. sugar

Cook the peas according to package directions. Meanwhile, in a saucepan, melt the butter. Stir in the flour, salt and pepper until blended; gradually add the milk and sugar. Bring to a boil; cook and stir until thickened, 1-2 minutes. Drain the peas; stir into the sauce and heat through.

½ cup: 110 cal., 4g fat (2g sat. fat), 12mg chol., 271mg sod., 14g carb. (6g sugars, 3g fiber), 5g pro.

BLUE CHEESE KALE SALAD

FARRO SALAD WITH CHARRED SHISHITO PEPPERS & CORN

I am lucky that my mom has a wonderful garden every summer and gives me all kinds of vegetables to try. I've found most shishito peppers to be mild in heat. After discarding the stems, I add the remaining chopped pepper, including the seeds, to this dish. The salad can be enjoyed warm or refrigerated and served cold.
—Tracy Kaifesh, Laguna Niguel, CA

Prep: 25 min. • **Cook:** 25 min.
Makes: 8 servings

- 1 cup farro, rinsed
- ¼ cup plus 2 tsp. olive oil, divided
- ¼ cup lime juice
- 1 tsp. garlic powder
- ½ tsp. ground cumin
- ½ tsp. kosher salt
- 4 oz. shishito peppers (about 20 peppers)
- 2 medium ears sweet corn, husked
- 1 cup chopped fresh tomatoes
- ½ cup crumbled Cotija cheese
- ½ cup sliced radishes
- ½ cup chopped green onions

1. Place the farro in a large saucepan; add water to cover. Bring to a boil. Reduce heat; cook, covered, until tender, 25-30 minutes.
2. Meanwhile, for dressing, whisk together ¼ cup oil, lime juice, garlic powder, cumin and salt; set aside. Preheat a grill pan over medium-high heat. Toss peppers with 1 tsp. oil. Cook 6-8 minutes or until all sides are blistered and blackened, turning occasionally with tongs. Transfer to a cutting board. Chop peppers; discard stems. Transfer to a large bowl.
3. Brush the corn with remaining 1 tsp. oil. Cook until lightly browned and tender, 10-12 minutes, turning occasionally. Cool slightly. Cut corn from the cobs; add to peppers. Drain farro; add to corn mixture. Stir in tomatoes, cheese, radishes, green onions and dressing; toss to coat. Serve warm or chilled.

¾ cup: 233 cal., 11g fat (2g sat. fat), 8mg chol., 240mg sod., 27g carb. (3g sugars, 5g fiber), 7g pro. **Diabetic exchanges:** 2 starch, 2 fat.

FARRO SALAD WITH CHARRED SHISHITO PEPPERS & CORN

"What's not to love about this healthy grain salad? It's fresh and colorful, and every bite is packed with different flavors and textures."
—SARAH FARMER, EXECUTIVE CULINARY DIRECTOR

MUSHROOM PANZANELLA

My fresh take on classic Italian bread salad pairs perfectly with grilled or roasted meats.
—Jennifer Beckman, Falls Church, VA

- -

Prep: 35 min. • **Makes:** 8 servings

- 4 cups cubed sourdough bread
- 6 Tbsp. olive oil, divided
- 1 tsp. salt, divided
- 1 lb. sliced fresh assorted mushrooms (such as shiitake, oyster and cremini)
- 1 garlic clove, minced
- 2 Tbsp. balsamic vinegar
- 1 Tbsp. stone-ground mustard
- 1 tsp. honey
- 4 cups fresh arugula
- 1 cup grape tomatoes, halved
- 2 Tbsp. pine nuts, toasted
- 2 Tbsp. golden raisins
- 2 oz. fresh goat cheese, crumbled

1. Preheat oven to 450°. In a large bowl, combine bread, 2 Tbsp. oil and ¼ tsp. salt; toss to coat. Transfer to an ungreased baking sheet. Bake until golden brown, 8-10 minutes. Cool to room temperature.
2. Combine the mushrooms, 2 Tbsp. oil, garlic and ¼ tsp. salt; transfer to a greased baking sheet. Bake for 10-12 minutes or until tender.
3. In another large bowl, whisk vinegar, mustard, honey, and remaining oil and salt. Add the arugula, tomatoes, pine nuts, raisins, toasted bread and mushrooms; toss to coat. Sprinkle with goat cheese. Serve immediately.

1 cup: 210 cal., 13g fat (2g sat. fat), 5mg chol., 506mg sod., 20g carb. (5g sugars, 2g fiber), 6g pro. **Diabetic exchanges:** 2 fat, 1 starch, 1 vegetable.

DIN TAI FUNG CHILLED CUCUMBER SALAD

My family and I are obsessed with Din Tai Fung, a famous Taiwanese restaurant in California, and its chilled cucumber salad. This is a copycat version I created at home.
—Andrea Potischman, Menlo Park, CA

- -

Prep: 35 min. + chilling
Makes: 4 servings

- 5 Persian or small cucumbers, cut into ½-in. rounds
- 4½ tsp. kosher salt
MARINADE
- 3 Tbsp. rice vinegar
- 2 Tbsp. mirin (sweet rice wine)
- 2 Tbsp. honey
- 2 tsp. canola oil
- 2 tsp. sesame oil
- ½ tsp. chili garlic sauce
- ½ tsp. kosher salt

1. Place cucumbers in a colander over a plate; sprinkle with salt and toss. Let stand 20 minutes. Rinse and blot dry with paper towels.
2. In a large bowl or shallow dish, combine marinade ingredients. Add cucumbers; turn to coat. Refrigerate, covered, at least 4 hours or overnight.
3. Drain the cucumbers, reserving ¼ cup marinade. Arrange the cucumbers on a serving plate; drizzle with the reserved marinade. Serve cold.

¾ cup: 66 cal., 3g fat (0 sat. fat), 0 chol., 439mg sod., 9g carb. (7g sugars, 1g fiber), 1g pro. **Diabetic exchanges:** 1 vegetable, ½ fat.

MUSHROOM PANZANELLA

CRUNCHY WALDORF SALAD

Lemon juice gives this easy Waldorf salad quite a zip, and the apples and nuts offer a nice crunch. It's light, refreshing and effortless to assemble.
—Chuck Hinz, Parma, OH

Takes: 30 min. • **Makes:** 9 servings

- 2 medium Red Delicious apples, chopped
- 2 medium Golden Delicious apples, chopped
- 2 Tbsp. lemon juice
- 2 celery ribs, chopped
- ¾ cup chopped walnuts
- ½ cup raisins
- 1 cup mayonnaise
  Optional: Ground cinnamon, ground nutmeg and lettuce leaves

In a large bowl, toss apples with lemon juice. Gently stir in the celery, walnuts, raisins and mayonnaise. Refrigerate until serving. If desired, sprinkle with cinnamon and nutmeg and serve on lettuce leaves.

¾ cup: 284 cal., 24g fat (3g sat. fat), 2mg chol., 133mg sod., 17g carb. (12g sugars, 3g fiber), 2g pro.

ASK SARAH

WHAT'S THE DIFFERENCE BETWEEN MAYONNAISE AND MIRACLE WHIP?

Miracle Whip has the same basic ingredients as mayonnaise (eggs, oil and vinegar) but also has extra sugar and spices.

CRUNCHY
WALDORF SALAD

SUMMER ORZO

SUMMER ORZO

I'm always looking for fun ways to use the fresh veggies that come in my Community Supported Agriculture box, and this salad is one of my favorite creations. I like to improvise with whatever I have on hand, so feel free to do the same here!
—Shayna Marmar, Philadelphia, PA

- -

Prep: 30 min. + chilling
Makes: 16 servings

- 1   pkg. (16 oz.) orzo pasta
- ¼   cup water
- 1½ cups fresh or frozen corn
- 24 cherry tomatoes, halved
- 2   cups crumbled feta cheese
- 1   medium cucumber, seeded and chopped
- 1   small red onion, finely chopped
- ¼   cup minced fresh mint
- 2   Tbsp. capers, drained and chopped, optional
- ½   cup olive oil
- ¼   cup lemon juice
- 1   Tbsp. grated lemon zest
- 1½ tsp. salt
- 1   tsp. pepper
- 1   cup sliced almonds, toasted

1. Cook the orzo according to package directions for al dente. Drain orzo; rinse with cold water and drain well. Transfer to a large bowl.

2. In a large nonstick skillet, heat ¼ cup water over medium heat. Add corn; cook and stir until crisp-tender, 3-4 minutes. Add to orzo; stir in tomatoes, feta cheese, cucumber, onion, mint and, if desired, capers. In a small bowl, whisk oil, lemon juice, lemon zest, salt and pepper until blended. Pour over orzo mixture; toss to coat. Refrigerate 30 minutes.

3. Just before serving, stir in almonds.

¾ cup: 291 cal., 15g fat (4g sat. fat), 15mg chol., 501mg sod., 28g carb. (3g sugars, 3g fiber), 11g pro.

CHEESY SUMMER SQUASH CASSEROLE

CHEESY SUMMER SQUASH CASSEROLE

Onion and cheddar cheese perk up the rich flavor of summer squash in this comforting casserole. A crispy cornflake-crumb topping adds a little crunch.
—Katherine Metz, Jacksonville, FL

- -

Prep: 10 min. • **Bake:** 25 min.
Makes: 2 servings

- 2   small yellow summer squash, sliced
- ¼   cup chopped onion
- ½   tsp. salt, divided
- 1   large egg
- ¼   cup mayonnaise
- 2   tsp. sugar
  Pepper to taste
- ¼   cup shredded cheddar cheese
- 2   Tbsp. crushed cornflakes
- 1½ tsp. butter, melted

1. In a small saucepan, combine squash, onion and ¼ tsp. salt. Cover with water. Bring to a boil. Reduce heat; simmer, uncovered, until squash is crisp-tender, about 2 minutes. Drain.

2. In a bowl, whisk the egg, mayonnaise, sugar, pepper and remaining salt until blended. Stir in the cheese and squash mixture. Transfer to a greased 2-cup baking dish. Toss cornflakes and butter; sprinkle over top.

3. Bake, uncovered, at 350° until golden brown and bubbly, 25-30 minutes.

¾ cup: 376 cal., 31g fat (8g sat. fat), 117mg chol., 937mg sod., 18g carb. (10g sugars, 2g fiber), 9g pro.

OLIVE & RED PEPPER LINGUINE

With 16 grandchildren, I find that someone is always hungry. This is a quick dish to fix. I sometimes serve garlic bread alongside it for an easy meatless meal.
—Betty Carpenter, Hookstown, PA

Takes: 20 min. • **Makes:** 8 servings

- 8 oz. uncooked linguine
- 1 medium sweet red pepper, chopped
- ¾ cup sliced fresh mushrooms
- ½ cup chopped onion
- 1½ tsp. minced garlic
- 1 Tbsp. canola oil
- 15 pimiento-stuffed olives, sliced
- 1 Tbsp. butter

Cook the linguine according to package directions. Meanwhile, in a large skillet, saute the red pepper, mushrooms, onion and garlic in oil until tender. Drain linguine; add to the skillet. Stir in olives and butter; heat through.

1 cup: 159 cal., 6g fat (1g sat. fat), 4mg chol., 221mg sod., 24g carb. (2g sugars, 2g fiber), 4g pro. **Diabetic exchanges:** 1½ starch, 1 fat.

VEGGIE MACARONI & CHEESE

VEGGIE MACARONI & CHEESE

This creamy mac and cheese definitely doesn't come from a box! Fresh veggies add crunch and color and will leave everyone asking for seconds!
—Marsha Morril, Harrisburg, OR

Prep: 30 min. • **Bake:** 15 min.
Makes: 12 servings

- 1½ cups uncooked elbow macaroni
- 3 cups fresh broccoli florets
- 2 cups fresh cauliflowerets
- 3 large carrots, halved lengthwise and thinly sliced
- 2 celery ribs, sliced
- 1 Tbsp. butter
- 1 medium onion, chopped
- ¼ cup all-purpose flour
- 1 cup 2% milk
- 1 cup chicken broth
- 3 cups shredded sharp cheddar cheese
- 1 Tbsp. Dijon mustard
- ¼ tsp. salt
- ⅛ tsp. pepper
- ¼ tsp. paprika

1. Preheat oven to 350°. In a 6-qt. stockpot, cook the macaroni according to package directions, adding broccoli, cauliflower, carrots and celery during last 6 minutes of cooking. Drain; transfer to a greased 13x9-in. baking dish.

2. Meanwhile, in a saucepan, heat butter over medium-high heat; saute onion until tender. Stir in flour until blended. Gradually stir in milk and broth; bring to a boil. Cook and stir until thickened, about 2 minutes; stir in cheese, mustard, salt and pepper.

3. Add sauce to the macaroni mixture, stirring to coat; sprinkle with paprika. Bake, uncovered, 15-20 minutes or until heated through.

1 cup: 200 cal., 11g fat (6g sat. fat), 33mg chol., 391mg sod., 15g carb. (3g sugars, 2g fiber), 10g pro.

PEPPERONI PASTA SALAD

Bottled Italian dressing and pepperoni add zip to this colorful combination. Serve it right away or assemble it ahead of time. The longer this salad chills, the yummier it is!
—Shannon Lommen, Kaysville, UT

- -

Takes: 30 min. • **Makes:** 6 servings

- 2 cups uncooked tricolor spiral pasta
- 1 cup cubed cheddar cheese
- 1 cup coarsely chopped cucumber
- 1 small tomato, chopped
- 2 green onions, chopped
- 28 pepperoni slices
- ½ cup zesty Italian salad dressing

Cook spiral pasta according to package directions; drain and rinse in cold water. In a large bowl, combine pasta, cheese, cucumber, tomato, onions and pepperoni. Add salad dressing and toss to coat. Cover and refrigerate until serving.

¾ cup: 287 cal., 15g fat (6g sat. fat), 31mg chol., 495mg sod., 25g carb. (3g sugars, 1g fiber), 11g pro.

TEST KITCHEN TIP

If you make this pasta salad hours ahead, freshen it by stirring in a little dressing before serving.

PEPPERONI PASTA SALAD

KENTUCKY COLESLAW

My crew enjoys a number of coleslaw recipes, but sometimes we just can't help but crave Kentucky Fried Chicken's version of the creamy side. We used to buy several pints at a time, but now that I've come up with this perfect copycat, we don't have to! If you have time, grate the cabbage by hand.
—Donna Gribbins, Shelbyville, KY

- -

Prep: 20 min. + chilling
Makes: 8 servings

- ½ cup buttermilk
- ½ cup mayonnaise
- ⅓ cup sugar
- 2 Tbsp. lemon juice
- 4½ tsp. white vinegar
- 1 tsp. salt
- ½ tsp. pepper
- 1 lb. finely chopped cabbage (about 8 cups)
- 2 medium carrots, finely chopped (about 2 cups)
- 3 Tbsp. grated onion

In a large bowl, whisk first 7 ingredients until combined. Add remaining ingredients; toss to coat. Refrigerate, covered, at least 2 hours and up to 3 days before serving.

¾ cup: 160 cal., 10g fat (2g sat. fat), 6mg chol., 421mg sod., 16g carb. (13g sugars, 3g fiber), 2g pro.

MASHED RED POTATOES

These simple-yet-satisfying chunky mashed potatoes are rich enough to stand on their own—but a big pat of butter on top sure never hurts.
—*Taste of Home* Test Kitchen

- -

Takes: 30 min. • **Makes:** 12 servings

- 4½ lbs. red potatoes,
  cut into 1-in. pieces
- 6 Tbsp. butter, cubed
- 1½ tsp. salt
- ¾ tsp. pepper
- 1 to 1⅓ cups heavy
  whipping cream, warmed

1. Place potatoes in a large saucepan or Dutch oven and cover with water. Bring to a boil. Reduce heat; cover and cook for 10-15 minutes or until tender. Drain.
2. In a large bowl, mash the potatoes with butter, salt, pepper and enough cream to achieve desired consistency.
¾ cup: 242 cal., 13g fat (8g sat. fat), 38mg chol., 356mg sod., 28g carb. (2g sugars, 3g fiber), 4g pro.

TARRAGON ASPARAGUS

I grow purple asparagus, so I'm always looking for new ways to prepare it. My husband and I recently discovered how wonderful any color of asparagus tastes when it's grilled.
—Sue Gronholz, Beaver Dam, WI

- -

Takes: 15 min. • **Makes:** 8 servings

- 2 lbs. fresh asparagus, trimmed
- 2 Tbsp. olive oil
- 1 tsp. salt
- ½ tsp. pepper
- ¼ cup honey
- 2 to 4 Tbsp. minced fresh tarragon

On a large plate, toss the asparagus with oil, salt and pepper. Grill, covered, over medium heat for 6-8 minutes or until crisp-tender, turning occasionally and basting frequently with honey during the last 3 minutes. Sprinkle with tarragon.
1 serving: 76 cal., 4g fat (1g sat. fat), 0 chol., 302mg sod., 11g carb. (10g sugars, 1g fiber), 2g pro. **Diabetic exchanges:** 1 vegetable, ½ starch, ½ fat.

SCALLOPED TATERS

This creamy, comforting slow-cooked side tastes marvelous with almost any main dish and is a snap to assemble with frozen hash browns. It's a good way to make potatoes when your oven is busy with other dishes.
—Lucinda Wolker, Somerset, PA

- -

Prep: 10 min. • **Cook:** 3 hours
Makes: 12 servings

- 1 pkg. (2 lbs.) frozen cubed
  hash brown potatoes
- 1 can (10¾ oz.) condensed
  cream of chicken soup, undiluted
- 1½ cups 2% milk
- 1 cup shredded cheddar cheese
- ½ cup plus 1 Tbsp. butter,
  melted, divided
- ¼ cup dried minced onion
- ½ tsp. salt
- ⅛ tsp. pepper
- ¾ cup crushed cornflakes

1. In a large bowl, combine hash browns, soup, milk, cheese, ½ cup butter, onion, salt and pepper. Pour into a greased 5-qt. slow cooker. Cover and cook on low until potatoes are tender, 3-4 hours.
2. Just before serving, combine cornflake crumbs and remaining butter in a pie plate. Bake at 350° 4-6 minutes or until golden brown. Stir the potatoes; sprinkle with crumb topping.
1 cup: 234 cal., 14g fat (8g sat. fat), 39mg chol., 500mg sod., 22g carb. (3g sugars, 1g fiber), 6g pro.

QUICK AMBROSIA FRUIT SALAD

I mix in a little coconut and just enough marshmallows so it tastes like the creamy ambrosia I grew up with. Now everyone in my home loves it too.
—Trisha Kruse, Eagle, ID

- -

Takes: 10 min. • **Makes:** 6 servings

- 1   can (8¼ oz.) fruit cocktail, drained
- 1   can (8 oz.) unsweetened pineapple chunks, drained
- 1   cup green grapes
- 1   cup seedless red grapes
- 1   cup miniature marshmallows
- 1   medium banana, sliced
- ¾   cup vanilla yogurt
- ½   cup sweetened shredded coconut

In a large bowl, combine all ingredients. Chill until serving.
¾ cup: 191 cal., 4g fat (3g sat. fat), 2mg chol., 48mg sod., 40g carb. (34g sugars, 2g fiber), 3g pro.

BALSAMIC ASIAGO SALAD

You can toss this tasty salad together in 10 minutes. Simply drizzle bottled dressing over the colorful blend of greens, tomato and pepper. Then add a quick sprinkle of garlic-seasoned cheese and serve!
—*Taste of Home* Test Kitchen

- -

Takes: 10 min. • **Makes:** 2 servings

- 2   cups torn mixed salad greens
- 1   plum tomato, cut into wedges
- ½   cup chopped sweet yellow pepper
- 2   Tbsp. balsamic vinaigrette
- 2   Tbsp. shredded Asiago cheese

In a small serving bowl, combine the salad greens, tomato and yellow pepper. Drizzle with vinaigrette and toss to coat. Sprinkle with cheese.
1 cup: 72 cal., 4g fat (1g sat. fat), 4mg chol., 169mg sod., 7g carb. (3g sugars, 2g fiber), 4g pro. **Diabetic exchanges:** 1 vegetable, 1 fat.

TEST KITCHEN TIP
This salad recipe can be easily increased to feed more people. And feel free to use any of your family's favorite veggies.

COWBOY CALICO BEANS

This is a tradition at the table when my friends and I go up north for a girls' weekend. The husbands and kids are left at home, but the slow cooker comes with us!
—Julie Butsch, Hartland, WI

- -

Prep: 30 min. • **Cook:** 4 hours
Makes: 8 servings

- 1   lb. lean ground beef (90% lean)
- 1   large sweet onion, chopped
- ½   cup packed brown sugar
- ¼   cup ketchup
- 3   Tbsp. cider vinegar
- 2   Tbsp. yellow mustard
- 1   can (16 oz.) butter beans, drained
- 1   can (16 oz.) kidney beans, rinsed and drained
- 1   can (15 oz.) pork and beans
- 1   can (15¼ oz.) lima beans, rinsed and drained

1. In a large skillet, cook beef and onion over medium heat until meat is no longer pink, breaking meat into crumbles; drain.
2. Transfer to a 3-qt. slow cooker. Combine the brown sugar, ketchup, vinegar and mustard; add to meat mixture. Stir in the beans. Cover and cook on low 4-5 hours or until heated through.
¾ cup: 326 cal., 5g fat (2g sat. fat), 35mg chol., 808mg sod., 52g carb. (22g sugars, 10g fiber), 22g pro.

ROCKY ROAD
RICE KRISPIES TREATS
PAGE 188

Cookies, Brownies & Bars

Our Test Kitchen staff loves to whip up blissful batches of bite-sized goodies for family and friends. And with these fun, flavorful recipes, you will too!

TWO-TONE CARAMEL BROWNIES

This dessert is a mashup of two bar recipes. A woman I worked with gave me the recipe for chocolate caramel brownies, and I had an easy recipe for bars made with yellow cake mix. I wondered what they would taste like if I baked them together, so I tried it. I've been making them ever since!
—Staci Perry Mergenthal, Verdi, MN

- -

Prep: 40 min.
Bake: 20 min. + cooling
Makes: 40 servings

- 1 pkg. chocolate cake mix (regular size)
- ¾ cup butter, melted
- 1 can (5 oz.) evaporated milk, divided
- 1 pkg. (11 oz.) Kraft caramel bits
- 1 cup semisweet chocolate chips
- 1 pkg. yellow cake mix (regular size)
- 1 large egg, room temperature
- ½ cup plus 1 Tbsp. butter, softened, divided
- 1 can (14 oz.) sweetened condensed milk
- 1 pkg. (11½ oz.) milk chocolate chips

1. Preheat oven to 350°. Line a 13x9-in. baking pan with parchment; grease paper. In a large bowl, beat chocolate cake mix, melted butter and ⅓ cup evaporated milk until blended; batter will be thick. Reserve ¼ cup batter for topping. Spread remaining batter into prepared pan. Bake 6 minutes.
2. Meanwhile, in a microwave, melt the caramel and remaining ⅓ cup evaporated milk; stir until smooth. Sprinkle the hot chocolate crust with semisweet chips; pour caramel mixture over top.
3. In another large bowl, beat the yellow cake mix, egg and ½ cup softened butter until combined; the batter will be thick. Reserve half for the topping. Crumble remaining mixture over caramel layer. Bake 6 minutes.
4. In a microwave, melt the sweetened condensed milk, milk chocolate chips and the remaining 1 Tbsp. softened butter; stir until smooth. Pour over yellow cake layer. Sprinkle with reserved yellow and chocolate cake batters. Bake until the top is golden brown, 20-25 minutes. Cool completely on a wire rack. Store in an airtight container.
1 brownie: 272 cal., 13g fat (8g sat. fat), 27mg chol., 260mg sod., 38g carb. (28g sugars, 1g fiber), 3g pro.

BUTTERFINGER COOKIES

These terrific cookies featuring a favorite candy don't last long—make a double batch!
—Carol Kitchens, Ridgeland, MS

- -

Prep: 15 min.
Bake: 10 min./batch + cooling
Makes: about 4 dozen

- ½ cup butter, softened
- ¾ cup sugar
- ⅔ cup packed brown sugar
- 2 large egg whites, room temperature
- 1¼ cups chunky peanut butter
- 1½ tsp. vanilla extract
- 1 cup all-purpose flour
- ½ tsp. baking soda
- ¼ tsp. salt
- 6 Butterfinger candy bars (1.9 oz. each), chopped

1. Preheat oven to 350°. Cream butter and sugars until light and fluffy, 5-7 minutes. Beat in egg whites. Beat in peanut butter and vanilla. In another bowl, combine flour, baking soda and salt; gradually beat into creamed mixture. Stir in candy bars.
2. Shape into 1½-in. balls and place 2 in. apart on greased baking sheets. Bake until golden brown, 10-12 minutes. Remove to wire racks to cool.
1 cookie: 122 cal., 7g fat (2g sat. fat), 5mg chol., 92mg sod., 15g carb. (10g sugars, 1g fiber), 2g pro.

TWO-TONE CARAMEL BROWNIES

SPRITZ COOKIES

It was a tradition to make these cookies with my grandmother every Christmas. Now my two daughters help me make them.
—Sharon Claussen, Wheat Ridge, CO

- -

Prep: 25 min. • **Bake:** 15 min./batch
Makes: 11 dozen

- 2 cups butter, softened
- 1 cup sugar
- 2 large eggs, room temperature
- 2 tsp. vanilla extract
- 4 cups all-purpose flour
- 1 tsp. baking powder
- ½ cup confectioners' sugar
- 1 to 2 Tbsp. water
  Colored sugar

1. Preheat oven to 325°. In a large bowl, cream butter and sugar until light and fluffy, 5-7 minutes. Add eggs, 1 at a time, beating well after each addition. Beat in vanilla. Combine flour and baking powder; add to creamed mixture and mix well.
2. Using a cookie press fitted with the disk of your choice, press dough 2 in. apart onto ungreased baking sheets. Bake until set, 11-12 minutes (do not brown). Remove to wire racks to cool.
3. Place confectioners' sugar in a small bowl; stir in enough water to reach desired consistency. Working with 1 cookie at a time, brush the glaze on the surface and sprinkle with sugar. Let stand until set.
1 cookie: 49 cal., 3g fat (2g sat. fat), 10mg chol., 28mg sod., 5g carb. (3g sugars, 0 fiber), 1g pro.

ASK SARAH

HOW CAN I QUICKLY SOFTEN BUTTER?
The fastest way to soften butter is to shred it with a box grater. You can also cut it into cubes.

SPRITZ
COOKIES

GLUTEN-FREE
BROWNIE BARS

GLUTEN-FREE BROWNIE BARS

I can't eat dairy or gluten, but I crave the delicious brownies I used to eat before these restrictions. This recipe sure is a satisfying substitute! The brownies will still seem soft from the oven. They're done when the edges are very lightly browned.
—Linda Speranza, Buckeye, AZ

- -

Prep: 20 min. • **Bake:** 30 min. + cooling
Makes: 16 servings

- 1   cup almond butter
- ½   cup agave nectar
- 1   large egg, room temperature
- ½   tsp. salt
- ½   tsp. baking powder
- 1   pkg. (10 oz.) dairy-free semisweet chocolate chips
- 1   cup chopped walnuts, lightly toasted

1. Preheat oven to 325°. Line an 8-in. square baking pan with parchment, letting ends extend up sides; set aside. In a large bowl, beat first 5 ingredients until blended. Stir in chocolate chips and walnuts. Spread into prepared pan.
2. Bake until edges begin to brown and a toothpick inserted in center comes out with moist crumbs (do not overbake), 30-35 minutes. Cool completely in pan on a wire rack, at least 2 hours. Lifting with parchment, remove brownies from pan. Cut into bars. Store in an airtight container.
1 bar: 266 cal., 19g fat (5g sat. fat), 12mg chol., 131mg sod., 23g carb. (17g sugars, 3g fiber), 6g pro.

THICK SUGAR COOKIES

THICK SUGAR COOKIES

This thick and cakelike sugar cookie is similar to those sold at bakeries. My children often request these for their birthdays and are always happy to help decorate them.
—Heather Biedler, Martinsburg, WV

- -

Prep: 25 min. + chilling
Bake: 10 min./batch + cooling
Makes: about 3 dozen

- 1   cup butter, softened
- 1   cup sugar
- 2   large eggs, room temperature
- 3   large egg yolks, room temperature
- 1½ tsp. vanilla extract
- ¾   tsp. almond extract
- 3½ cups all-purpose flour
- 1½ tsp. baking powder
- ¼   tsp. salt

FROSTING
- 4   cups confectioners' sugar
- ½   cup butter, softened
- ½   cup shortening
- 1   tsp. vanilla extract
- ½   tsp. almond extract
- 2   to 3 Tbsp. 2% milk
     Assorted colored sprinkles, optional

1. In a large bowl, cream butter and sugar until light and fluffy, 5-7 minutes. Beat in eggs, egg yolks and extracts. In another bowl, whisk flour, baking powder and salt; gradually beat into the creamed mixture. Shape into a disk; wrap and refrigerate 1 hour or until firm enough to roll.
2. Preheat oven to 375°. On a lightly floured surface, roll dough to ½-in. thickness. Cut with a floured 2-in. cookie cutter. Place 1 in. apart on ungreased baking sheets.
3. Bake until the edges begin to brown, 10-12 minutes. Cool on pans 5 minutes. Remove to wire racks to cool completely.
4. For the frosting, in a large bowl, beat confectioners' sugar, butter, shortening, extracts and enough milk to reach desired consistency. Spread over the cookies. If desired, sprinkle with nonpareils.
1 frosted cookie: 219 cal., 11g fat (6g sat. fat), 49mg chol., 92mg sod., 28g carb. (18g sugars, 0 fiber), 2g pro.

"This is the cookie I make for all my cutout needs, whether it's for Christmas or another holiday. Almond extract can be a little polarizing, so I usually leave it out and just add the vanilla."
—PEGGY WOODWARD, SENIOR FOOD EDITOR

APPLE KUCHEN BARS

This recipe is about family, comfort and simplicity. My mom made this delicious sweet treat many a winter night and served it warm with some of her homemade ice cream. I like to make a double batch and pass on the love!
—Elizabeth Monfort, Celina, OH

- -

Prep: 35 min. • **Bake:** 1 hour + cooling
Makes: 2 dozen

   3   cups all-purpose flour, divided
   ¼   tsp. salt
   1½ cups cold butter, divided
   4   to 5 Tbsp. ice water
   8   cups thinly sliced peeled
       tart apples (about 8 medium)
   2   cups sugar, divided
   2   tsp. ground cinnamon

1. Preheat oven to 350°. Place 2 cups flour and the salt in a food processor; pulse until blended. Add 1 cup butter; pulse until the butter is the size of peas. While pulsing, add just enough ice water to form moist crumbs. Press mixture onto bottom of a greased 13x9-in. baking pan. Bake until edges are lightly browned, 20-25 minutes. Cool on a wire rack.
2. In a large bowl, combine apples, 1 cup sugar and cinnamon; toss to coat. Spoon over crust. Place remaining flour, butter and sugar in food processor; pulse until coarse crumbs form. Sprinkle over apples. Bake until golden brown and apples are tender, 60-70 minutes. Cool completely on a wire rack. Cut into bars.
1 bar: 240 cal., 12g fat (7g sat. fat), 30mg chol., 106mg sod., 33g carb. (21g sugars, 1g fiber), 2g pro.

BERRY-PATCH BROWNIE PIZZA

BERRY-PATCH BROWNIE PIZZA

I just love the combination of fruit, almonds and chocolate that makes this brownie so distinctive. The fruit lightens the chocolate a bit and makes it feel as though you're eating something both decadent and healthy.
—Sue Kauffman, Columbia City, IN

- -

Prep: 20 min. + chilling
Bake: 15 min. + cooling
Makes: 12 servings

   1   pkg. fudge brownie mix
       (13x9-in. pan size)
   ⅓   cup chopped unblanched almonds
   1   tsp. almond extract
TOPPING
   1   pkg. (8 oz.) cream cheese, softened
   1   Tbsp. sugar
   1   tsp. vanilla extract
   ½   tsp. grated lemon zest
   2   cups whipped topping

       Assorted fresh berries
       Optional: Fresh mint leaves
       and coarse sugar

1. Preheat oven to 375°. Prepare brownie batter according to package directions for fudgelike brownies, adding almonds and almond extract. Spread into a greased 14-in. pizza pan.
2. Bake until a toothpick inserted in the center comes out clean, 15-18 minutes. Cool completely on a wire rack.
3. Beat first 4 topping ingredients until smooth; fold in whipped topping. Spread over the crust to within ½ in. of edge; refrigerate, loosely covered, 2 hours.
4. To serve, cut into 12 pieces; top with berries of choice. If desired, top with mint and sprinkle with coarse sugar.
1 piece: 404 cal., 26g fat (8g sat. fat), 51mg chol., 240mg sod., 39g carb. (26g sugars, 2g fiber), 5g pro.

AUDREY'S LEMON MERINGUE BARS

We have a prolific lemon tree in our backyard and are forever trying to find new ways to incorporate lemons into our culinary endeavors. My daughter, Audrey, knows my love of all things sweet and decided to test her baking skill by combining two of my lemony favorites: lemon bars and lemon meringue pie. After hours in the kitchen, these delicious bars were born.
—Monica Fearnside,
Rancho Palos Verdes, CA

Prep: 35 min. + cooling
Bake: 40 min. + chilling • **Makes:** 2 dozen

2 cups all-purpose flour
½ cup sugar
¼ tsp. salt
1 cup cold butter

FILLING

1⅓ cups sugar
½ cup lemon juice
4 large eggs
¼ cup all-purpose flour
2 Tbsp. grated lemon zest

MERINGUE

3 large egg whites, room temperature
1 tsp. grated lemon zest
¼ tsp. cream of tartar
7 Tbsp. sugar

1. Preheat oven to 350°. Line a 13x9-in. baking pan with parchment, letting ends extend up sides.

2. In a large bowl, combine flour, sugar and salt; cut in butter until mixture resembles coarse crumbs. Press into the bottom of the prepared pan. Bake until light golden brown, 20-25 minutes. Cool completely on a wire rack.

3. For filling, in another large bowl, mix sugar, lemon juice, eggs, flour and zest until combined. Pour over crust. Bake until set and top is dry, 22-27 minutes.

4. Meanwhile, for meringue, in a large bowl, beat egg whites with lemon zest and cream of tartar on medium speed until foamy. Gradually add sugar, 1 Tbsp. at a time, beating on high after each addition until the sugar is dissolved. Continue beating until stiff glossy peaks form. Spread or pipe over hot filling.

5. Bake until meringue is golden brown, 15-18 minutes. Cool 1 hour on a wire rack. Refrigerate at least 4 hours before serving. Lifting with parchment, remove from pan. Cut into bars.

1 bar: 200 cal., 9g fat (5g sat. fat), 51mg chol., 105mg sod., 29g carb. (19g sugars, 0 fiber), 3g pro.

"These may be the best lemon meringue bars I've ever had! They are so pretty and always impress wherever I take them."
—MARGARET KNOEBEL, ASSOCIATE RECIPE EDITOR/ TEST COOK

AUDREY'S LEMON MERINGUE BARS

CHOCOLATE MARSHMALLOW COOKIES

What fun—these double-chocolaty delights have a surprise bit of marshmallow. Kids love them!

—June Formanek, Belle Plaine, IA

Prep: 25 min.
Bake: 10 min./batch + cooling
Makes: 3 dozen

½ cup butter, softened
1 cup sugar
1 large egg, room temperature
¼ cup 2% milk
1 tsp. vanilla extract
1¾ cups all-purpose flour
⅓ cup baking cocoa
½ tsp. baking soda
½ tsp. salt
18 large marshmallows
ICING
6 Tbsp. butter, softened
2 Tbsp. baking cocoa
¼ cup 2% milk
1¾ cups confectioners' sugar
½ tsp. vanilla extract
Pecan halves

1. In a large bowl, cream the butter and sugar. Add the egg, milk and vanilla; mix well. Combine flour, cocoa, baking soda and salt; beat into creamed mixture.
2. Drop by tablespoonfuls onto ungreased baking sheets. Bake at 350° for 8 minutes. Meanwhile, cut marshmallows in half. Press a marshmallow half, cut side down, onto each cookie. Return to the oven for 2 minutes. Cool completely on a wire rack.
3. For icing, in a small saucepan, combine the butter, cocoa and milk. Bring to a boil; boil for 1 minute, stirring constantly. Cool slightly; transfer to a small bowl. Beat in the confectioners' sugar and vanilla until smooth. Spread over the cooled cookies. Top each with a pecan half.
1 cookie: 125 cal., 5g fat (3g sat. fat), 17mg chol., 92mg sod., 20g carb. (14g sugars, 0 fiber), 1g pro.

CHOCOLATE
MARSHMALLOW
COOKIES

PEANUT BUTTER COOKIES

It is amazing how much flavor is in these simple cookies. I make them often because I always have the ingredients on hand. It's nice that the recipe makes a little batch.
—Maggie Schimmel, Wauwatosa, WI

- -

Takes: 30 min. • **Makes:** 2 dozen

- 1 large egg, room temperature, beaten
- 1 cup sugar
- 1 cup creamy peanut butter

1. In a large bowl, mix all the ingredients. Scoop level tablespoonfuls and roll into balls. Place on ungreased baking sheets and flatten with a fork.
2. Bake at 350° until set, about 18 minutes. Remove to wire racks to cool.
1 cookie: 99 cal., 6g fat (1g sat. fat), 8mg chol., 48mg sod., 11g carb. (10g sugars, 1g fiber), 3g pro.

DID YOU KNOW?
Peanut butter cookies can be a bit dense. Adding a criss-cross pattern with a fork flattens them so they bake more evenly.

LOADED M&M OREO COOKIE BARS

We're all so busy and pressed for time. I find myself creating recipes that are fast to prepare and deliver fabulous results, proving you don't have to spend all day in the kitchen. Here's a favorite of mine that combines chocolate candies and cookies into one wonderful bar.
—Averie Sunshine, San Diego, CA

- -

Prep: 15 min. • **Bake:** 25 min. + cooling
Makes: 9 bars

- 1 large egg, room temperature
- 1 cup packed light brown sugar
- ½ cup unsalted butter, melted
- 3 tsp. vanilla extract
- ¼ tsp. baking soda, optional
- ¼ tsp. salt, optional
- 1 cup all-purpose flour
- 18 Oreo cookies, coarsely chopped
- ½ cup milk chocolate M&M's

1. Preheat oven to 350°. Line an 8-in. square baking pan with foil, letting the ends extend up sides of pan; grease foil.
2. In a large bowl, whisk the egg, brown sugar, butter and vanilla until blended. If desired, add baking soda and salt to flour; add flour to brown sugar mixture. Stir in chopped cookies.
3. Spread into prepared pan; sprinkle with M&M's. Bake for 25-30 minutes or until a toothpick inserted in center comes out with moist crumbs (do not overbake). Cool completely in pan on a wire rack. Lifting with foil, remove from pan. Cut into bars. Store in an airtight container.
Note: For a chewier cookie bar texture, add the baking soda and salt.
1 bar: 403 cal., 18g fat (9g sat. fat), 49mg chol., 117mg sod., 58g carb. (40g sugars, 1g fiber), 3g pro.

"My family loves these bars. We swap out the M&M colors for a quick and easy holiday treat."
—RAEANN THOMPSON, ASSOCIATE CREATIVE DIRECTOR

LOADED M&M
OREO COOKIE BARS

GRANDMA KRAUSE'S COCONUT COOKIES

GRANDMA KRAUSE'S COCONUT COOKIES

When my two daughters were young, their great-grandma made them cookies with oats and coconut. Thankfully, she shared the recipe.
—Debra J. Dorn, Dunnellon, FL

Prep: 40 min. + freezing
Bake: 10 min./batch
Makes: about 3½ dozen

1 cup shortening
1 cup sugar
1 cup packed brown sugar
2 large eggs, room temperature
1 tsp. vanilla extract
2 cups all-purpose flour
1 tsp. baking powder
1 tsp. baking soda
¼ tsp. salt
1 cup old-fashioned oats
1 cup sweetened shredded coconut

1. In a large bowl, beat the shortening and sugars until blended. Beat in eggs and vanilla. In another bowl, whisk flour, baking powder, baking soda and salt; gradually beat into sugar mixture. Stir in oats and coconut.

2. Divide the dough into 4 portions. On a lightly floured surface, shape each into a 6-in.-long log. Wrap in waxed paper; freeze 2 hours or until firm.

3. Preheat oven to 350°. Unwrap and cut the dough crosswise into ½-in. slices, reshaping as needed. Place 2 in. apart on ungreased baking sheets. Bake for 10-12 minutes or until golden brown. Cool on pans 5 minutes. Remove to wire racks to cool.

1 cookie: 124 cal., 6g fat (2g sat. fat), 9mg chol., 66mg sod., 17g carb. (11g sugars, 0 fiber), 1g pro.

STRAWBERRY & PEACH LIME CUSTARD BARS

After I baked, my dad would always find his way to the kitchen and ask if he could try what I made. I enjoyed asking him to taste test different creations, such as these bars. He was always ready with a compliment. Other fruits can be arranged over the custard, depending on what's in season.
—Carlin Tou, Chandler, AZ

Prep: 20 min. + cooling
Bake: 20 min. + chilling • **Makes:** 2 dozen

2 cups graham cracker crumbs
1 cup all-purpose flour
¾ cup butter, softened
½ cup plus 2 Tbsp. sugar, divided
5 large egg yolks
4 oz. cream cheese, softened
1 can (14 oz.) sweetened condensed milk
½ cup lime juice
2 Tbsp. grated lime zest, divided
1 Tbsp. vanilla bean paste
2½ cups fresh strawberries, halved
1 can (15 oz.) peach halves in light syrup, drained and thinly sliced
2 tsp. ground cinnamon

1. Preheat oven to 350°. Line a 13x9-in. baking pan with nonstick foil; set aside. In a large bowl, beat cracker crumbs, flour, butter and ½ cup sugar until combined. Press onto bottom of prepared pan. Bake until lightly browned, 10-15 minutes. Cool on a wire rack.

2. In a large bowl, beat the egg yolks and cream cheese until smooth. Beat in the milk and lime juice until blended. Stir in 1 Tbsp. lime zest and vanilla paste; pour over the cooled crust. Alternately arrange strawberries and peaches in closely spaced rows over the filling. Combine cinnamon and remaining 2 Tbsp. sugar; sprinkle over fruit.

3. Bake 20-25 minutes or until custard looks set. Cool completely on a wire rack. Cover and refrigerate at least 2 hours or overnight. Sprinkle with remaining 1 Tbsp. lime zest; cut into bars.

1 bar: 226 cal., 11g fat (6g sat. fat), 64mg chol., 123mg sod., 30g carb. (20g sugars, 1g fiber), 4g pro.

STRAWBERRY & PEACH
LIME CUSTARD BARS

BANANA NUT BROWNIES

This recipe comes from my Grandma Schlientz. Anytime there are ripe bananas around our house, it's banana brownie time! People are always surprised to learn bananas are the secret ingredient.
—Christine Mol, Grand Rapids, MI

Prep: 10 min. • **Bake:** 40 min. + cooling
Makes: 16 brownies

- ½ cup butter, melted, cooled
- 1 cup sugar
- 3 Tbsp. baking cocoa
- 2 large eggs, room temperature, lightly beaten
- 1 Tbsp. 2% milk
- 1 tsp. vanilla extract
- ½ cup all-purpose flour
- 1 tsp. baking powder
- ¼ tsp. salt
- 1 cup mashed ripe bananas (2½ to 3 medium)
- ½ cup chopped walnuts
  Confectioners' sugar, optional

1. In a bowl, combine butter, sugar and cocoa. Stir in eggs, milk and vanilla. Blend in flour, baking powder and salt. Stir in bananas and nuts.
2. Pour into a greased 9-in. square baking pan. Bake at 350° until a toothpick comes out with moist crumbs, 40-45 minutes. Cool on a wire rack. Just before serving, dust with confectioners' sugar if desired.
1 brownie: 163 cal., 9g fat (4g sat. fat), 42mg chol., 128mg sod., 20g carb. (15g sugars, 1g fiber), 3g pro.

FIRST-PLACE COCONUT MACAROONS

These coconut macaroon cookies earned me a first-place ribbon at the county fair. They remain my husband's favorites— whenever I make them to give away, he asks me where his batch is! I especially like the fact that this recipe makes a small enough batch for the two of us to nibble on.
—Penny Ann Habeck, Shawano, WI

Prep: 10 min. • **Bake:** 20 min./batch
Makes: about 1½ dozen

- 1⅓ cups sweetened shredded coconut
- ⅓ cup sugar
- 2 Tbsp. all-purpose flour
- ⅛ tsp. salt
- 2 large egg whites, room temperature
- ½ tsp. vanilla extract

1. Preheat oven to 325°. In a small bowl, combine the coconut, sugar, flour and salt. Add egg whites and vanilla; mix well.
2. Drop by rounded teaspoonfuls onto greased baking sheets. Bake until golden brown, 18-20 minutes. Cool on a wire rack.
1 cookie: 54 cal., 2g fat (2g sat. fat), 0 chol., 41mg sod., 8g carb. (7g sugars, 0 fiber), 1g pro. **Diabetic exchanges:** ½ starch, ½ fat.

BANANA NUT BROWNIES

WYOMING
COWBOY COOKIES

GOOEY BUTTER COOKIES

As a native of St. Louis, I wanted to make a cookie version of the famous gooey butter cake. And although many gooey butter cake recipes use a cake mix, these cookies are made from scratch.
—Julia TenHoeve, Richmond, VA

Prep: 25 min. + chilling
Bake: 10 min./batch • **Makes:** 5 dozen

- ½ cup butter, softened
- 1 pkg. (8 oz.) cream cheese, softened
- 1½ cups sugar
- 1 large egg, room temperature
- 1¼ tsp. vanilla extract
- 2¼ cups all-purpose flour
- ½ cup nonfat dry milk powder
- 3 tsp. baking powder
- ½ cup confectioners' sugar

1. Preheat oven to 350°. Beat butter, cream cheese and sugar until blended. Beat in egg and vanilla. In another bowl, whisk flour, milk powder and baking powder; gradually beat into creamed mixture. Chill the dough 30 minutes or until slightly firm.
2. Scoop level tablespoons of dough; roll in confectioners' sugar. Place 1 in. apart on parchment-lined baking sheets. Bake until light brown, 10-12 minutes. Remove from pans to wire racks to cool.
1 cookie: 70 cal., 3g fat (2g sat. fat), 11mg chol., 50mg sod., 10g carb. (6g sugars, 0 fiber), 1g pro.

WYOMING COWBOY COOKIES

These cookies are very popular here in Wyoming. Mix up a batch and see why!
—Patsy Steenbock, Shoshoni, WY

Prep: 25 min. • **Bake:** 15 min.
Makes: 6 dozen

- 1 cup sweetened shredded coconut
- ¾ cup chopped pecans
- 1 cup butter, softened
- 1½ cups packed brown sugar
- ½ cup sugar
- 2 large eggs, room temperature
- 1½ tsp. vanilla extract
- 2 cups all-purpose flour
- 1 tsp. baking soda
- ½ tsp. salt
- 2 cups old-fashioned oats
- 2 cups chocolate chips

1. Preheat oven to 350°. Place coconut and pecans on a 15x10x1-in. baking pan. Bake for 6-8 minutes or until toasted, stirring every 2 minutes. Set aside to cool.
2. In a large bowl, cream butter and sugars until light and fluffy, 5-7 minutes. Add eggs and vanilla; beat well. In another bowl, combine the flour, baking soda and salt. Add to creamed mixture; beat well. Stir in the oats, chocolate chips, and toasted coconut and pecans.
3. Drop by rounded teaspoonfuls onto greased baking sheets. Bake at 350° until browned, about 12 minutes. Remove to wire racks to cool.
1 cookie: 105 cal., 6g fat (3g sat. fat), 12mg chol., 61mg sod., 14g carb. (9g sugars, 1g fiber), 1g pro.

TEST KITCHEN TIP

For hearty appetites, double the size of these cookies. Just make sure to increase the baking time until they're golden brown. Don't overbake, though. You want them crunchy on the outside and chewy on the inside.

BACK-TO-SCHOOL COOKIES

These have become a favorite for almost anyone who tries them, and they make a delicious after-school treat, especially with a glass of ice-cold milk.
—Frances Pierce, Waddington, NY

Prep: 30 min. • **Bake:** 10 min./batch
Makes: 6½ dozen

- 1   cup butter-flavored shortening
- 1   cup creamy peanut butter
- 2   cups packed brown sugar
- 4   large egg whites
- 1   tsp. vanilla extract
- 2   cups all-purpose flour
- 1   tsp. baking soda
- ½   tsp. baking powder
- 2   cups crisp rice cereal
- 1½   cups chopped nuts
- 1   cup sweetened shredded coconut
- 1   cup quick-cooking oats

1. Preheat oven to 375°. In a large bowl, cream the shortening, peanut butter and brown sugar until light and fluffy, about 5 minutes. Beat in egg whites and vanilla. Combine the flour, baking soda and baking powder; gradually add to creamed mixture and mix well. Stir in cereal, nuts, coconut and oats.

2. Drop by rounded tablespoonfuls 2 in. apart onto ungreased baking sheets. Bake 7-8 minutes or until golden brown. Remove to wire racks.

1 cookie: 103 cal., 6g fat (1g sat. fat), 0 chol., 49mg sod., 11g carb. (6g sugars, 1g fiber), 2g pro.

TEST KITCHEN TIP
Get creative with your mix-ins! Try chocolate or butterscotch chips and dried cranberries.

LEMON LOVER'S COOKIES

With butter and confectioners' sugar, these light cookies will melt in your mouth. They're sure to be a hit wherever you serve them.
—Virginia Dillard, Whitmire, SC

Prep: 20 min. + chilling
Bake: 10 min./batch + cooling
Makes: About 3½ dozen

- ¾   cup butter, softened
- ⅓   cup confectioners' sugar
- 2   tsp. lemon juice
- 1   cup all-purpose flour
- ½   cup cornstarch
- 1   tsp. grated lemon zest

LEMON FROSTING
- ¼   cup butter, softened
- 1   cup confectioners' sugar
- 2   tsp. lemon juice
- 1   tsp. grated lemon zest

GARNISH
   Additional grated lemon zest, optional

1. In a small bowl, cream butter and sugar until light and fluffy, 5-7 minutes. Beat in lemon juice. Combine the flour, cornstarch and lemon zest; gradually add to creamed mixture and mix well.

2. Shape into a 1½-in. roll; securely wrap in waxed paper. Refrigerate for 1 hour or until firm. Unwrap and cut into ¼-in. slices. Place 2 in. apart on greased baking sheets.

3. Bake at 350° until the edges are golden brown, 10-12 minutes. Gently remove to wire racks to cool completely.

4. For frosting, in a small bowl, beat butter until fluffy. Add the confectioners' sugar, lemon juice and zest; beat until smooth. Spread over cooled cookies; sprinkle with additional lemon zest if desired. Let stand until set. Store in an airtight container.

1 cookie: 74 cal., 5g fat (3g sat. fat), 12mg chol., 37mg sod., 8g carb. (4g sugars, 0 fiber), 0 pro. **Diabetic exchanges:** 1 fat, ½ starch.

BACK-TO-SCHOOL COOKIES

PEANUT BUTTER CHOCOLATE BARS

These chewy bars are the perfect no-fuss contribution to a potluck or bake sale. I've discovered the trick is to get them into the refrigerator so the chocolate can set before they disappear!
—Lorri Speer, Centralia, WA

Prep: 30 min. + chilling • **Makes:** 2 dozen

- 1 **cup sugar**
- 1 **cup light corn syrup**
- 1 **cup peanut butter**
- 6 **cups crisp rice cereal**
- 2 **cups semisweet chocolate chips, melted**

In a large saucepan, combine sugar, corn syrup and peanut butter. Cook and stir over medium-low heat until the sugar is dissolved. Remove from the heat; stir in cereal. Spread into a greased 13x9-in. pan; press lightly. Spread the melted chocolate over top; refrigerate until set. Cut into bars.

1 bar: 302 cal., 14g fat (6g sat. fat), 0 chol., 96mg sod., 46g carb. (37g sugars, 2g fiber), 4g pro.

TEST KITCHEN TIP

If you're looking to cut some sugar in these bars, feel free to substitute all-natural peanut butter for regular.

PEANUT BUTTER CHOCOLATE BARS

CHOCOLATE PECAN
SKILLET COOKIE

CHOCOLATE PECAN SKILLET COOKIE

Bake up the ultimate shareable cookie! For variety, swap the chocolate chips for an equal quantity of M&M's or chocolate chunks. Or go super fancy by mixing the chocolate chips and pecans into the dough, then gently folding in fresh raspberries.
—James Schend, Deputy Culinary Editor, *Taste of Home*

- -

Prep: 15 min. • **Bake:** 35 min.
Makes: 12 servings

1	cup butter
1	cup sugar
1	cup packed brown sugar
2	large eggs, room temperature
2	tsp. vanilla extract
3	cups all-purpose flour
1½	tsp. baking soda
½	tsp. kosher salt
1	cup 60% cacao bittersweet chocolate baking chips
1	cup chopped pecans, toasted Vanilla ice cream, optional

1. Preheat oven to 350°. In a 12-in. cast-iron skillet, heat butter in oven as it preheats. Meanwhile, in a large bowl, stir together sugar and brown sugar. When butter is almost melted, remove skillet from oven and swirl butter until completely melted. Stir the butter into sugar mixture; set skillet aside.
2. Beat eggs and vanilla into sugar mixture. In another bowl, whisk together the flour, baking soda and salt; gradually beat into sugar mixture. Stir in chocolate chips and nuts. Spread mixture into buttered skillet.
3. Bake until toothpick inserted in center comes out with moist crumbs and top is golden brown, 35-40 minutes. Serve warm, with vanilla ice cream if desired.
1 serving: 528 cal., 27g fat (13g sat. fat), 72mg chol., 378mg sod., 69g carb. (43g sugars, 3g fiber), 6g pro.

TEST KITCHEN TIP
This cookie can be prepared in four 6-in. cast-iron skillets. Just brush skillets with melted butter before adding dough. Bake 25-30 minutes.

HOMEMADE HONEY GRAHAMS

HOMEMADE HONEY GRAHAMS

The way my boys eat them, I would spend a fortune on honey graham crackers at the grocery store. So I decided to make a homemade version that is less processed—and less expensive. These are wonderful, although they still don't last long.
—Crystal Jo Bruns, Iliff, CO

- -

Prep: 15 min. + chilling
Bake: 10 min./batch • **Makes:** 32 crackers

1	cup whole wheat flour
¾	cup all-purpose flour
½	cup toasted wheat germ
2	Tbsp. dark brown sugar
1	tsp. baking powder
1	tsp. ground cinnamon
½	tsp. salt
½	tsp. baking soda
6	Tbsp. cold butter, cubed
¼	cup honey
4	Tbsp. ice water

1. In a bowl, whisk the first 8 ingredients; cut in butter until crumbly. In another bowl, whisk honey and water; gradually add to dry ingredients, tossing with a fork until dough holds together when pressed.
2. Divide dough in half. Shape each into a disk; cover and refrigerate until firm enough to roll, about 30 minutes.
3. Preheat oven to 350°. On a lightly floured surface, roll each portion of dough to an 8-in. square. Using a knife or fluted pastry wheel, cut each portion into sixteen 2-in. squares. If desired, prick holes with a fork. Place 1 in. apart on parchment-lined baking sheets.
4. Bake until the edges are light brown, 10-12 minutes. Remove from pans to wire racks to cool. Store in an airtight container.
1 cracker: 60 cal., 2g fat (1g sat. fat), 6mg chol., 89mg sod., 9g carb. (3g sugars, 1g fiber), 1g pro. **Diabetic exchanges:** ½ starch, ½ fat.

ROCKY ROAD RICE KRISPIES TREATS

Piled high with chocolate chunks, gooey marshmallows and crushed graham crackers, this rocky road treat recipe is perfect for those with a sweet tooth.
—Taste of Home Test Kitchen

Prep: 20 min. + chilling • **Makes:** 2 dozen

- 2 pkg. (10 oz. each) miniature marshmallows, divided
- 3 Tbsp. canola oil
- 5 cups Rice Krispies
- 5 whole graham crackers, crumbled
- 1¼ cups salted roasted almonds, chopped and divided
- 2 pkg. (11½ oz. each) semisweet chocolate chunks, divided

In a microwave or a large saucepan over low heat, melt 1 package of marshmallows in oil; stir until smooth. Remove from heat; stir in cereal, graham crackers, 1 cup almonds and 1 cup chocolate chunks. Press the mixture into a lightly greased 13x9-in. baking pan, using waxed paper or a lightly greased spatula. Cool to room temperature. Melt 1 package chocolate chunks in microwave; spread over top. Sprinkle with the remaining package of marshmallows and the remaining almonds and chocolate chunks. If desired, toast marshmallows using a kitchen torch. Cut into bars.
1 bar: 318 cal., 16g fat (5g sat. fat), 0 chol., 124mg sod., 46g carb. (30g sugars, 3g fiber), 4g pro.

RANGER COOKIES

RANGER COOKIES

These golden brown cookies are crispy on the outside and cakelike on the inside. You won't be able to eat just one!
—Mary Lou Boyce, Wilmington, DE

Prep: 25 min. • **Bake:** 10 min./batch
Makes: 7½ dozen

- 1 cup shortening
- 1 cup sugar
- 1 cup packed brown sugar
- 2 large eggs, room temperature
- 1 tsp. vanilla extract
- 2 cups all-purpose flour
- 1 tsp. baking soda
- ½ tsp. baking powder
- ½ tsp. salt
- 2 cups quick-cooking oats
- 2 cups crisp rice cereal
- 1 cup sweetened shredded coconut

1. Preheat oven to 350°. In a large bowl, cream shortening and sugars until light and fluffy, 5-7 minutes. Beat in eggs and vanilla. Combine flour, baking soda, baking powder and salt; gradually add to creamed mixture and mix well. Stir in oats, cereal and coconut.
2. Drop by rounded tablespoonfuls 2 in. apart onto ungreased baking sheets. Bake until golden brown, 7-9 minutes. Remove from pans to wire racks to cool.
1 cookie: 63 cal., 3g fat (1g sat. fat), 5mg chol., 40mg sod., 9g carb. (5g sugars, 0 fiber), 1g pro.

TEST KITCHEN TIP
To make Peanut Butter Ranger Cookies, add 1 cup creamy peanut butter to shortening and sugar mixture; cream as directed.

POMEGRANATE MAGIC BARS

Pomegranates make dessert festive and bright with a burst of juicy sweetness. These pomegranate bars are no exception.
—Lisa Keys, Kennet Square, PA

Prep: 45 min. • **Bake:** 25 min. + cooling
Makes: 3 dozen

- 1¼ cups all-purpose flour
- ¾ cup sugar
- ¼ cup baking cocoa
- ¾ cup cold butter, cubed
- 1 large egg, room temperature
- ½ tsp. vanilla extract
- 1 Tbsp. sesame seeds, toasted
- 1 cup sweetened shredded coconut, toasted
- ½ cup slivered almonds, toasted
- 2 cups (12 oz.) semisweet chocolate chips
- 1 can (14 oz.) sweetened condensed milk
- 1 cup pomegranate seeds

1. Preheat oven to 350°. Line a 13x9-in. pan with parchment, letting the ends extend up sides. Lightly grease the parchment with cooking spray. In a food processor, combine flour, sugar and cocoa; pulse until combined. Add butter; pulse until mixture appears sandy. Add egg and vanilla; pulse just until combined. Press dough into prepared pan.

2. Sprinkle dough with sesame seeds. Bake until top appears dry and toothpick comes out clean, 20-25 minutes. Remove from oven; sprinkle evenly with coconut, almonds and chocolate chips. Pour the condensed milk evenly over top; return to oven. Bake 25-30 minutes or until golden brown. Cool on wire rack 10 minutes.

3. Sprinkle with the pomegranate seeds; press gently into warm topping with back of a spoon. Cool completely in pan on wire rack. Lifting with parchment, remove from pan. Cut into bars.

1 bar: 176 cal., 10g fat (6g sat. fat), 19mg chol., 55mg sod., 22g carb. (17g sugars, 1g fiber), 3g pro.

"These are a really colorful twist on traditional magic bars. I like the little burst of juicy flavor from the pomegranate seeds and how they look like little ruby jewels on top."
—MARK NEUFANG, CULINARY ASSISTANT

POMEGRANATE MAGIC BARS

GOOEY CHOCOLATE CARAMEL BARS

These rich, gooey bars are my most-requested treats. They're popular at school functions, family barbecues and picnics. We like them alone or topped with a scoop of ice cream.
—Betty Hagerty, Philadelphia, PA

- -

Prep: 25 min. • **Bake:** 20 min. + cooling
Makes: about 4½ dozen

2¼ cups all-purpose flour, divided
2 cups quick-cooking oats
1½ cups packed brown sugar
1 tsp. baking soda
½ tsp. salt
1½ cups cold butter, cubed
2 cups semisweet chocolate chips
1 cup chopped pecans
1 jar (12 oz.) caramel ice cream topping

1. Preheat oven to 350°. In a large bowl, combine 2 cups flour, oats, brown sugar, baking soda and salt. Cut in butter until crumbly. Set half aside for topping.
2. Press the remaining crumb mixture into a greased 13x9-in. baking pan. Bake 15 minutes. Sprinkle with the chocolate chips and pecans.
3. Whisk caramel topping and remaining flour until smooth; drizzle over the top. Sprinkle with reserved crumb mixture. Bake for 18-20 minutes or until golden brown. Cool on a wire rack for 2 hours before cutting.
1 bar: 156 cal., 9g fat (5g sat. fat), 14mg chol., 110mg sod., 20g carb. (13g sugars, 1g fiber), 2g pro.

AMISH SUGAR COOKIES

These easy-to-make cookies simply melt in your mouth. I've passed the recipe around to many friends. After I gave the recipe to my sister, she entered the cookies in a local fair and won the best of show prize!
—Sylvia Ford, Kennett, MO

- -

Prep: 10 min. • **Bake:** 10 min./batch
Makes: about 5 dozen

1 cup butter, softened
1 cup canola oil
1 cup sugar
1 cup confectioners' sugar
2 large eggs
1 tsp. vanilla extract
4½ cups all-purpose flour
1 tsp. baking soda
1 tsp. cream of tartar

1. Preheat oven to 375°. In a large bowl, beat butter, oil and sugars. Beat in eggs until well blended. Beat in vanilla. Combine the flour, baking soda and cream of tartar; gradually add to creamed mixture.
2. Drop by teaspoonfuls onto ungreased baking sheets. Bake for 8-10 minutes or until lightly browned. Remove to wire racks to cool.
1 cookie: 117 cal., 7g fat (2g sat. fat), 14mg chol., 48mg sod., 13g carb. (5g sugars, 0 fiber), 1g pro.

> **TEST KITCHEN TIP**
> For a little more sweetness, you can sprinkle the cookies with coarse sugar before baking.

PEANUT BUTTER COOKIE CUPS

I'm a busy schoolteacher and pastor's wife. I wouldn't dare show my face at a church dinner or bake sale without these tempting peanut butter treats. They're quick, easy to make and always a hit.
—Kristi Tackett, Banner, KY

- -

Prep: 35 min. • **Bake:** 15 min. + cooling
Makes: 3 dozen

1 pkg. (17½ oz.) peanut butter cookie mix
36 miniature peanut butter cups, unwrapped

1. Preheat oven to 350°. Prepare cookie mix according to package directions. Roll dough into thirty-six 1-in. balls. Place in greased miniature muffin cups. Press dough evenly onto bottom and up sides of each cup.
2. Bake for 11-13 minutes or until set. Immediately place a peanut butter cup in each cup; press down gently. Cool 10 minutes; carefully remove from pans.
Note: Substitute 2¼ cups peanut butter cookie dough of your choice for the cookie mix.
1 cookie cup: 119 cal., 7g fat (2g sat. fat), 6mg chol., 89mg sod., 13g carb. (3g sugars, 1g fiber), 2g pro.

CHEERY CHERRY COOKIES

With a tall glass of ice-cold milk, a couple of these cookies really hit the spot for a snack or dessert. The coconut and bits of cherries provide a fun look and texture.
—Judy Clark, Elkhart, IN

Prep: 10 min. • **Bake:** 10 min./batch
Makes: 4 dozen

- 1 cup packed brown sugar
- ¾ cup butter, softened
- 1 large egg
- 2 Tbsp. 2% milk
- 1 tsp. vanilla extract
- 2 cups all-purpose flour
- ½ tsp. salt
- ½ tsp. baking soda
- ½ cup maraschino cherries, well drained and chopped
- ½ cup sweetened shredded coconut
- ½ cup chopped pecans

1. In a large bowl, cream brown sugar and butter until light and fluffy. Beat in the egg, milk and vanilla. In another bowl, mix the flour, salt and baking soda; gradually beat into creamed mixture. Stir in the cherries, coconut and pecans.
2. Drop by teaspoonfuls onto ungreased baking sheets. Bake at 375° 10-12 minutes or until golden brown. Remove from pans to wire racks to cool.
1 cookie: 81 cal., 4g fat (2g sat. fat), 12mg chol., 74mg sod., 10g carb. (6g sugars, 0 fiber), 1g pro.

LIME & GIN COCONUT MACAROONS

I took these lime and coconut macaroons to our annual cookie exchange, where we name a queen each year. These won me the crown!
—Milissa Kirkpatrick, Palestine, TX

Prep: 20 min.
Bake: 15 min./batch + cooling
Makes: about 2½ dozen

- 4 large egg whites
- ⅔ cup sugar
- 3 Tbsp. gin
- 1½ tsp. grated lime zest
- ¼ tsp. salt
- ¼ tsp. almond extract
- 1 pkg. (14 oz.) sweetened shredded coconut
- ½ cup all-purpose flour
- 8 oz. white baking chocolate, melted

1. Preheat oven to 350°. Whisk the first 6 ingredients until blended. In another bowl, toss coconut with flour; stir in egg white mixture.
2. Drop by tablespoonfuls 2 in. apart onto greased baking sheets. Bake until tops are light brown, 15-18 minutes. Remove from pans to wire racks to cool completely.
3. Dip bottoms of macaroons into melted chocolate, allowing the excess to drip off. Place on waxed paper; let stand until set. Store in an airtight container.
1 cookie: 133 cal., 7g fat (6g sat. fat), 0 chol., 67mg sod., 17g carb. (15g sugars, 1g fiber), 2g pro.

SOUTH DAKOTA FRITO TREATS

Yep, they're made with corn chips! These salty sweets were a staple after meetings at the quilt guild I belonged to in South Dakota.
—Carol Tramp, Wynot, NE

Prep: 15 min. + standing • **Makes:** 2 dozen

- 2 pkg. (9¾ oz. each) corn chips, divided
- 2 cups semisweet chocolate chips, divided
- 1 cup sugar
- 1 cup light corn syrup
- 1 cup creamy peanut butter

1. Spread 1 package corn chips on the bottom of a greased 13x9-in. baking pan; sprinkle 1 cup chocolate chips over the top.
2. In a large heavy saucepan, combine the sugar and corn syrup. Bring to a boil; cook and stir 1 minute. Remove from heat; stir in the peanut butter. Pour half the peanut butter mixture over chip mixture. Top with remaining corn chips and chocolate chips; drizzle with the remaining peanut butter mixture. Let stand until set. Cut into bars.
1 bar: 337 cal., 18g fat (5g sat. fat), 0 chol., 196mg sod., 43g carb. (29g sugars, 2g fiber), 5g pro.

**CHOCOLATE-STRAWBERRY
CELEBRATION CAKE PAGE 210**

Cakes & Pies

Whether you need a layered cake for a birthday or a pleasing pie to showcase the season's finest fruit, these treats will turn any event into a special celebration!

LEMON-ROSEMARY LAYER CAKE

Tall and impressive, this unique dessert is a treat for the senses with flecks of lemon zest and fresh rosemary. Just wait till you taste it!
—Mary Fraser, Surprise, AZ

Prep: 20 min. • **Bake:** 25 min. + cooling
Makes: 16 servings

1	cup plus 2 Tbsp. butter, softened
2½	cups sugar
4	large eggs, room temperature
1	large egg yolk, room temperature
4	cups all-purpose flour
3	tsp. baking powder
1½	tsp. salt
¼	tsp. plus ⅛ tsp. baking soda
1½	cups sour cream
6	Tbsp. lemon juice
3	tsp. grated lemon zest
3	tsp. minced fresh rosemary

FROSTING

2	pkg. (8 oz. each) cream cheese, softened
8¼	cups confectioners' sugar
3	tsp. grated lemon zest
2¼	tsp. lemon juice
	Optional: Candied lemon and rosemary sprigs

1. Preheat oven to 350°. In a large bowl, cream butter and sugar until light and fluffy, 5-7 minutes. Add eggs, 1 at a time, and yolk, beating well after each addition. Combine flour, baking powder, salt and baking soda; add to creamed mixture alternately with sour cream, beating well after each addition. Beat in lemon juice, zest and rosemary.

2. Transfer the batter to 3 greased and floured 9-in. round baking pans. Bake for 25-30 minutes or until the edges begin to brown. Cool for 10 minutes before removing from the pans to wire racks to cool completely.

3. For the frosting, in a large bowl, beat cream cheese until fluffy. Add the confectioners' sugar, lemon zest and juice; beat until smooth.

4. Spread frosting between layers and over top and sides of cake. If desired, decorate with candied lemon and rosemary. Refrigerate leftovers.

1 piece: 756 cal., 28g fat (17g sat. fat), 146mg chol., 527mg sod., 119g carb. (90g sugars, 1g fiber), 8g pro.

TEST KITCHEN TIP

For a perfectly frosted cake, start with a crumb coat, which is simply the first layer of frosting. Then refrigerate the cake until chilled before adding your second coat.

LEMON-ROSEMARY LAYER CAKE

MIXED BERRY SHORTCAKE

This fruit-filled summer dessert looks so pretty served in parfait glasses. Strawberries, blueberries and a cool custard sauce are layered between tender cubes of homemade shortcake.
—*Taste of Home* Test Kitchen

Prep: 25 min. • **Bake:** 15 min.
Makes: 8 servings

½ cup plus ⅓ cup sugar, divided
3 Tbsp. cornstarch
2¾ cups fat-free milk
2 large egg yolks, lightly beaten
1 tsp. vanilla extract
2 cups all-purpose flour
1 tsp. baking powder
¼ tsp. baking soda
¼ tsp. salt
6 Tbsp. cold butter
⅔ cup buttermilk
4 cups sliced fresh strawberries
4 cups fresh blueberries
8 whole strawberries, halved
½ cup reduced-fat whipped topping
Fresh mint

1. In a heavy saucepan, combine ½ cup sugar and cornstarch. Stir in milk until blended. Bring to a boil over medium-low heat; cook and stir for 1-2 minutes or until thickened. Remove from the heat. Stir a small amount into egg yolks; return all to the pan, stirring constantly. Remove from the heat; stir in vanilla. Transfer to a bowl; press a piece of plastic wrap on top of custard. Refrigerate.

2. In a bowl, combine flour, baking powder, baking soda, salt and remaining sugar. Cut in butter until mixture resembles coarse crumbs. Stir in the buttermilk until a soft dough forms. Pat gently into a 9-in. square baking pan coated with cooking spray. Bake at 400° for 15-20 minutes or until lightly browned. Cool on a wire rack.

3. Cut the shortcake into ¾-in. cubes. In parfait glasses, alternate the layers of shortcake, custard, sliced strawberries and blueberries. Garnish with halved strawberries, a dollop of whipped topping and mint.

1 serving: 417 cal., 11g fat (7g sat. fat), 72mg chol., 321mg sod., 72g carb. (39g sugars, 5g fiber), 9g pro.

MIXED BERRY SHORTCAKE

WHITE CHOCOLATE
FRUIT TART

WHITE CHOCOLATE FRUIT TART

It takes a little time to make, but this tart is absolutely marvelous, especially in summer when fresh fruit is in abundance.
—Claire Dailey, New Castle, DE

- -

Prep: 30 min. • **Bake:** 25 min. + chilling
Makes: 16 servings

- ¾ cup butter, softened
- ½ cup confectioners' sugar
- 1½ cups all-purpose flour

FILLING
- 1 pkg. (10 to 12 oz.) white baking chips, melted and cooled
- ¼ cup heavy whipping cream
- 1 pkg. (8 oz.) cream cheese, softened
- 1 can (11 oz.) mandarin oranges
- 1 can (8 oz.) pineapple chunks
- 1 pint fresh strawberries, sliced
- 2 kiwifruit, peeled and sliced

GLAZE
- 3 Tbsp. sugar
- 2 tsp. cornstarch
- ½ tsp. lemon juice
  Optional: Minced fresh basil or fresh mint

1. In a small bowl, cream the butter and confectioners' sugar until light and fluffy. Gradually add flour and mix well.
2. Press into an ungreased 11-in. fluted tart pan with removable bottom or 12-in. pizza pan with sides. Bake at 300° until lightly browned, 25-30 minutes. Cool on a wire rack.
3. For filling, beat the melted chips and cream. Add cream cheese; beat until smooth. Spread over crust. Refrigerate for 30 minutes.
4. Drain oranges and pineapple, reserving ½ cup fruit juices. Arrange the oranges, pineapple, strawberries and kiwi over the filling.
5. For glaze, in a small saucepan, combine sugar and cornstarch. Stir in lemon juice and reserved fruit juices until smooth. Bring to a boil over medium heat; cook and stir 2 minutes or until thickened. Cool.
6. Brush glaze over the fruit. Refrigerate 1 hour before serving. If desired, sprinkle with basil or mint. Refrigerate leftovers.
1 piece: 335 cal., 21g fat (13g sat. fat), 45mg chol., 133mg sod., 35g carb. (24g sugars, 1g fiber), 4g pro.

OATMEAL CAKE
WITH CARAMEL ICING

OATMEAL CAKE WITH CARAMEL ICING

This lightened-up version of a classic dessert is full of flavor. The icing sets up quickly, so make it right before you frost the cake.
—Summer Marks, Louisville, KY

- -

Prep: 30 min. • **Bake:** 20 min. + cooling
Makes: 20 servings

- 1¼ cups boiling water
- 1 cup quick-cooking oats
- ¼ cup butter, softened
- 1 cup packed brown sugar
- ½ cup sugar
- 2 large eggs, room temperature
- ¼ cup unsweetened applesauce
- 1 tsp. vanilla extract
- 1½ cups all-purpose flour
- 2 tsp. baking powder
- ¾ tsp. ground cinnamon
- ½ tsp. baking soda
- ½ tsp. salt
- ¼ tsp. ground nutmeg

ICING
- ½ cup packed brown sugar
- ¼ cup butter, cubed
- ¼ cup fat-free milk
- ½ tsp. vanilla extract
- ⅛ tsp. salt
- 1½ cups confectioners' sugar

1. In a small bowl, pour boiling water over oats; let stand 10 minutes.
2. Meanwhile, preheat oven to 350°. In a large bowl, beat butter and sugars until crumbly, about 2 minutes. Add eggs, 1 at a time, beating well after each addition. Beat in applesauce and vanilla. Combine flour, baking powder, cinnamon, baking soda, salt and nutmeg. Gradually add to the creamed mixture. Stir in the oats. Pour into a greased 13x9-in. baking pan.
3. Bake 18-22 minutes or until a toothpick inserted in center comes out with moist crumbs. Cool completely on a wire rack.
4. For icing, in a small saucepan, combine brown sugar and butter. Bring to a boil over medium heat, stirring constantly. Cook and stir 1 minute. Gradually whisk in the milk. Return to a boil. Cook and stir 1 minute. Transfer to a small bowl. Stir in the vanilla and salt. Gradually beat in the confectioners' sugar until smooth. Immediately spread icing over cake. Let stand until set.
1 piece: 218 cal., 5g fat (3g sat. fat), 31mg chol., 203mg sod., 41g carb. (30g sugars, 1g fiber), 2g pro.

BLOOD ORANGE & GOAT CHEESE GALETTE

I made this galette for my mother-in-law's birthday, and it was a sensational hit. It's an easy yet elegant dessert.
—Tia Laws, Enterprise, OR

Prep: 1 hour + freezing
Bake: 1 hour + cooling
Makes: 8 servings (²/₃ cup sauce)

- 1 cup all-purpose flour
- 2 Tbsp. sugar
- ½ tsp. salt
- ⅓ cup cold butter, cubed
- ¼ cup quick-cooking oats
- 4 to 6 Tbsp. ice water

FILLING
- 10 medium blood oranges
- ¾ cup crumbled goat cheese
- 3 oz. cream cheese, softened
- ⅓ cup sour cream
- ¼ cup honey
- 2 large egg yolks, divided use
- ¼ tsp. salt
- 3 Tbsp. coarse sugar, divided
- 1 Tbsp. butter
- 1 Tbsp. water

SAUCE
- ¼ cup butter, cubed
- ½ cup packed brown sugar
- 2 Tbsp. half-and-half cream
- 2 Tbsp. honey
- ½ tsp. ground cinnamon

1. In a large bowl, mix flour, sugar and salt; cut in butter until crumbly. Stir in the oats. Gradually add ice water, tossing with a fork until dough holds together when pressed. Shape into a disk; cover and refrigerate for 1 hour or overnight.

2. On a lightly floured surface, roll dough to a 13-in. circle. Transfer to a parchment-lined 14-in. pizza pan. Refrigerate, covered, while preparing filling.

3. For filling, cut a thin slice from the top and bottom of oranges; stand oranges upright on a cutting board. With a knife, cut peel and outer membrane from oranges. Cut along the membrane of each segment to remove fruit from 8 oranges. Thinly slice remaining 2 oranges; remove seeds. Place the orange segments and slices between layers of paper towels to remove excess moisture; let stand while preparing filling.

4. In a small bowl, beat goat cheese, cream cheese, sour cream, honey, 1 egg yolk and salt until smooth. Spread over the crust to within 2 in. of edge. Arrange orange segments over cheese mixture. Sprinkle with 2 Tbsp. coarse sugar; dot with butter.

5. Fold crust edge over filling, pleating as you go and leaving an opening in center. Whisk the remaining egg yolk and 1 Tbsp. water; brush over folded crust. Arrange orange slices over crust to within 1 in. of edge. Sprinkle with the remaining 1 Tbsp. coarse sugar. Freeze, covered, overnight.

6. Preheat oven to 375°. Bake until crust is golden and filling is bubbly, 60-70 minutes. Transfer tart to a wire rack to cool.

7. For sauce, in a small saucepan, melt butter over medium heat. Add the brown sugar, cream, honey and cinnamon; bring to a boil. Boil 1 minute, stirring constantly to dissolve sugar. Serve with galette.

BLOOD ORANGE & GOAT CHEESE GALETTE

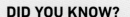

1 piece: 488 cal., 25g fat (15g sat. fat), 79mg chol., 434mg sod., 63g carb. (46g sugars, 4g fiber), 6g pro.

DID YOU KNOW?
Blood oranges have a sweeter taste (and fewer seeds) than naval oranges.

MARGARITA CUPCAKES

My hobby is cake decorating, and this is my most-requested recipe. It is delicious! If you are unable to find Key lime juice, you can use regular lime juice.
—Kerri McMillan, Sylvester, GA

Prep: 15 min. • **Bake:** 15 min.
Makes: 20 servings

- 1 pkg. yellow cake mix (regular size)
- ¾ cup frozen nonalcoholic margarita mix, thawed
- ⅓ cup canola oil
- 3 large eggs, room temperature
- **KEY LIME FROSTING**
- 3 to 4 Tbsp. Key lime juice, divided
- 1 Tbsp. meringue powder
- 1 tsp. water
- 3½ to 4 cups confectioners' sugar
- 1 cup vegetable shortening
  Optional: Lime zest and lime slices

1. Preheat oven to 350°. Line 20 muffin cups with paper liners. Combine the first 4 ingredients. Beat on low speed for 30 seconds; beat on medium 2 minutes.

2. Fill prepared cups half full. Bake until a toothpick inserted in the center comes out clean, 15-20 minutes. Cool in pans 10 minutes before removing to wire racks to cool completely.

3. For frosting, in a bowl, combine 2 Tbsp. lime juice, meringue powder and water. Whisk until frothy. Add the confectioners' sugar, shortening and remaining lime juice. Beat until smooth; frost cupcakes. If desired, garnish with lime zest and lime slices.

1 cupcake: 309 cal., 15g fat (4g sat. fat), 28mg chol., 170mg sod., 43g carb. (34g sugars, 1g fiber), 2g pro.

> "I'm not a huge fan of cupcakes, but these are super flavorful and delicious! They're the perfect ending to your family's favorite Mexican meal."
>
> —MARGARET KNOEBEL, ASSOCIATE RECIPE EDITOR/ TEST COOK

SPECIAL RAISIN PIE

When I first made this pie, I thought it was terrific. Then I entered it at the county fair, and I guess the judges thought it was wonderful, too, since it won first place.
—Laura Fall-Sutton, Buhl, ID

Prep: 40 min. • **Bake:** 35 min. + cooling
Makes: 8 servings

- 2½ cups raisins
- 2 cups water
- ⅓ cup packed brown sugar
- ⅓ cup sugar
- ⅛ tsp. salt
- 2 Tbsp. plus 1½ tsp. cornstarch
- ¼ cup cold water
- 2 Tbsp. lemon juice
- 1 Tbsp. orange juice
- 2 tsp. grated orange zest
- 1 tsp. grated lemon zest
- ½ tsp. rum extract
  2 sheets refrigerated pie crust
- 2 Tbsp. butter

1. In a small saucepan, combine raisins and water. Bring to a boil; cook 2 minutes. Add sugars and salt; cook until sugars are dissolved. Combine cornstarch and cold water until smooth; gradually stir into the pan. Cook and stir for 2 minutes or until thickened and bubbly. Remove from the heat; stir in the juices, zests and extract.

2. Roll out half the pie dough to fit a 9-in. pie plate; transfer to pie plate. Fill with raisin mixture. Dot with butter.

3. Roll out remaining dough; make a lattice crust. Trim, seal and flute edge. Bake at 375° until crust is golden brown and filling is bubbly, 35-40 minutes, covering edge with foil during the last 10 minutes. Cool on a wire rack. Refrigerate leftovers.

1 piece: 481 cal., 17g fat (8g sat. fat), 18mg chol., 266mg sod., 82g carb. (46g sugars, 2g fiber), 3g pro.

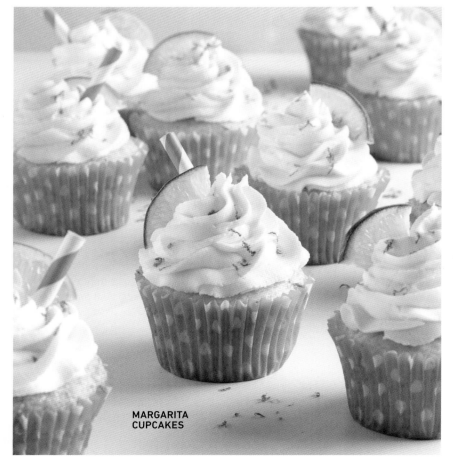

MARGARITA CUPCAKES

HUMMINGBIRD CUPCAKES

Turn the traditional hummingbird cake—flavored with pineapple, bananas and walnuts—into a bite-sized treat with these moist cupcakes.
—Jessie Oleson, Santa Fe, NM

Prep: 40 min. • **Bake:** 20 min. + cooling
Makes: 2 dozen

- 1 cup butter, softened
- 2 cups sugar
- 3 large eggs, room temperature
- 2 tsp. vanilla extract
- 2 cups mashed ripe bananas
- ½ cup drained canned crushed pineapple
- 3 cups all-purpose flour
- 1 tsp. baking soda
- 1 tsp. ground cinnamon
- ½ tsp. salt
- 1 cup sweetened shredded coconut
- 1 cup chopped walnuts

CREAM CHEESE FROSTING
- 1 pkg. (8 oz.) cream cheese, softened
- ½ cup butter, softened
- 3¾ cups confectioners' sugar
- 1 tsp. vanilla extract

1. In a large bowl, cream butter and sugar until light and fluffy, 5-7 minutes. Add eggs, 1 at a time, beating well after each addition. Beat in vanilla. In a small bowl, combine bananas and pineapple.

2. Combine flour, baking soda, cinnamon and salt; add to the creamed mixture alternately with banana mixture, beating well after each addition. Fold in coconut and walnuts.

3. Fill 24 paper-lined muffin cups about two-thirds full. Bake at 350° 20-25 minutes or until a toothpick inserted in the center comes out clean. Cool the cupcakes for 10 minutes before removing from pans to wire racks to cool completely.

4. In a small bowl, beat the cream cheese and butter until fluffy. Add confectioners' sugar and vanilla; beat until smooth. Frost the cupcakes.

1 cupcake: 410 cal., 20g fat (11g sat. fat), 67mg chol., 230mg sod., 56g carb. (39g sugars, 2g fiber), 4g pro.

HUMMINGBIRD CUPCAKES

PEANUT BUTTER SILK PIE

My son wanted pies at his wedding, and this was one of his requests!
—Lee Steinmetz, Lansing, MI

- -

Prep: 10 min. + chilling
Makes: 8 servings

- ¾ cup peanut butter
- 4 oz. cream cheese, softened
- 1 cup confectioners' sugar
- 1 carton (8 oz.) frozen whipped topping, thawed
- 1 graham cracker crust (9 in.)
  Salted chopped peanuts
  Optional: Chocolate syrup and peanut butter ice cream topping

In a large bowl, beat the peanut butter, cream cheese and confectioners' sugar until smooth. Fold in whipped topping; pour into prepared crust. Refrigerate at least 2 hours before serving. Sprinkle with peanuts. If desired, garnish with chocolate syrup, peanut butter ice cream topping and additional whipped topping.

1 piece: 434 cal., 27g fat (11g sat. fat), 16mg chol., 276mg sod., 40g carb. (29g sugars, 2g fiber), 8g pro.

> "I love French silk pie, and I love peanut butter desserts, so this incredible treat was an instant favorite for me."
> —MARK HAGEN, CONTENT DIRECTOR

OLD-FASHIONED WHOOPIE PIES

Who can resist soft chocolate sandwich cookies filled with a layer of fluffy white frosting? Mom has made these for years. They're a treat that never lasted very long with me and my two brothers around.
—Maria Costello, Monroe, NC

- -

Prep: 35 min. + chilling
Bake: 10 min./batch + cooling
Makes: 2 dozen

- ½ cup baking cocoa
- ½ cup hot water
- ½ cup shortening
- 1½ cups sugar
- 2 large eggs, room temperature
- 1 tsp. vanilla extract
- 2⅔ cups all-purpose flour
- 1 tsp. baking powder
- 1 tsp. baking soda
- ¼ tsp. salt
- ½ cup buttermilk

FILLING
- 3 Tbsp. all-purpose flour
  Dash salt
- 1 cup 2% milk
- ¾ cup shortening
- 1½ cups confectioners' sugar
- 2 tsp. vanilla extract

1. Preheat oven to 350°. In a small bowl, combine the cocoa and water. Cool for 5 minutes. In a large bowl, cream the shortening and sugar until light and fluffy, 5-7 minutes. Beat in the eggs, vanilla and cocoa mixture. Combine dry ingredients; gradually add to the creamed mixture alternately with buttermilk, beating well after each addition

2. To form each cookie, drop 2 Tbsp. 2 in. apart onto greased baking sheets. Bake 10-12 minutes or until firm to the touch. Remove to wire racks to cool.

3. For filling, in a small saucepan, combine flour and salt. Gradually whisk in milk until smooth; cook and stir over medium-high heat until thickened, 5-7 minutes. Remove from heat. Cover and refrigerate until completely cool.

4. In a small bowl, cream the shortening, sugar and vanilla until light and fluffy, 5-7 minutes. Add milk mixture; beat until fluffy, about 7 minutes. Spread filling on half the cookies; top with the remaining cookies. Store in the refrigerator.

1 whoopie pie: 244 cal., 11g fat (3g sat. fat), 19mg chol., 116mg sod., 33g carb. (20g sugars, 1g fiber), 3g pro.

OLD-FASHIONED WHOOPIE PIES

COCONUT TRES LECHES
CUPCAKES

HOT MILK CAKE

When I think back on my mom's delicious meals, her milk cake always comes to mind as the perfect dessert. The simple, old-fashioned treat tastes so good, it will surprise you!
—Rosemary Pryor, Pasadena, MD

- -

Prep: 20 min. • **Bake:** 30 min.
Makes: 16 servings

- 4 large eggs, room temperature
- 2 cups sugar
- 1 tsp. vanilla extract
- 2¼ cups all-purpose flour
- 2¼ tsp. baking powder
- 1¼ cups 2% milk
- 10 Tbsp. butter, cubed

1. Preheat oven to 350°. In a large bowl, beat eggs on high speed for 5 minutes or until thick and lemon-colored. Gradually add sugar, beating until mixture is light and fluffy. Beat in vanilla. Combine flour and baking powder; gradually add to batter, beating on low speed until smooth.
2. In a small saucepan, heat the milk and butter just until butter is melted. Gradually add to batter; beat just until combined.
3. Pour into a greased 13x9-in. baking pan. Bake until a toothpick inserted in center comes out clean, 30-35 minutes. Cool on a wire rack.

1 piece: 254 cal., 9g fat (5g sat. fat), 75mg chol., 154mg sod., 39g carb. (26g sugars, 0 fiber), 4g pro.

> ### TEST KITCHEN TIP
> If you have leftover cake, cube it and layer it into a trifle with berries and cream.

COCONUT TRES LECHES CUPCAKES

Three types of milk wonderfully moisten these cupcakes. Toasted coconut on top adds an elegant touch.
—*Taste of Home* Test Kitchen

- -

Prep: 35 min. + chilling
Bake: 20 min. + cooling
Makes: about 1½ dozen

- ½ cup butter, softened
- 1½ cups sugar
- 1½ tsp. vanilla extract
- 4 large egg whites, room temperature
- 2 cups all-purpose flour
- 1 tsp. baking powder
- ½ tsp. baking soda
- ¼ tsp. salt
- 1⅓ cups buttermilk
- 1 can (14 oz.) sweetened condensed milk
- ⅔ cup evaporated milk
- ½ cup coconut milk

WHIPPED CREAM
- 1½ cups heavy whipping cream
- ⅓ cup confectioners' sugar
  Toasted sweetened shredded coconut

1. Preheat oven to 350°. Line 18 muffin cups with paper liners.
2. Cream butter and sugar until light and fluffy, 5-7 minutes. Beat in vanilla; add egg whites, 1 at a time, beating well after each addition. In another bowl, whisk together flour, baking powder, baking soda and salt; add to the creamed mixture alternately with the buttermilk, beating after each addition.
3. Fill prepared cups about two-thirds full. Bake until a toothpick inserted in the center comes out clean, 17-20 minutes. Cool 10 minutes. Remove cupcakes to a 15x10x1-in. pan.
4. In a bowl, mix sweetened condensed, evaporated and coconut milks. Poke holes in cupcakes, about ½ in. apart, with a skewer. Slowly spoon milk mixture over top, allowing it to absorb into cake. Refrigerate, covered, at least 2 hours.
5. To serve, beat cream until it begins to thicken. Add confectioners' sugar; beat until soft peaks form. Spread or pipe over cupcakes. Top with coconut. Store in the refrigerator.

1 cupcake: 342 cal., 16g fat (11g sat. fat), 47mg chol., 226mg sod., 44g carb. (33g sugars, 0 fiber), 6g pro.

HOT MILK CAKE

CHOCOLATE MAYONNAISE CAKE

Mom always made this special chocolate mayo cake for my birthday dessert. It is very moist and has a nice light chocolate taste. Plus, the frosting is the perfect topping.
—Deborah Amrine, Fort Myers, FL

Prep: 15 min. • **Bake:** 30 min. + cooling
Makes: 12 servings

- 1 cup water
- 1 cup mayonnaise
- 1 tsp. vanilla extract
- 2 cups all-purpose flour
- 1 cup sugar
- 3 Tbsp. baking cocoa
- 2 tsp. baking soda
BROWN SUGAR FROSTING
- ½ cup packed brown sugar
- ¼ cup butter, cubed
- 2 Tbsp. 2% milk
- 1¾ cups confectioners' sugar

1. In a large bowl, combine the water, mayonnaise and vanilla until well blended. In another large bowl, combine the flour, sugar, cocoa and baking soda; gradually beat dry ingredients into mayonnaise mixture until blended.

2. Pour into a greased 9-in. square or 11x7-in. baking pan. Bake at 350° until a toothpick inserted in center comes out clean, 30-35 minutes. Cool completely.

3. For frosting, in a small saucepan, cook and stir the brown sugar in butter until bubbly. Remove from the heat; stir in milk. Gradually add confectioners' sugar; beat until smooth. Frost cake.

1 piece: 416 cal., 19g fat (4g sat. fat), 17mg chol., 354mg sod., 60g carb. (42g sugars, 1g fiber), 3g pro.

ALMOND CAKE WITH RASPBERRY SAUCE

The drizzle of raspberry sauce adds to the overall experience of this beautiful dessert.
—Joan Sullivan, Gambrills, MD

Prep: 30 min. • **Bake:** 40 min. + cooling
Makes: 12 servings (¼ cup sauce)

- 1 can (8 oz.) almond paste
- ¾ cup plus 1 Tbsp. sugar, divided
- ½ cup butter, softened
- 3 large eggs, room temperature, lightly beaten
- 1 Tbsp. orange liqueur
- ¼ tsp. almond extract
- ¼ cup all-purpose flour
- ¼ tsp. plus ⅛ tsp. baking powder
- ¼ cup confectioners' sugar
- 1 pkg. (10 oz.) frozen sweetened raspberries, thawed

1. Line an 8-in. round baking pan with parchment; coat paper with cooking spray and set aside.

2. In a large bowl, combine almond paste, ¾ cup sugar and butter; beat for 2 minutes until blended. Beat in eggs, liqueur and extract. Combine flour and baking powder; add to paste mixture just until combined.

3. Spread into prepared pan. Bake at 350° for 40-45 minutes or until a toothpick inserted in the center comes out clean. Cool completely on a wire rack.

4. Invert the cake onto a cake plate; remove parchment. Sprinkle with confectioners' sugar.

5. Place raspberries in a food processor; cover and process until pureed. Strain, reserving juice; discard seeds. In a small saucepan over medium heat, cook the raspberry juice and remaining sugar for 15-18 minutes or until mixture is reduced to ¼ cup. Serve with cake.

1 slice with 1 tsp. sauce: 272 cal., 14g fat (6g sat. fat), 73mg chol., 84mg sod., 34g carb. (28g sugars, 2g fiber), 4g pro.

> "This cake is so tender and delicious. Plus, the recipe conveniently calls for just one ordinary 8-inch pan."
> —SARAH FARMER, EXECUTIVE CULINARY DIRECTOR

ALMOND CAKE WITH RASPBERRY SAUCE

INCREDIBLE COCONUT CAKE

I found this recipe in a newspaper many years ago and modified it to suit my taste. This is my all-time favorite cake, and family and friends absolutely love it.
—Lynne Bassler, Indiana, PA

Prep: 35 min.
Bake: 25 min. + chilling
Makes: 16 servings

- 5 large eggs, separated
- 2 cups sugar
- ½ cup butter, softened
- ½ cup canola oil
- 2¼ cups cake flour
- 1 tsp. baking powder
- ½ tsp. baking soda
- ¼ tsp. salt
- 1 cup buttermilk
- 2 cups sweetened shredded coconut, chopped
- 1 tsp. coconut extract
- ½ tsp. vanilla extract
- ¼ tsp. almond extract
- ¼ tsp. cream of tartar

FROSTING
- 11 oz. cream cheese, softened
- ⅔ cup butter, softened
- 4⅓ cups confectioners' sugar
- 1¼ tsp. coconut extract
- 2 cups sweetened shredded coconut, toasted

1. Place egg whites in a large bowl; let stand at room temperature for 30 minutes.
2. Preheat oven to 325°. In another large bowl, beat sugar, butter and oil until well blended. Add egg yolks, 1 at a time, beating well after each addition.
3. Combine flour, baking powder, baking soda and salt; add to creamed mixture alternately with buttermilk, beating well after each addition. Stir in the coconut and extracts.
4. Add cream of tartar to egg whites; with clean beaters, beat on medium until stiff peaks form. Fold a fourth of the egg whites into batter, then fold in remaining whites.
5. Transfer to 3 greased and floured 9-in. round baking pans. Bake 25-30 minutes or until a toothpick inserted in center comes out clean. Cool 10 minutes before removing from pans to wire racks to cool completely.
6. For the frosting, beat cream cheese and butter until fluffy. Add confectioners' sugar and extract; beat until smooth.

7. Place 1 cake layer on a serving plate; spread with ½ cup frosting and sprinkle with ⅓ cup coconut. Repeat. Top with remaining cake layer. Spread remaining frosting over the top and sides of cake; sprinkle with the remaining coconut. Refrigerate for 2 hours before cutting. Store in the refrigerator.
1 piece: 689 cal., 37g fat (21g sat. fat), 123mg chol., 353mg sod., 85g carb. (64g sugars, 1g fiber), 6g pro.

INCREDIBLE COCONUT CAKE

DID YOU KNOW?
Cake flour, which is perfect for making light and tender cakes, is finely milled and has a lower protein content than all-purpose flour.

HONEY LEMON MERINGUE PIE

My husband especially enjoys this lemon meringue pie recipe that comes together quickly. His mother made a similar treat for him when he was a child, but it was rewarding for me to create a recipe of my own that he loves so much!
—Portia Gorman, Los Angeles, CA

- -

Prep: 20 min. • **Cook:** 35 min. + chilling
Makes: 8 servings

  1   Tbsp. honey
  3   Tbsp. butter, melted, divided
  1   graham cracker crust (9 in.)
  1   can (14 oz.) sweetened
      condensed milk
  ½   cup lemon juice
  ¼   cup sugar
  3   large eggs, separated,
      room temperature
MERINGUE
  ¼   tsp. cream of tartar
  ½   tsp. vanilla extract
  6   Tbsp. sugar

1. Preheat oven to 350°. Drizzle the honey and 1 Tbsp. melted butter in bottom of crust. In a medium bowl, beat sweetened condensed milk, lemon juice, sugar, egg yolks and remaining 2 Tbsp. melted butter until blended. Pour into the crust; bake for 20 minutes.
2. Meanwhile, in a small bowl, beat egg whites and cream of tartar until frothy. Add vanilla; gradually beat in sugar, 1 Tbsp. at a time, on high until stiff glossy peaks form and sugar is dissolved. Spread evenly over the hot filling, sealing edges to crust. Bake until the meringue is golden brown, about 15 minutes. Cool on a wire rack for 1 hour. Refrigerate at least 3 hours before serving. Refrigerate leftovers.
1 piece: 458 cal., 17g fat (8g sat. fat), 104mg chol., 268mg sod., 69g carb. (65g sugars, 0 fiber), 9g pro.

> "Honey makes the bottom crust caramelized and slightly chewy, and it pairs beautifully with the brightness of the citrus."
> — SARAH TRAMONTE, CULINARY PRODUCER

HONEY LEMON MERINGUE PIE

BOSTON CREAM CUPCAKES

Boston cream Bismarcks have been my favorite bakery treat since I was a child, so I put together this easy cupcake version.
—Jeanne Holt, St. Paul, MN

- -

Prep: 25 min. • **Bake:** 15 min. + cooling
Makes: ½ dozen

  3   Tbsp. shortening
  ⅓   cup sugar
  1   large egg, room temperature
  ½   tsp. vanilla extract
  ½   cup all-purpose flour
  ½   tsp. baking powder
  ¼   tsp. salt
  3   Tbsp. 2% milk
  ⅔   cup prepared vanilla pudding
  ½   cup semisweet chocolate chips
  ¼   cup heavy whipping cream

1. Preheat oven to 350°. In a small bowl, cream shortening and sugar until light and fluffy, 5-7 minutes. Beat in egg and vanilla. Combine the flour, baking powder and salt; add to creamed mixture alternately with milk, beating well after each addition.
2. Fill paper-lined muffin cups half full. Bake until a toothpick inserted in the center comes out clean, 15-20 minutes. Cool 10 minutes before removing from pan to a wire rack to cool completely.
3. Cut small hole in the corner of a pastry bag; insert a small tip. Fill with pudding. Push tip through top to fill each cupcake.
4. Place chocolate chips in a small bowl. In a small saucepan, bring cream just to a boil. Pour over chocolate; whisk until smooth. Cool, stirring occasionally, to room temperature or until the ganache thickens slightly, about 10 minutes. Spoon over cupcakes. Let stand until set. Store in an airtight container in the refrigerator.
1 cupcake: 283 cal., 15g fat (7g sat. fat), 45mg chol., 204mg sod., 34g carb. (20g sugars, 1g fiber), 4g pro.

ZUCCHINI WALNUT CAKE

What gardener doesn't have extra zucchini? When it is abundant, I shred and freeze plenty so I have it on hand to bake this moist sheet cake all year long. The cream cheese frosting is yummy, and the big panful always goes fast at a picnic or potluck.
—Marie Hoyer, Hodgenville, KY

Prep: 20 min. • **Bake:** 35 min. + cooling
Makes: 24 servings

- 2 **cups shredded zucchini**
- 2 **cups sugar**
- 1 **cup canola oil**
- 4 **large eggs**
- 2½ **cups all-purpose flour**
- 1½ **tsp. ground cinnamon**
- 1 **tsp. salt**
- ½ **tsp. baking powder**
- ½ **tsp. baking soda**
- ½ **cup chopped toasted walnuts, optional**

FROSTING
- 3 **oz. cream cheese, softened**
- ¼ **cup butter, softened**
- 1 **Tbsp. 2% milk**
- 1 **tsp. vanilla extract**
- 2 **cups confectioners' sugar**
  Chopped toasted walnuts, optional

1. Preheat oven to 350°. Grease a 13x9-in. baking pan; set aside.
2. In a large bowl, beat zucchini, sugar, oil and eggs until well blended. Combine flour, cinnamon, salt, baking powder and baking soda; gradually beat into zucchini mixture until blended. Fold in walnuts if desired.
3. Pour into prepared pan. Bake until a toothpick inserted in the center comes out clean, 35-40 minutes. Cool completely on a wire rack.
4. For frosting, in a small bowl, beat the cream cheese, butter, milk and vanilla until smooth. Add confectioners' sugar and mix well. Frost the cake. Sprinkle with nuts if desired. Store in the refrigerator.
1 piece: 275 cal., 13g fat (3g sat. fat), 45mg chol., 174mg sod., 37g carb. (26g sugars, 1g fiber), 3g pro.

ZUCCHINI WALNUT CAKE

BLUEBERRY
PUDDING CAKE

BLUEBERRY PUDDING CAKE

We have many acres of blueberry bushes in the area where we live. My father-in-law has a number near his house, so I have an abundant supply every year. I am always looking for new ways to use the berries. This is a new recipe I found, and it's been very popular.
—Jan Bamford, Sedgwick, ME

Prep: 15 min. • **Bake:** 45 min.
Makes: 9 servings

- 2 cups fresh or frozen blueberries
- 1 tsp. ground cinnamon
- 1 tsp. lemon juice
- 1 cup all-purpose flour
- ¾ cup sugar
- 1 tsp. baking powder
- ½ cup 2% milk
- 3 Tbsp. butter, melted

TOPPING
- ¾ cup sugar
- 1 Tbsp. cornstarch
- 1 cup boiling water
  Whipped cream, optional

1. Preheat oven to 350°. Toss blueberries with cinnamon and lemon juice; pour into a greased 8-in. square baking dish. In a small bowl, combine the flour, sugar and baking powder; stir in milk and butter. Spoon over berries.
2. Combine sugar and cornstarch; sprinkle over batter. Slowly pour boiling water over all. Bake 45-50 minutes or until a toothpick inserted into the cake portion comes out clean. Serve warm. If desired, top with whipped cream and additional berries.
1 serving: 244 cal., 4g fat (3g sat. fat), 11mg chol., 91mg sod., 51g carb. (37g sugars, 1g fiber), 2g pro.

TEST KITCHEN TIP
If you're using frozen blueberries in this recipe, there's no need to thaw them first.

FAVORITE
DUTCH APPLE PIE

FAVORITE DUTCH APPLE PIE

Everything about this dessert makes it the top request for family gatherings. The delightful crust cuts beautifully to reveal a filling of diced apple. At harvest time or any time, you cannot beat this delectable pie.
—Brenda DuFresne, Midland, MI

Prep: 20 min. • **Bake:** 40 min. + cooling
Makes: 8 servings

- 2 cups all-purpose flour
- 1 cup packed brown sugar
- ½ cup quick-cooking oats
- ¾ cup butter, melted

FILLING
- ⅔ cup sugar
- 3 Tbsp. cornstarch
- 1¼ cups cold water
- 4 cups chopped peeled tart apples (about 2 large)
- 1 tsp. vanilla extract
  Optional: Vanilla ice cream and caramel sundae syrup

1. Preheat oven to 350°. Mix flour, brown sugar, oats and butter; reserve ¾ cup mixture for topping. Press remaining mixture onto bottom and up sides of an ungreased 9-in. pie plate.
2. In a saucepan, mix sugar, cornstarch and water until smooth; bring to a boil. Cook and stir until thickened, about 2 minutes. Remove from heat; stir in apples and vanilla. Pour into the crust. Crumble topping over filling.
3. Bake until crust is golden brown and filling is bubbly, 40-45 minutes. Cover edges with foil during last 20 minutes to prevent overbrowning if necessary. Cool on a wire rack. If desired, serve with ice cream and caramel.
1 piece: 494 cal., 18g fat (11g sat. fat), 46mg chol., 146mg sod., 81g carb. (49g sugars, 2g fiber), 4g pro.

CARAMEL NUT CRUNCH PIE

This cool and creamy pie has a lot going for it. It's easy to make, it can be assembled well in advance to save time, and it's impressive enough to serve guests. To make it even more decadent and delicious, you can chop extra peanuts and candy bars and crumble a few more cookies to sprinkle over the top.
—Andrea Bolden, Unionville, TN

- -

Prep: 25 min. + freezing
Makes: 8 servings

- 20 Oreo cookies, finely crushed (about 2 cups)
- ½ cup honey-roasted peanuts, chopped
- ¼ cup butter, melted
- 6 Snickers candy bars (1.86 oz. each), chopped
- 6 cups vanilla ice cream, slightly softened
- ¼ cup hot caramel ice cream topping
- ¼ cup hot fudge ice cream topping, warmed
  Optional: Additional hot caramel and hot fudge ice cream topping

1. Preheat oven to 375°. In a bowl, mix the cookie crumbs and peanuts; stir in butter. Press onto the bottom and up sides of a greased 9-in. pie plate. Bake until set, 10-12 minutes. Cool on a wire rack.
2. Fold candy bars into ice cream; spread into prepared crust. Drizzle with caramel and fudge toppings. Loosely cover and freeze until firm, at least 8 hours. If not serving right away, cover securely after it's frozen firm. If desired, drizzle with additional caramel and fudge toppings before serving.
1 piece: 733 cal., 39g fat (17g sat. fat), 64mg chol., 487mg sod., 88g carb. (66g sugars, 4g fiber), 11g pro.

TEST KITCHEN TIP
A store-bought Oreo pie crust makes this treat even easier. Sprinkle the chopped peanuts over the top of the prepared crust, then follow the recipe beginning at the second step.

CHOCOLATE-STRAWBERRY CELEBRATION CAKE

CHOCOLATE-STRAWBERRY CELEBRATION CAKE

Although I have some wonderful from-scratch recipes, this one uses a boxed mix with plenty of doctoring. It has become a popular groom's cake that gets more attention than the wedding cake.
—Nora Fitzgerald, Sevierville, TN

- -

Prep: 30 min. • **Bake:** 30 min. + cooling
Makes: 16 servings

- 1 pkg. chocolate cake mix (regular size)
- 1 pkg. (3.9 oz.) instant chocolate pudding mix
- 4 large eggs
- 1 cup sour cream
- ¾ cup water
- ¼ cup canola oil
- 4 oz. semisweet chocolate, melted

FROSTING
- 2 cups butter, softened
- 4 cups confectioners' sugar
- ¾ cup baking cocoa
- ½ cup 2% milk

GARNISHES
- 4 oz. semisweet chocolate, chopped
- ½ cup heavy whipping cream

- 1 lb. fresh strawberries, hulled
  Seedless strawberry jam, warmed, optional

1. Preheat oven to 350°. Combine the first 7 ingredients; beat on low speed for 30 seconds. Beat on medium for 2 minutes. Transfer to 2 greased and floured 9-in. round baking pans.
2. Bake until a toothpick inserted in the center comes out clean, 28-32 minutes. Cool 10 minutes before removing from pans to wire racks to cool completely.
3. In a large bowl, cream the butter, confectioners' sugar and cocoa until light and fluffy. Beat in the milk until smooth. Spread the frosting between layers and over top and sides of cake.
4. For ganache, place chocolate in a small bowl. Heat cream just to a boil; pour over chocolate and whisk until smooth. Drizzle over top of the cake, allowing ganache to drape down sides. Arrange strawberries on top of cake. If desired, brush jam onto strawberries.
1 piece: 666 cal., 40g fat (23g sat. fat), 120mg chol., 485mg sod., 69g carb. (50g sugars, 2g fiber), 6g pro.

CAST-IRON CHERRY-BERRY PEACH PIE

I had an overabundant supply of cherries one year, so I adapted several recipes to use them up. This one was a keeper.
—Amy Hartke, Elgin, IL

Prep: 30 min. + chilling
Bake: 50 min. + cooling
Makes: 8 servings

- 2½ cups all-purpose flour
- 2 Tbsp. sugar
- ½ tsp. salt
- 1 cup cold butter, cubed
- 6 to 8 Tbsp. cold water

FILLING

- 2 cups fresh or frozen sliced peaches, thawed
- 1¾ cups pitted fresh dark sweet cherries or 1 can (15 oz.) pitted dark sweet cherries, drained
- 1 cup fresh or frozen blueberries, thawed
- 1 tsp. vanilla extract
- ½ tsp. almond extract
- 1½ cups sugar
- ¼ cup all-purpose flour
- ¼ cup quick-cooking tapioca
- ½ tsp. salt
- ½ tsp. ground nutmeg
- 1 Tbsp. butter

1. In a large bowl, mix flour, sugar and salt; cut in butter until crumbly. Gradually add water, tossing with a fork until dough holds together when pressed. Divide dough into 2 portions. Shape each into a disk; cover and refrigerate for 1 hour or overnight.

2. In a large bowl, combine peaches, cherries, blueberries and extracts. Combine sugar, flour, tapioca, salt and nutmeg; sprinkle over fruit and gently toss to coat. Let stand for 15 minutes.

3. Preheat oven to 375°. On a lightly floured surface, roll half the dough to a ⅛-in.-thick circle; transfer to a 9-in. cast-iron skillet. Trim to ½ in. beyond rim of plate. Add filling; dot with butter.

4. Roll remaining dough to a ⅛-in.-thick circle; cut into ½-in.-wide strips. Arrange over filling in a lattice pattern. Trim and seal strips to edge of bottom crust; flute edge. Bake until crust is golden brown and filling is bubbly, 50-55 minutes. Cover edges with foil during the last 15 minutes to prevent overbrowning, if necessary. Cool on a wire rack.

1 piece: 601 cal., 25g fat (16g sat. fat), 65mg chol., 491mg sod., 91g carb. (49g sugars, 2g fiber), 5g pro.

CAST-IRON CHERRY-BERRY PEACH PIE

ASK SARAH

HOW DO I CLEAN MY CAST-IRON SKILLET AFTER USE?

Rinse the cool pan with hot water, using a stiff nylon brush to remove residue. Dry and apply a light coat of oil while the pan is still warm.

TOFFEE POKE CAKE

This cake recipe is a favorite among my family and friends. I love making it because it is so simple.
—Jeanette Hoffman, Oshkosh, WI

- -

Prep: 25 min. • **Bake:** 25 min. + chilling
Makes: 15 servings

- 1   pkg. chocolate cake mix (regular size)
- 1   jar (17 oz.) butterscotch-caramel ice cream topping
- 1   carton (12 oz.) frozen whipped topping, thawed
- 3   Heath candy bars (1.4 oz. each), chopped

1. Prepare and bake cake according to package directions, using a greased 13x9-in. baking pan. Cool on a wire rack.
2. Using the handle of a wooden spoon, poke holes in cake. Pour ¾ cup caramel topping into holes. Spoon remaining caramel over cake. Top with whipped topping. Sprinkle with candy. Refrigerate for at least 2 hours before serving.
1 piece: 404 cal., 16g fat (8g sat. fat), 48mg chol., 322mg sod., 60g carb. (39g sugars, 1g fiber), 4g pro.

BLACKBERRY APPLE PIE

My mother made this pie so often she could do it with her eyes closed! We picked the berries ourselves, and the apples came from the trees in our orchard.
—Fran Stanfield, Wilmington, OH

- -

Prep: 20 min. • **Bake:** 50 min.
Makes: 8 servings

- 2   sheets refrigerated pie crust
- 5   cups thinly sliced peeled tart apples (about 5 medium)
- 1   pint fresh blackberries, rinsed and drained
- 1   Tbsp. lemon juice
- ¾   cup sugar
- 2   Tbsp. cornstarch
- 2   Tbsp. butter
- 1   large egg
- 1   Tbsp. water or milk

1. On a lightly floured surface, roll out half the dough to fit a 9-in. pie plate; trim to 1 in. beyond rim of plate. Top with a thin layer of apples. In a large bowl, combine the blackberries and remaining apples; sprinkle with lemon juice. In a small bowl, combine sugar and cornstarch. Add to fruit mixture; toss gently to coat. Spoon into crust; dot with butter.
2. Roll out the remaining dough; make a lattice crust. Trim, seal and flute edges. Beat egg with water; brush over lattice top and pie edges.
3. Bake at 375° for 50 minutes or until filling is bubbly and apples are tender. Cool on a wire rack. Serve warm or at room temperature.
1 piece: 415 cal., 18g fat (8g sat. fat), 44mg chol., 238mg sod., 62g carb. (32g sugars, 2g fiber), 3g pro.

PINEAPPLE PUDDING CAKE

My mother used to love making this easy dessert in the summertime. It's so cool and refreshing that it never lasts very long!
—Kathleen Worden, North Andover, MA

- -

Prep: 25 min. • **Bake:** 15 min. + chilling
Makes: 20 servings

- 1   pkg. (9 oz.) yellow cake mix
- 1½ cups cold fat-free milk
- 1   pkg. (1 oz.) sugar-free instant vanilla pudding mix
- 1   pkg. (8 oz.) reduced-fat cream cheese
- 1   can (20 oz.) unsweetened crushed pineapple, well drained
- 1   carton (8 oz.) frozen reduced-fat whipped topping, thawed
- ¼   cup chopped walnuts, toasted
- 20 maraschino cherries, well drained

1. Preheat oven to 350°. Prepare cake mix batter according to package directions; pour into a greased 13x9-in. baking pan. Bake until a toothpick inserted near the center comes out clean, 15-20 minutes. Cool completely on a wire rack.
2. In a large bowl, whisk milk and pudding mix for 2 minutes. Let stand 2 minutes or until soft-set.
3. In a small bowl, beat cream cheese until smooth. Beat in pudding mixture until blended. Spread evenly over cake. Sprinkle with pineapple; spread with whipped topping. Sprinkle with walnuts and garnish with cherries. Refrigerate until serving.
1 piece: 152 cal., 5g fat (3g sat. fat), 18mg chol., 173mg sod., 22g carb. (15g sugars, 1g fiber), 3g pro. **Diabetic exchanges:** 1½ starch, ½ fat.

SOUR CREAM POUND CAKE

I enjoy baking, especially desserts such as this one. It tastes amazing as is, or tuck it under ice cream and chocolate syrup like a hot fudge sundae!
—Karen Conrad, East Troy, WI

- -

Prep: 15 min. • **Bake:** 1¼ hours + cooling
Makes: 20 servings

1	cup butter, softened
3	cups sugar
6	large eggs, room temperature
3	cups all-purpose flour
¼	tsp. baking soda
¼	tsp. salt
1	cup sour cream
2	tsp. vanilla extract
	Confectioners' sugar, optional

1. In a bowl, cream butter and sugar until light and fluffy, 5-7 minutes. Add eggs, 1 at a time, beating well after each addition. Combine flour, baking soda and salt; add to creamed mixture alternately with sour cream and vanilla. Beat on low just until blended. Pour into a greased and floured 10-in. fluted tube pan.
2. Bake at 325° for 1¼-1½ hours or until a toothpick inserted near the center comes out clean. Cool cake in the pan 15 minutes before removing to a wire rack to cool completely. Sprinkle with confectioners' sugar if desired.
1 piece: 311 cal., 13g fat (7g sat. fat), 96mg chol., 163mg sod., 45g carb. (30g sugars, 1g fiber), 4g pro.

CHOCOLATE ZUCCHINI CUPCAKES

Our grandkids love these cupcakes and don't believe us when we tell them there are veggies in them!
—Carole Fraser, North York, ON

- -

Prep: 25 min. • **Bake:** 20 min. + cooling
Makes: 21 cupcakes

1¼	cups butter, softened
1½	cups sugar
2	large eggs, room temperature
1	tsp. vanilla extract
2½	cups all-purpose flour
¾	cup baking cocoa
1	tsp. baking powder
1	tsp. baking soda
½	tsp. salt
½	cup plain yogurt
1	cup grated zucchini
1	cup grated carrots
1	can (16 oz.) chocolate frosting

1. In a large bowl, cream butter and sugar until light and fluffy, 5-7 minutes. Add eggs, 1 at a time, beating well after each addition. Stir in vanilla. Combine flour, baking cocoa, baking powder, baking soda and salt; add to the creamed mixture alternately with yogurt, beating well after each addition. Fold in zucchini and carrots.
2. Fill paper-lined muffin cups two-thirds full. Bake at 350° for 18-22 minutes or until a toothpick inserted in center comes out clean. Cool 10 minutes before removing from pans to wire racks to cool completely. Frost cupcakes.
1 cupcake: 326 cal., 17g fat (9g sat. fat), 50mg chol., 288mg sod., 40g carb. (25g sugars, 1g fiber), 3g pro.

PATRIOTIC ICE CREAM CUPCAKES

These frosty cupcakes are practically a fireworks display on their own. The little treats feature red velvet cake, blue moon ice cream, a creamy white topping and star-spangled sprinkles.
—*Taste of Home* Test Kitchen

- -

Prep: 30 min. + freezing
Bake: 15 min. + cooling • **Makes:** 3 dozen

1	pkg. red velvet cake mix (regular size)
1½	qt. blue moon ice cream, softened if necessary
1	jar (7 oz.) marshmallow creme
3	cups heavy whipping cream
	Red, white and blue sprinkles

1. Preheat oven to 350°. Line 36 muffin cups with paper liners.
2. Prepare cake batter according to package directions. Fill prepared cups about one-third full. Bake until a toothpick inserted in the center comes out clean, 11-14 minutes. Cool 10 minutes before removing from the pans to wire racks; cool completely.
3. Working quickly, spread ice cream onto cupcakes. Freeze until firm, at least 1 hour.
4. Place marshmallow creme in a large bowl. Add whipping cream; beat until blended and stiff peaks form. Pipe or spread over cupcakes. Decorate with sprinkles. Serve immediately or freeze until firm.
Note: The blue moon ice cream may be substituted with vanilla ice cream tinted with blue food coloring.
1 cupcake: 220 cal., 13g fat (6g sat. fat), 46mg chol., 139mg sod., 21g carb. (16g sugars, 0 fiber), 4g pro.

DOUBLE CHOCOLATE ESPRESSO
CHEESECAKE PAGE 221

Desserts

Say hello to sweet endings! Family and friends will leave room for dessert when they catch sight of these knock-'em-dead treats.

NONNI'S FRITOLE

My Italian grandmother was famous for her fritole and made these treats for her family and friends. Years later we found her recipe card, but we tried making them without success. We finally figured out the missing part of the recipe—the self-rising flour! Now we can have these as often as we like. They bring back so many wonderful memories of our grandmother.
—Ann Marie Eberhart, Gig Harbor, WA

- -

Prep: 15 min. • **Cook:** 5 min./batch
Makes: 4 dozen

- 4 cups self-rising flour
- ½ cup sugar
- 3 large eggs, room temperature
- 1 cup whole milk
- 3 oz. whiskey, rum or orange juice
- 2 medium apples, peeled and grated
- 8 tsp. grated orange zest
  Oil for deep-fat frying
  Confectioners' sugar

1. In a large bowl, whisk the flour and sugar. In another bowl, whisk eggs, milk and whiskey until blended. Add to the dry ingredients, stirring just until moistened. Fold in apples and zest.

2. In an electric skillet or deep fryer, heat oil to 375°. Drop batter by tablespoonfuls, a few at a time, into hot oil. Fry for about 2 minutes on each side or until golden brown. Drain on paper towels. Dust with confectioners' sugar.

1 fritter: 69 cal., 2g fat (0 sat. fat), 12mg chol., 131mg sod., 11g carb. (3g sugars, 0 fiber), 2g pro.

TEST KITCHEN TIP

If you don't have self-rising flour on hand, make your own! For each cup needed, place 1½ tsp. baking powder and ½ tsp. salt in a measuring cup. Then add all-purpose flour to measure 1 cup.

POTS DE CREME

Looking for an easy dessert recipe that's guaranteed to impress? Served in pretty stemmed glasses, this classic chocolate custard really sets the tone.
—Connie Dreyfoos, Cincinnati, OH

- -

Prep: 15 min. + chilling
Makes: 5 servings

- 1 large egg
- 2 Tbsp. sugar
  Dash salt
- ¾ cup half-and-half cream
- 1 cup semisweet chocolate chips
- 1 tsp. vanilla extract
  Optional: Whipped cream and assorted fresh fruit

1. In a small saucepan, combine egg, sugar and salt. Whisk in cream. Cook and stir over medium heat until mixture reaches 160° and coats the back of a metal spoon.

2. Remove from the heat; whisk in the chocolate chips and vanilla until smooth. Pour into small dessert dishes. Cover and refrigerate, 8 hours or overnight. If desired, garnish with whipped cream and fruit.

⅓ cup: 246 cal., 15g fat (9g sat. fat), 55mg chol., 66mg sod., 28g carb. (25g sugars, 2g fiber), 4g pro.

NONNI'S FRITOLE

COCONUT MILK STRAWBERRY-BANANA POPS

These four-ingredient freezer pops are a delicious way to use up a pint of fresh strawberries. You'll love the hint of tropical flavor, thanks to the coconut milk.
—*Taste of Home* Test Kitchen

Prep: 10 min. + freezing
Makes: 12 servings

- 1 can (13.66 oz.) coconut milk
- 1 pint fresh strawberries, chopped, divided
- 1 medium banana, sliced
- 2 Tbsp. maple syrup
- 12 freezer pop molds or 12 paper cups (3 oz. each) and wooden pop sticks

Place coconut milk, 1½ cups strawberries, banana and syrup in a blender; cover and process until smooth. Divide remaining strawberries among 12 molds or paper cups. Pour the pureed mixture into molds or cups, filling ¾ full. Top the molds with holders. If using cups, top with foil and insert sticks through foil. Freeze until firm, at least 4 hours.

1 pop: 51 cal., 3g fat (3g sat. fat), 0 chol., 5mg sod., 7g carb. (5g sugars, 1g fiber), 1g pro.

TEST KITCHEN TIP
These frozen pops can be stored for up to 6 weeks.

COCONUT MILK
STRAWBERRY-BANANA
POPS

BANANA CRUMB
PUDDING

BANANA CRUMB PUDDING

Friends and family ask me to make my thick and creamy banana pudding for all occasions. They can't get enough of the wonderful flavor of the fruit and the vanilla wafer crumbs. You can also top the classic southern treat with meringue instead of whipped cream.
—Yvonnia Butner, Pinnacle, NC

Prep: 15 min. • **Cook:** 20 min. + chilling
Makes: 15 servings

- 1 cup sugar
- ½ cup cornstarch
- 6 cups 2% milk
- 5 large egg yolks
- ¼ cup butter, cubed
- 2 tsp. vanilla extract
- 1 tsp. kosher salt
- 2 pkg. (11 oz. each) vanilla wafers
- 7 medium bananas, sliced

TOPPING
- 2 cups heavy whipping cream
- 6 Tbsp. sugar

1. In a large heavy saucepan, mix sugar and cornstarch. Whisk in milk. Cook and stir over medium heat until thickened and bubbly. Reduce heat to low; cook and stir 2 minutes longer. Remove from heat.
2. In a bowl, whisk a small amount of hot mixture into egg yolks; return all to pan, whisking constantly. Bring to a gentle boil; cook and stir 2 minutes. Remove from the heat. Stir in butter, vanilla and salt. Cool 15 minutes, stirring occasionally.
3. Reserve 1 cup whole vanilla wafers and 1 banana for topping. Crush 2 cups wafers and set aside. In a 13x9-in. baking dish, place a single layer of whole wafers, filling gaps with crushed wafers. Layer with a third of the bananas and pudding. Repeat layers twice. Press waxed paper onto surface of the pudding. Refrigerate, covered, overnight.
4. In a bowl, beat the heavy cream until it begins to thicken. Add sugar; beat until soft peaks form (do not overmix). Just before serving, remove paper and spread whipped cream over pudding; top with reserved banana and whole wafers.
¾ cup: 535 cal., 27g fat (13g sat. fat), 121mg chol., 370mg sod., 70g carb. (46g sugars, 1g fiber), 7g pro.

CHOCOLATE & VANILLA
CREME BRULEE

CHOCOLATE & VANILLA CREME BRULEE

For a truly delicious dessert that will impress every guest, try this fancy recipe. It tastes so delicious!
—*Taste of Home* Test Kitchen

Prep: 30 min. • **Bake:** 35 min. + chilling
Makes: 8 servings

- 4 cups heavy whipping cream
- 9 large egg yolks
- 1 cup sugar, divided
- 1 tsp. vanilla extract
- ½ cup semisweet chocolate chips

1. In a large saucepan, heat cream until bubbles form around sides of pan. In a small bowl, whisk egg yolks and ¾ cup sugar. Remove cream from the heat; stir a small amount of hot cream into egg yolk mixture. Return all to pan, stirring constantly. Stir in vanilla. Set aside.
2. In a microwave, melt the chocolate chips; stir until smooth. Slowly whisk in 2 cups cream mixture until smooth. Transfer to 8 ungreased 6-oz. ramekins or custard cups.
3. Slowly pour remaining cream mixture over the back of a small spoon into the ramekins, forming layers. Place ramekins in a baking pan; add 1 in. boiling water to the pan.
4. Bake, uncovered, at 325° 35-40 minutes or until centers are just set (mixture will jiggle). Remove ramekins from water bath; cool for 10 minutes. Cover and refrigerate for at least 4 hours.
5. If using a creme brulee torch, sprinkle custards with remaining sugar; heat until caramelized. Serve immediately.
6. If broiling the custards, place ramekins on a baking sheet and let stand at room temperature for 15 minutes. Sprinkle with remaining sugar. Broil 8 in. from heat for 4-7 minutes or until caramelized. Refrigerate for 1-2 hours or until chilled.
1 dessert: 619 cal., 52g fat (31g sat. fat), 343mg chol., 43mg sod., 36g carb. (34g sugars, 1g fiber), 7g pro.
Vanilla Creme Brulee: Omit the chocolate chips.
Chocolate Creme Brulee: Increase chocolate chips to 1 cup and whisk entire custard mixture into the melted chips.

JAM-TOPPED MINI CHEESECAKES

We turned cheesecake into irresistible bite-sized snacks with these cute little treats. Feel free to swap in a favorite flavor jam.
—*Taste of Home* Test Kitchen

Prep: 20 min. • **Bake:** 15 min. + chilling
Makes: 9 servings

- ⅔ cup graham cracker crumbs
- 2 Tbsp. butter, melted
- 1 pkg. (8 oz.) cream cheese, softened
- ⅓ cup sugar
- 1 tsp. vanilla extract
- 1 large egg, room temperature
- 3 Tbsp. assorted jams, warmed

1. In a small bowl, combine the graham cracker crumbs and butter. Press gently onto the bottoms of 9 paper-lined muffin cups. In another small bowl, beat cream cheese, sugar and vanilla until smooth. Add the egg; beat on low speed just until combined. Spoon over crusts.
2. Bake at 350° until the centers are set, 15-16 minutes. Cool for 10 minutes before removing from pan to a wire rack to cool completely. Refrigerate for at least 1 hour.
3. Remove the paper liners and top each cheesecake with 1 tsp. jam.

1 mini cheesecake: 198 cal., 13g fat (7g sat. fat), 53mg chol., 141mg sod., 19g carb. (14g sugars, 0 fiber), 3g pro.

DIRT DESSERT

DIRT DESSERT

My mom used to serve this yummy dessert, and I just loved it. It's so fun to eat and a snap to make. Add some gummy worms on top for the kids if you'd like.
—Kristi Linton, Bay City, MI

Prep: 30 min. + chilling
Makes: 20 servings

- 1 pkg. (8 oz.) cream cheese, softened
- ¼ cup butter, softened
- 1 cup confectioners' sugar
- 3½ cups cold 2% milk
- 2 pkg. (3.4 oz. each) instant vanilla pudding mix
- 1 carton (12 oz.) frozen whipped topping, thawed
- 1 pkg. (15½ oz.) Oreo cookies, crushed
  Shaved white chocolate, optional

1. In a large bowl, beat cream cheese, butter and confectioners' sugar until smooth. In another large bowl, whisk milk and pudding mixes for 2 minutes; let stand for 2 minutes or until soft-set. Gradually stir into cream cheese mixture. Fold in whipped topping.
2. Spread 1⅓ cups crushed cookies into an ungreased 13x9-in. dish. Layer with half the pudding mixture and half the remaining cookies. Repeat the layers. Refrigerate for at least 1 hour before serving. Serve with shaved white chocolate if desired.

½ cup: 278 cal., 13g fat (7g sat. fat), 16mg chol., 316mg sod., 38g carb. (26g sugars, 1g fiber), 3g pro.

TEST KITCHEN TIP
For even more indulgence, use chocolate pudding mix instead of vanilla.

DOUBLE CHOCOLATE ESPRESSO CHEESECAKE

Every slice of this creamy cheesecake is a standout. The classic pairing of chocolate and coffee is sure to please partygoers.
—Cheryl Perry, Hertford, NC

Prep: 35 min. • **Bake:** 1 hour + chilling
Makes: 16 servings

- 1½ cups crushed vanilla wafers (about 45)
- ¼ cup butter, melted
- 2 Tbsp. sugar
- ¼ tsp. instant espresso powder

FILLING
- 1 cup sour cream, room temperature
- ¼ cup half-and-half cream, room temperature
- 1 cup 60% cacao bittersweet chocolate baking chips, melted
- 1½ tsp. instant espresso powder
- 1 tsp. vanilla extract
- 4 pkg. (8 oz. each) cream cheese, softened
- 1½ cups sugar
- ½ cup baking cocoa
- 1 Tbsp. all-purpose flour
- 5 large eggs, room temperature, lightly beaten

TOPPING
- 1 cup coffee liqueur
- 1 Tbsp. half-and-half cream
- 1 cup heavy whipping cream
- 2 Tbsp. confectioners' sugar
- ½ cup 60% cacao bittersweet chocolate baking chips, chopped
- 16 chocolate-covered coffee beans

1. Preheat oven to 350°. Place a greased 9-in. springform pan on a double thickness of heavy-duty foil (about 18 in. square). Securely wrap foil around pan.

2. In a large bowl, combine wafer crumbs, butter, sugar and espresso powder. Press onto the bottom and 1 in. up the sides of prepared pan.

3. In a small bowl, stir together the sour cream, half-and-half and melted chocolate until blended; set aside. In second bowl, combine espresso powder and vanilla extract; set aside.

4. In a large bowl, beat the cream cheese and sugar; add chocolate mixture, cocoa and flour until smooth. Stir in the espresso mixture. Add eggs; beat on low speed just until combined. Pour into the crust. Place springform pan in a large baking pan; add 1 in. hot water to larger pan.

5. Bake until the center is just set and top appears dull, 60-70 minutes. Remove the springform pan from water bath. Cool on a wire rack 10 minutes. Carefully run a knife around edge of pan to loosen; cool 1 hour longer. Refrigerate overnight. Remove sides of pan.

6. In a small saucepan, combine liqueur and half-and-half. Bring to a boil; cook until liquid is reduced by half. Meanwhile, in a large bowl, beat whipping cream until it begins to thicken. Add the confectioners' sugar; beat until stiff peaks form.

7. Drizzle cheesecake with coffee syrup; garnish with whipped cream, chocolate and coffee beans.

1 piece: 610 cal., 40g fat (23g sat. fat), 170mg chol., 259mg sod., 52g carb. (41g sugars, 2g fiber), 9g pro.

> "This was a hit the moment my mom set it on the table for a family get-together. We've all enjoyed it many times since. It's really a delicious showstopper."
> —MARK HAGEN, CONTENT DIRECTOR

DOUBLE CHOCOLATE ESPRESSO CHEESECAKE

MIXED BERRY TIRAMISU

Because I love tiramisu, I came up with this deliciously refreshing twist on the traditional coffee-flavored Italian dessert. Fresh berries star with crisp ladyfinger cookies and mascarpone cheese. Serve it from a glass bowl or in clear dishes to show off the luscious layers.
—Najmussahar Ahmed, Ypsilanti, MI

Prep: 35 min. + chilling
Makes: 12 servings

　3　cups fresh raspberries
　3　cups fresh blackberries
　2　cups fresh blueberries
　2　cups fresh strawberries, sliced
1⅓　cups sugar, divided
　4　tsp. grated orange zest
　1　cup orange juice
　1　cup heavy whipping cream
　2　cartons (8 oz. each)
　　　mascarpone cheese
　1　tsp. vanilla extract
　2　pkg. (7 oz. each) crisp
　　　ladyfinger cookies

1. Place berries in a large bowl. Mix ⅓ cup sugar, orange zest and orange juice; toss gently with berries. Refrigerate, covered, 45 minutes.
2. Beat cream until soft peaks form. In another bowl, mix mascarpone cheese, vanilla and the remaining sugar. Fold in the whipped cream, a third at a time.
3. Drain berries over a shallow bowl, reserving juices. Dip the ladyfingers in reserved juices, allowing excess to drip off; arrange ladyfingers in a single layer on bottom of a 13x9-in. dish. Layer with half the berries and half the mascarpone mixture; repeat layers, starting with the ladyfingers. Refrigerate, covered, overnight.
1 piece: 501 cal., 26g fat (14g sat. fat), 105mg chol., 77mg sod., 63g carb. (45g sugars, 5g fiber), 8g pro.

MIXED BERRY TIRAMISU

SOPAIPILLAS

Light, crispy pastry puffs, sopaipillas are a sweet way to round out a spicy meal. We love to serve them warm and to top them off with honey or sugar.
—Mary Anne McWhirter, Pearland, TX

Prep: 15 min. + standing • **Cook:** 25 min.
Makes: 1 dozen

- 1 cup all-purpose flour
- 1½ tsp. baking powder
- ¼ tsp. salt
- 1 Tbsp. shortening
- ⅓ cup warm water
  Oil for deep-fat frying
  Optional: Confectioners' sugar and honey

1. In a large bowl, combine flour, baking powder and salt. Cut in shortening until mixture resembles fine crumbs. Gradually add water, tossing with a fork until a loose ball forms (dough will be crumbly).
2. On a lightly floured surface, knead the dough for 3 minutes or until smooth. Cover and let rest for 10 minutes. Roll out into a 12x10-in. rectangle. Cut into 12 square shapes with a knife or cut into 12 circles using a round biscuit cutter.
3. In a deep-fat fryer, heat 2 in. oil to 375°. Fry sopaipillas for 1-2 minutes on each side. Drain on paper towels; keep warm. If desired, dust with confectioners' sugar and/or serve with honey.
1 sopaipilla: 57 cal., 2g fat (0 sat. fat), 0 chol., 109mg sod., 8g carb. (0 sugars, 0 fiber), 1g pro.

MANGO GLACE WITH PINEAPPLE POMEGRANATE SALSA

I'd like to say this dish was a brilliant idea that came from expert planning. But the truth is that between the quickly ripening fruit on my counter and the 100-degree heat, it pretty much invented itself! Very ripe fruit eliminates the need for added sugar.
—Jodi Taffel, Altadena, CA

Prep: 45 min. + freezing • **Makes:** 1 dozen

- 4 medium ripe mangoes, peeled and chopped
- 1 fresh ripe pineapple, peeled and cut into ½-in. pieces
- 2 Tbsp. lime juice

SALSA

- 1 cup finely chopped fresh pineapple
- 2 Tbsp. pomegranate seeds
- 1 Tbsp. minced fresh mint

1. Combine the mangoes, pineapple and lime juice in a blender. Cover and process until smooth. Strain through a fine-mesh strainer into a large bowl. Pour into 1¾-in. silicone ice cube trays. Freeze until firm, 8 hours or overnight.
2. Combine salsa ingredients; cover and refrigerate overnight.
3. Take cubes out of freezer 10 minutes before serving. Run a small spatula around edge of each fruit cube to loosen; remove from trays. Serve with salsa.
1 cube with 4 tsp. salsa: 114 cal., 1g fat (0 sat. fat), 0 chol., 2mg sod., 29g carb. (24g sugars, 3g fiber), 1g pro.

MANGO GLACE WITH PINEAPPLE POMEGRANATE SALSA

COCONUT MANGO BREAD PUDDING WITH RUM SAUCE

RAINBOW GELATIN CUBES

These perky gelatin cubes are fun to serve and to eat! I vary the colors to match the occasion—pink and blue for a baby shower, school colors for a graduation party, etc. Kids of all ages snap them up.
—Deanna Pietrowicz, Bridgeport, CT

- -

Prep: 30 min. + chilling • **Makes:** 9 dozen

  4 pkg. (3 oz. each) assorted
     flavored gelatin, divided
  6 envelopes unflavored
     gelatin, divided
  5¾ cups boiling water, divided
  1 can (14 oz.) sweetened
     condensed milk
  ¼ cup cold water

1. In a bowl, combine 1 package flavored gelatin and 1 envelope unflavored gelatin. Stir in 1 cup boiling water until dissolved. Pour into a 13x9-in. dish coated with cooking spray; refrigerate until set but not firm, about 20 minutes.
2. In another bowl, combine condensed milk and 1 cup boiling water. In another bowl, sprinkle 2 envelopes unflavored gelatin over cold water; let stand for 1 minute. Stir in ¾ cup boiling water. Add to the milk mixture. Spoon 1 cup creamy gelatin mixture over the first flavored gelatin layer. Refrigerate until set but not firm, about 25 minutes.
3. Repeat from beginning of recipe twice, alternating flavored gelatin with creamy gelatin layers. Chill each layer until set but not firm before spooning next layer on top. Make final flavored gelatin layer; spoon over top. Refrigerate at least 1 hour after completing last layer before cutting into 1-in. squares.
1 piece: 25 cal., 0 fat (0 sat. fat), 1mg chol., 13mg sod., 5g carb. (5g sugars, 0 fiber), 1g pro.

TEST KITCHEN TIP
Spooning, not pouring, each color of gelatin onto the previous layer helps keep the layers intact.

COCONUT MANGO BREAD PUDDING WITH RUM SAUCE

All the fun flavors of Puerto Rico come together in a dessert that's both exotic and familiar. Topped with a brown sugar rum sauce, it's even better with vanilla ice cream or whipped cream.
—Jennifer Jackson, Keller, TX

- -

Prep: 30 min. • **Cook:** 3 hours
Makes: 6 servings

  4 large eggs, beaten
  1 can (13.66 oz.) coconut milk
  ⅓ cup packed brown sugar
  1 tsp. rum extract
  ½ tsp. vanilla extract
  ½ tsp. ground cinnamon
  4 cups torn French bread
  ⅓ cup chopped dried mangoes
  ¼ cup unsweetened
     coconut flakes, toasted
SAUCE
  ¼ cup butter
  ½ cup packed brown sugar
  2 Tbsp. water
  1 large egg yolk, beaten
  ½ tsp. rum extract
     Toasted unsweetened
     coconut flakes, optional

1. In a large bowl, whisk first 6 ingredients until blended. Gently stir in the bread, mangoes and coconut flakes. Transfer to a greased 3-qt. slow cooker. Cook, covered, on low until puffed and edges are dark golden, about 3 hours.
2. In a small heavy saucepan, heat butter and brown sugar over medium-low heat until blended. Whisk in water and yolk. Cook and stir until the mixture is slightly thickened and a thermometer reads 175°, about 10 minutes. Do not allow to boil. Immediately transfer to a bowl; stir in rum extract. Serve warm bread pudding with the rum sauce. If desired, top with additional toasted coconut.
¾ cup with 2 Tbsp. sauce: 447 cal., 24g fat (18g sat. fat), 175mg chol., 285mg sod., 49g carb. (37g sugars, 1g fiber), 8g pro.

CONTEST-WINNING STRAWBERRY PRETZEL DESSERT

I love the sweet-salty flavor of this pretty layered dessert. Sliced strawberries and gelatin top a smooth cream cheese filling and crispy pretzel crust. I think it's best when eaten within a day of being made.
—Wendy Weaver, Leetonia, OH

Prep: 15 min. + chilling
Makes: 2 servings

- ⅓ cup crushed pretzels
- 2 Tbsp. butter, softened
- 2 oz. cream cheese, softened
- ¼ cup sugar
- ¾ cup whipped topping
- 2 Tbsp. plus 1½ tsp. strawberry gelatin
- ½ cup boiling water
- 1 cup sliced fresh strawberries
  Optional: Whipped topping and pretzel twists

1. Preheat oven to 375°. In a large bowl, combine pretzels and butter. Press onto the bottom of 2 greased 10-oz. custard cups. Bake until set, 6-8 minutes. Cool on a wire rack.
2. In a small bowl, combine cream cheese and sugar until smooth. Fold in whipped topping. Spoon over crust. Refrigerate for 30 minutes.
3. Meanwhile, in a small bowl, dissolve the gelatin in boiling water. Cover and refrigerate for 20 minutes or until slightly thickened. Fold in strawberries. Carefully spoon over filling. Cover and refrigerate at least 3 hours. If desired, top with whipped topping and pretzel twists.
1 serving: 516 cal., 27g fat (18g sat. fat), 62mg chol., 458mg sod., 64g carb. (47g sugars, 2g fiber), 6g pro.

PEACH CRUMBLE DESSERT

We save our forks after dinner so we can enjoy this yummy, old-fashioned dessert. It's delicious, so easy to make and wonderful with ice cream.
—Nancy Horsburgh, Everett, ON

Prep: 15 min. • **Bake:** 35 min.
Makes: 12 servings

- 6 cups sliced peeled ripe peaches
- ¼ cup packed brown sugar
- 3 Tbsp. all-purpose flour
- 1 tsp. lemon juice
- ½ tsp. grated lemon zest
- ½ tsp. ground cinnamon

TOPPING
- 1 cup all-purpose flour
- 1 cup sugar
- 1 tsp. baking powder
- ¼ tsp. salt
- ¼ tsp. ground nutmeg
- 1 large egg, lightly beaten
- ½ cup butter, melted and cooled
  Vanilla ice cream, optional

1. Preheat oven to 375°. Place the peaches in a greased shallow 2½-qt. Dutch oven, cast-iron pan or 2½-qt. ovenproof baking dish. In a bowl, combine the brown sugar, flour, lemon juice, zest and cinnamon; sprinkle over the peaches.
2. Combine flour, sugar, baking powder, salt and nutmeg. Stir in egg until mixture resembles coarse crumbs. Sprinkle over peaches. Pour butter evenly over topping.
3. Bake 35-40 minutes. If desired, serve with ice cream.
1 serving: 237 cal., 8g fat (5g sat. fat), 38mg chol., 167mg sod., 40g carb. (28g sugars, 2g fiber), 2g pro.

"I make this fruity dessert a couple of times each summer, and it's always a hit!"
— JAMES SCHEND, DEPUTY CULINARY EDITOR

PEACH CRUMBLE DESSERT

CHOCOLATE-GLAZED RASPBERRY ECLAIRS

I first made choux pastry in high school for a French class assignment, and I was fascinated. I loved watching it puff up in the oven and enjoyed eating my delicious eclairs! Since then, eclairs have been my favorite pastry to make. They're not as tricky as they seem, and you can make so many amazing flavors.

—Elisabeth Larsen, Pleasant Grove, UT

CHOCOLATE-GLAZED RASPBERRY ECLAIRS

Prep: 1 hour + chilling
Bake: 25 min. + cooling
Makes: 1 dozen

- ½ cup sugar
- ¼ cup cornstarch
- 2 cups whole milk
- 4 large egg yolks
- 2 Tbsp. unsalted butter

PASTRY
- ½ cup water
- 6 Tbsp. unsalted butter, cubed
- ¼ cup whole milk
- 2 tsp. sugar
- ¼ tsp. salt
- ¾ cup all-purpose flour
- 3 large eggs

GLAZE
- ⅔ cup semisweet chocolate chips
- ½ cup heavy whipping cream
- 1 Tbsp. light corn syrup
- 1 cup fresh raspberries

1. In a small heavy saucepan, mix sugar and cornstarch. Whisk in milk. Cook and stir over medium heat until thickened and bubbly. Reduce heat to low; cook and stir 2 minutes longer. Remove from heat.

2. In a small bowl, whisk a small amount of hot mixture into egg yolks; return all to pan, whisking constantly. Bring to a gentle boil; cook and stir 2 minutes. Immediately transfer to a clean bowl; stir in the butter. Press plastic wrap onto surface of filling; refrigerate until cold.

3. Preheat oven to 425°. For pastry, in a large saucepan, bring water, butter, milk, sugar and salt to a rolling boil. Add flour all at once and beat until blended. Cook over medium heat, stirring vigorously until the mixture pulls away from the side of pan and forms a ball. Remove from heat; let stand 5 minutes.

4. Add the eggs, 1 at a time, beating well after each addition until smooth. Continue beating until mixture is smooth and shiny. Transfer to a piping bag with a large round tip. Pipe twelve 4½-in. strips about 3 in. apart on parchment-lined baking sheets. Bake for 15 minutes. Reduce the oven temperature to 350°; bake until golden brown, 8-10 minutes longer. Pierce the side of each eclair with tip of knife. Cool completely on wire racks. Split eclairs open. Pull out and discard the soft dough from inside tops and bottoms.

5. For the glaze, in a microwave, melt chocolate chips, cream and corn syrup; stir until smooth. Stir raspberries into chilled pastry filling, mashing berries lightly. Fill eclairs just before serving. Dip tops in chocolate glaze; replace tops. Top with additional fresh raspberries. Let stand until set. Refrigerate leftovers.

Freeze option: Freeze unfilled, unglazed eclairs in an airtight container for up to 2 months. Thaw, fill and glaze eclairs just before serving.

1 eclair: 295 cal., 18g fat (11g sat. fat), 144mg chol., 96mg sod., 29g carb. (19g sugars, 1g fiber), 6g pro.

DID YOU KNOW?
The choux pastry and the filling can both be made a day in advance. Store the baked, unfilled eclairs in an airtight container overnight. Fill the eclairs the day you plan on serving them.

LEMON DREAM CHEESECAKE

This cheesecake bakes like a dream with no cracks. Plus it cuts well and everyone loves the light lemon flavor—a refreshing treat any time of year.
—Bonnie Jost, Manitowoc, WI

Prep: 30 min. • **Bake:** 55 min. + chilling
Makes: 16 servings

- 2 cups graham cracker crumbs
- 6 Tbsp. butter, melted
- ¼ cup sugar

FILLING

- 4 pkg. (8 oz. each) cream cheese, softened
- 1 cup sugar
- ½ cup heavy whipping cream
- ¼ cup lemon juice
- 2 Tbsp. all-purpose flour
- 1 Tbsp. grated lemon zest
- 2½ tsp. vanilla extract
- 1 tsp. lemon extract
- 10 drops yellow food coloring, optional
- 5 large eggs, room temperature, lightly beaten

1. Preheat oven to 325°. In a small bowl, combine the cracker crumbs, butter and sugar. Press onto bottom and 1-2 in. up the inside of a greased 10-in. springform pan. Place pan on a baking sheet. Bake 10 minutes. Cool on a wire rack.

2. In a large bowl, beat cream cheese and sugar until smooth. Beat in cream, lemon juice, flour, lemon zest, extracts and, if desired, food coloring. Add eggs; beat on low speed just until combined. Pour into the crust. Return the pan to baking sheet.

3. Bake 55-65 minutes or until center is almost set. Cool on a wire rack 10 minutes. Carefully run a knife around edge of pan to loosen; cool 1 hour. Refrigerate overnight. Remove side of pan.

1 piece: 396 cal., 29g fat (18g sat. fat), 150mg chol., 286mg sod., 27g carb. (19g sugars, 0 fiber), 7g pro.

PINA COLADA ICEBOX CAKE

This icebox cake has all the flavors of a pina colada. It takes just one bite to escape to a tropical island!
—Rachel Lewis, Danville, VA

Prep: 25 min. + chilling
Makes: 12 servings

- 1 pkg. (8 oz.) cream cheese, softened
- ½ cup confectioners' sugar
- ½ tsp. rum extract
- 1 can (13.66 oz.) coconut milk, divided
- 1 pkg. (3.4 oz.) instant vanilla pudding mix
- 1 container (8 oz.) frozen whipped topping, thawed
- 15 whole graham crackers
- 1 can (20 oz.) crushed pineapple, drained
- 1 cup sweetened shredded coconut, toasted

1. In a large bowl, beat cream cheese, confectioners' sugar and extract until smooth. Gradually beat in 1 cup coconut milk. Add pudding mix; beat on low speed until smooth. Fold in whipped topping.

2. Pour the remaining coconut milk into a shallow dish. Quickly dip half the graham crackers into milk; allow excess to drip off. Arrange crackers in a single layer in the bottom of a 13x9-in. baking dish, breaking to fit as needed. Layer with half each of the cream cheese mixture, pineapple and coconut. Repeat layers. Refrigerate, covered, at least 4 hours before serving.

1 piece: 377 cal., 20g fat (15g sat. fat), 19mg chol., 259mg sod., 47g carb. (33g sugars, 1g fiber), 3g pro.

LEMON DREAM CHEESECAKE

ICE CREAM CONE TREATS

I came up with this recipe as a way for my grandkids to enjoy Rice Krispies treats without getting sticky hands. You can also pack the cereal mixture into paper cups and insert a wooden pop stick to create cute pops.

—Mabel Nolan, Vancouver, WA

Takes: 20 min. • **Makes:** 12 dozen

12 ice cream sugar cones
    Melted semisweet chocolate,
    optional
    Colored sprinkles
4   cups miniature marshmallows
3   Tbsp. butter
6   cups Rice Krispies

1. If desired, dip ice cream cones in melted chocolate to coat the edges; stand in juice glasses or coffee mugs.

2. Place sprinkles in a shallow bowl. In a microwave or in a large saucepan over low heat, melt marshmallows and butter; stir until smooth. Remove from the heat; stir in the cereal.

3. Working quickly, use buttered hands to shape mixture into 12 balls; pack firmly into cones. Dip tops in sprinkles.

1 serving: 174 cal., 4g fat (2g sat. fat), 8mg chol., 142mg sod., 34g carb. (14g sugars, 0 fiber), 2g pro.

TEST KITCHEN TIP

Decorate these cones with colored sprinkles fit for various occasions: red and green for Christmas, red and pink for Valentine's Day, green and white for St. Patrick's Day, or black and orange for Halloween.

ICE CREAM CONE
TREATS

LEMON BREAD
PUDDING

LEMON BREAD PUDDING

Sweet raisins and a smooth lemon sauce make this bread pudding extra special.
—Mildred Sherrer, Fort Worth, TX

- -

Prep: 15 min. • **Bake:** 50 min.
Makes: 6 servings

- 3 slices day-old bread, cubed
- ¾ cup raisins
- 2 cups 2% milk
- ½ cup sugar
- 2 Tbsp. butter
- ¼ tsp. salt
- 2 large eggs
- 1 tsp. vanilla extract

LEMON SAUCE

- ¾ cup sugar
- 2 Tbsp. cornstarch
- 1 cup water
- 2 tsp. grated lemon zest
- 3 Tbsp. lemon juice
- 1 Tbsp. butter

1. Preheat oven to 350°. Toss bread and raisins in a greased 1½-qt. baking dish. In a small saucepan, combine milk, sugar, butter and salt; cook and stir until butter melts. Remove from the heat. Whisk eggs and vanilla in a small bowl. Stir a small amount of hot milk mixture into the egg mixture; return all to the pan, stirring constantly. Pour over bread and raisins.
2. Place dish in a larger baking pan. Fill larger pan with hot water to a depth of 1 in. Bake, uncovered, 50-60 minutes or until a knife inserted in the center comes out clean.
3. For sauce, in a small saucepan, combine sugar and cornstarch. Stir in water until smooth. Bring to a boil over medium heat; cook and stir until thickened, 1-2 minutes. Remove from the heat. Stir in the lemon zest, juice and butter until butter is melted. Serve sauce over warm or cold pudding. Refrigerate leftovers.
1 cup: 385 cal., 10g fat (5g sat. fat), 84mg chol., 280mg sod., 71g carb. (58g sugars, 1g fiber), 7g pro.

BEST BANANA ICE CREAM

BEST BANANA ICE CREAM

My son-in-law says this is the best ice cream. It appears at many gatherings.
—Donna Robbins, Skiatook, OK

- -

Prep: 15 min. + chilling
Process: 20 min./batch + freezing
Makes: 3 qt.

- 4 cups half-and-half cream
- 2½ cups sugar
  Dash salt
- 4 large eggs, room temperature, lightly beaten
- 4 cups heavy whipping cream
- 1 can (5 oz.) evaporated milk
- 3 tsp. vanilla extract
- 2 cups mashed ripe bananas (4 to 5 medium)

1. In a large heavy saucepan, heat the half-and-half to 175°; stir in sugar and salt until dissolved. Whisk a small amount of hot mixture into eggs. Return all to the pan, whisking constantly. Cook and stir over low heat until mixture reaches 160° and coats the back of a metal spoon.

2. Remove from the heat. Cool quickly by placing pan in a bowl of ice water; stir for 2 minutes. Stir in the whipping cream, milk and vanilla. Press plastic wrap onto the surface of the custard. Refrigerate for several hours or overnight.
3. Stir in bananas. Fill cylinder of ice cream freezer two-thirds full; freeze according to manufacturer's directions. Refrigerate remaining mixture until ready to freeze. When the ice cream is frozen, transfer to a freezer container; freeze for 2-4 hours before serving.
½ cup: 308 cal., 20g fat (12g sat. fat), 98mg chol., 55mg sod., 28g carb. (26g sugars, 0 fiber), 4g pro.

> **"This banana ice cream is so creamy and delicious. You can easily customize it by adding whatever mix-ins you'd like, but it's perfect as is."**
> —SARAH TRAMONTE, CULINARY PRODUCER

ORANGE CREAM POPS

For a lower-fat alternative to pops filled with ice cream, try this citrus novelty. The tangy orange flavor will make your taste buds tingle, while the silky smooth texture offers cool comfort.
—*Taste of Home* Test Kitchen

Prep: 10 min. + freezing
Makes: 10 ice pops

- 1   pkg. (3 oz.) orange gelatin
- 1   cup boiling water
- 1   cup vanilla yogurt
- ½   cup 2% milk
- ½   tsp. vanilla extract
- 10 freezer pop molds or 10 paper cups (3 oz. each) and wooden pop sticks

In a large bowl, dissolve gelatin in boiling water. Cool to room temperature. Stir in the yogurt, milk and vanilla. Pour ¼ cup into each mold or paper cup. Top molds with holders. If using cups, top with foil and insert sticks through foil. Freeze until firm.

1 pop: 58 cal., 1g fat (0 sat. fat), 2mg chol., 41mg sod., 11g carb. (11g sugars, 0 fiber), 2g pro. **Diabetic exchanges:** 1 starch.

AIR-FRYER
CARIBBEAN
WONTONS

AIR-FRYER CARIBBEAN WONTONS

I first served these fresh and fruity treats as an appetizer at a summer luau. My family and friends now enjoy them as a dessert for special occasions throughout the year.
—*Melissa Pelkey Hass, Waleska, GA*

Prep: 30 min. • **Cook:** 10 min./batch
Makes: 2 dozen (1¼ cups sauce)

- 4   oz. cream cheese, softened
- ¼   cup sweetened shredded coconut
- ¼   cup mashed ripe banana
- 2   Tbsp. chopped walnuts
- 2   Tbsp. canned crushed pineapple
- 1   cup marshmallow creme
- 24 wonton wrappers
     Cooking spray

SAUCE
- 1   lb. fresh strawberries, hulled
- ¼   cup sugar
- 1   tsp. cornstarch
     Confectioners' sugar and ground cinnamon

1. Preheat air fryer to 350°. In a small bowl, beat cream cheese until smooth. Stir in coconut, banana, walnuts and pineapple. Fold in marshmallow creme.
2. Position a wonton wrapper with 1 point toward you. Keep remaining wrappers covered with a damp paper towel until ready to use. Place 2 tsp. filling in the center of wrapper. Moisten edges with water; fold opposite corners together over filling and press to seal. Repeat with the remaining wrappers and filling.
3. In batches, arrange wontons in a single layer on greased tray in air-fryer basket; spritz with cooking spray. Cook until golden brown and crisp, 10-12 minutes.
4. Meanwhile, place strawberries in a food processor; cover and process until pureed. In a small saucepan, combine sugar and cornstarch. Stir in pureed strawberries. Bring to a boil; cook and stir 2 minutes or until thickened. If desired, strain mixture, reserving sauce; discard seeds. Sprinkle wontons with confectioners' sugar and cinnamon. Serve with sauce.

1 wonton with 1½ tsp. sauce: 83 cal., 3g fat (1g sat. fat), 5mg chol., 67mg sod., 13g carb. (7g sugars, 1g fiber), 1g pro.

CHOCOLATE CHIP COOKIE DOUGH CHEESECAKE

I created this recipe to combine two of my all-time favorites—cheesecake and chocolate chip cookie dough.
—Julie Craig, Kewaskum, WI

Prep: 25 min. • **Bake:** 45 min. + chilling
Makes: 14 servings

- 1¾ cups crushed chocolate chip cookies or chocolate wafer crumbs
- ¼ cup sugar
- ⅓ cup butter, melted

FILLING
- 3 pkg. (8 oz. each) cream cheese, softened
- 1 cup sugar
- 1 cup sour cream
- ½ tsp. vanilla extract
- 3 large eggs, lightly beaten

COOKIE DOUGH
- ¼ cup butter, softened
- ¼ cup sugar
- ¼ cup packed brown sugar
- 1 Tbsp. water
- 1 tsp. vanilla extract
- ½ cup all-purpose flour
- 1½ cups miniature semisweet chocolate chips, divided

1. In a small bowl, combine cookie crumbs and sugar; stir in butter. Press onto the bottom and 1 in. up the side of a greased 9-in. springform pan. Place the pan on a baking sheet.

2. In a large bowl, beat cream cheese and sugar until smooth. Beat in sour cream and vanilla. Add eggs; beat on low speed just until combined. Pour over crust.

3. In another bowl, cream the butter and sugars until light and fluffy, 5-7 minutes. Add water and vanilla. Gradually add flour and mix well. Stir in 1 cup chocolate chips.

4. Drop dough by teaspoonfuls over filling, gently pushing dough below the surface (the dough should be completely covered by the filling).

5. Bake at 350° until center is almost set, 45-55 minutes. Cool on a wire rack for 10 minutes. Carefully run a knife around edge of pan to loosen; cool 1 hour longer. Refrigerate overnight.

6. Remove sides of the pan. Sprinkle the top with remaining ½ cup chips. Refrigerate leftovers.

1 piece: 551 cal., 36g fat (22g sat. fat), 131mg chol., 328mg sod., 52g carb. (37g sugars, 2g fiber), 8g pro.

ASK SARAH

HOW CAN I TELL WHEN A CHEESECAKE IS DONE BAKING?

Tap the side of your cake pan with a wooden spoon. If the cake ripples a lot, it needs more time in the oven. If it wobbles a bit without ripples, it's just right. The cake will continue to bake and firm up when it comes out of the oven.

CHOCOLATE CHIP COOKIE DOUGH CHEESECAKE

SPECIAL STUFFED STRAWBERRIES

These sweet bites can be made ahead of time—and they look really colorful on a tray. I sometimes sprinkle the piped filling with finely chopped pistachio nuts.
—Marcia Orlando, Boyertown, PA

- -

Takes: 20 min. • **Makes:** 2 dozen

- 24 **large fresh strawberries**
- ½ **cup spreadable strawberry cream cheese**
- 3 **Tbsp. sour cream**
  Graham cracker crumbs

1. Place strawberries on a cutting board and cut off tops; remove bottom tips so they sit flat. Using a small paring knife, hull out the center of each berry.
2. In a small bowl, beat cream cheese and sour cream until smooth. Pipe or spoon filling into each berry. Top with crushed graham crackers. Refrigerate until serving.
1 strawberry: 18 cal., 1g fat (1g sat. fat), 4mg chol., 22mg sod., 1g carb. (1g sugars, 0 fiber), 1g pro.

IRISH CREME CHOCOLATE TRIFLE

I was given a bottle of Irish cream liqueur as a gift and had leftover peppermint candy, so I created this delicious trifle. It's always rich and decadent.
—Margaret Wilson, San Bernardino, CA

- -

Prep: 20 min. + chilling
Bake: 30 min. + cooling
Makes: 16 servings

- 1 **pkg. devil's food cake mix (regular size)**
- 1 **cup refrigerated Irish creme nondairy creamer**
- 3½ **cups 2% milk**
- 2 **pkg. (3.9 oz. each) instant chocolate pudding mix**
- 3 **cups whipped topping**
- 12 **mint Andes candies, chopped**

1. Prepare and bake cake mix according to package directions using a 13x9-in. pan. Cool in pan on a wire rack 1 hour.
2. With a meat fork or wooden skewer, poke holes in cake about 2 in. apart. Slowly pour the creamer over cake; refrigerate, covered, 1 hour.
3. In a large bowl, whisk milk and pudding mixes 2 minutes; let stand until soft-set, about 2 minutes.
4. Cut cake into 1½-in. cubes. In a 3-qt. trifle or glass bowl, layer a third of each of the following: cake cubes, pudding, whipped topping and candies. Repeat layers twice. Refrigerate until serving.
1 serving: 343 cal., 14g fat (5g sat. fat), 39mg chol., 363mg sod., 49g carb. (32g sugars, 1g fiber), 5g pro.

PEAR-BLACKBERRY CRISP

I love making this recipe in the fall when I have an abundance of fresh pears from a nearby orchard. The unique combination of pears and blackberries really makes this dessert special.
—Beth Fleming, Downers Grove, IL

- -

Prep: 25 min. • **Bake:** 45 min.
Makes: 12 servings

- 10 **medium pears (about 4 lbs.), peeled and sliced**
- 2 **cups fresh or frozen blackberries**
- ⅓ **cup sugar**
- ¼ **cup all-purpose flour**
TOPPING
- 1⅓ **cups all-purpose flour**
- 1⅓ **cups quick-cooking oats**
- 1 **cup packed brown sugar**
- 1 **tsp. ground cinnamon**
- ½ **tsp. salt**
- 1 **cup cold butter, cubed**

1. Preheat oven to 375°. Place pears and blackberries in a large bowl. Mix sugar and flour; toss with fruit. Transfer to a greased 13x9-in. baking dish.
2. In a bowl, mix first 5 topping ingredients; cut in butter until crumbly. Sprinkle over filling. Bake until the filling is bubbly and topping is golden brown, 45-50 minutes.
1 serving: 415 cal., 16g fat (10g sat. fat), 41mg chol., 228mg sod., 67g carb. (39g sugars, 7g fiber), 4g pro.

SUGAR COOKIE FRUIT PIZZAS

Purchased sugar cookies create a sweet crust for these colorful pizzas. Make them throughout the year using a variety of fresh and canned fruits.
—Marge Hodel, Roanoke, IL

- -

Prep: 45 min. + chilling • **Makes:** 1 dozen

- ½ cup sugar
- 1 Tbsp. cornstarch
- ½ cup unsweetened pineapple juice
- ¼ cup water
- 2 Tbsp. lemon juice
- 4 oz. cream cheese, softened
- ¼ cup confectioners' sugar
- 1¾ cups whipped topping
- 12 sugar cookies (3 in.)
- 1 cup fresh blueberries
- 1 cup chopped peeled kiwifruit
- ½ cup chopped fresh strawberries

1. For glaze, in a small saucepan, combine sugar, cornstarch, pineapple juice, water and lemon juice until smooth. Bring to a boil; cook and stir for 2 minutes or until thickened. Transfer to a bowl; refrigerate until cooled but not set.
2. In a small bowl, beat cream cheese and confectioners' sugar until smooth; fold in the whipped topping. Spread over tops of cookies. Arrange fruit on top; drizzle with glaze. Refrigerate for 1 hour or until chilled.
1 pizza: 198 cal., 8g fat (4g sat. fat), 10mg chol., 99mg sod., 30g carb. (20g sugars, 2g fiber), 2g pro.

FROZEN CHOCOLATE MONKEY TREATS

Everyone needs a fun, friendly way for kids to play with food. These bites are nutty and yummy. Just coat bananas in chocolate and dip them into peanuts, sprinkles or coconut.
—Susan Hein, Burlington, WI

- -

Prep: 20 min. + freezing
Makes: 1½ dozen

- 3 medium bananas
- 1 cup dark chocolate chips
- 2 tsp. shortening
  Optional toppings: Chopped peanuts, toasted sweetened shredded coconut and colored jimmies

1. Cut each banana crosswise into 6 pieces (about 1 in. thick). Insert a toothpick into each piece; transfer to a waxed paper-lined baking sheet. Freeze until completely firm, about 1 hour.
2. In a microwave, melt the chocolate and shortening; stir until smooth. Dip banana pieces in chocolate mixture; allow excess to drip off. Dip pieces in the toppings as desired; return to baking sheet. Freeze for at least 30 minutes before serving.
1 treat: 72 cal., 4g fat (2g sat. fat), 0 chol., 0 sod., 10g carb. (7g sugars, 1g fiber), 1g pro. **Diabetic exchanges:** 1 fat, ½ starch.

GINGER-GLAZED GRILLED HONEYDEW

If you've never grilled fruit before, you're in for a real treat! I love the idea of cooking everything from appetizers to desserts on the grill. This is sweet and really light.
—Jacqueline Correa, Landing, NJ

- -

Takes: 25 min. • **Makes:** 6 servings

- ¼ cup peach preserves
- 1 Tbsp. lemon juice
- 1 Tbsp. finely chopped crystallized ginger
- 2 tsp. grated lemon zest
- ⅛ tsp. ground cloves
- 1 medium honeydew melon, cut into 2-in. cubes

1. In a small bowl, combine the first 5 ingredients. Thread honeydew onto 6 metal or soaked wooden skewers; brush with half the glaze.
2. On a lightly oiled rack, grill honeydew, covered, over medium-high heat just until the melon begins to soften and brown, 4-6 minutes, turning and basting frequently with the remaining glaze.
1 skewer: 101 cal., 0 fat (0 sat. fat), 0 chol., 18mg sod., 26g carb. (23g sugars, 1g fiber), 1g pro. **Diabetic exchanges:** 1 fruit, ½ starch.

DID YOU KNOW?
These honeydew skewers are a sweet (and delicious) way to get a healthy dose of vitamin C and potassium.

Cutting Techniques

MINCING AND CHOPPING

Holding the handle of a chef's knife with one hand, rest the fingers of your other hand on the top of the blade near the tip. Using the handle to guide and apply pressure, move knife in an arc across the food with a rocking motion until pieces of food are the desired size. Mincing results in pieces no larger than ⅛ in. and chopping produces ¼- to ½-in. pieces.

DICING AND CUBING

Using a utility knife, trim each side of the frui, vegetable or other food, squaring it off. Cut lengthwise into evenly spaced strips. The narrower the strips, the smaller the pieces will be. Stack the strips and cut lengthwise into uniformly sized strips. Arrange the square-shaped strips into a pile and cut widthwise into uniform pieces.

MAKING BIAS OR DIAGONAL CUTS

Holding a chef's knife at an angle to the length of the food slice as thick or thin as desired. This technique is often used in stir-fry recipes.

MAKING JULIENNE STRIPS

Using a utility knife, cut a thin strip from one side of vegetable. Turn so flat side is down. Cut into 2-in. lengths, then cut each piece lengthwise into thin strips. Stack the strips and cut lengthwise into thinner strips.

CUTTING WEDGES

Using a chef's knife or serrated knife cut the produce in half from stem end to blossom end. Lay halves cut side down on a cutting board. Set knife at the center of one the halves and cut in half vertically, then cut each quarter in half vertically. Repeat with other half.

ZESTING

Pull a citrus zester across limes, lemons or oranges being careful not to remove the bitter white pith. The small holes in the zester will yield thin, narrow strips of zest. Use full strips to garnish or, if recipe instructs, chop into fine pieces and use as directed.

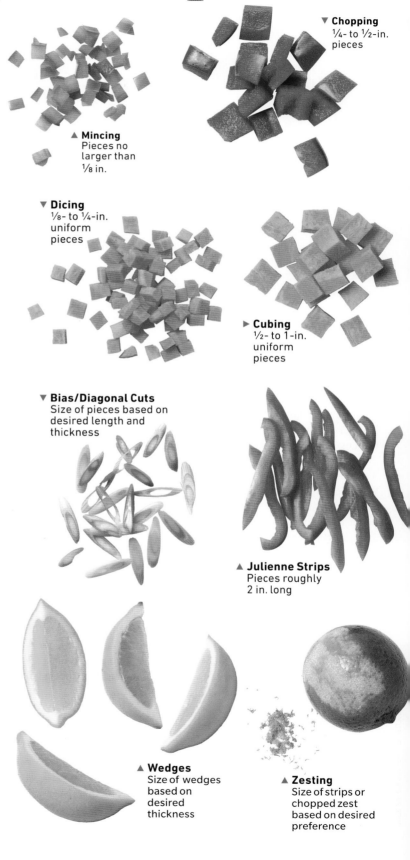

▼ **Chopping**
¼- to ½-in. pieces

▲ **Mincing**
Pieces no larger than ⅛ in.

▼ **Dicing**
⅛- to ¼-in. uniform pieces

► **Cubing**
½- to 1-in. uniform pieces

▼ **Bias/Diagonal Cuts**
Size of pieces based on desired length and thickness

▲ **Julienne Strips**
Pieces roughly 2 in. long

▲ **Wedges**
Size of wedges based on desired thickness

▲ **Zesting**
Size of strips or chopped zest based on desired preference

Equivalents & Substitutions

EQUIVALENT MEASURES

3 teaspoons = 1 tablespoon	**16 tablespoons** = 1 cup
4 tablespoons = ¼ cup	**2 cups** = 1 pint
5⅓ tablespoons = ⅓ cup	**4 cups** = 1 quart
8 tablespoons = ½ cup	**4 quarts** = 1 gallon

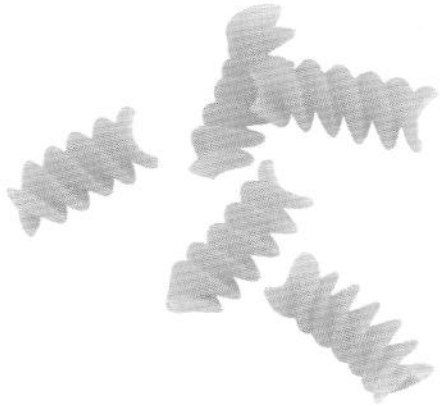

FOOD EQUIVALENTS

Macaroni	1 cup (3½ ounces) uncooked = 2½ cups cooked
Noodles Medium	3 cups (4 ounces) uncooked = 4 cups cooked
Popcorn	⅓-½ cup unpopped = 8 cups popped
Rice Long Grain	1 cup uncooked = 3 cups cooked
Rice Quick-Cooking	1 cup uncooked = 2 cups cooked
Spaghetti	8 ounces uncooked = 4 cups cooked

Bread	1 slice = ¾ cup soft crumbs or ¼ cup fine dry crumbs
Graham Crackers	7 squares = ½ cup finely crushed
Buttery Round Crackers	12 crackers = ½ cup finely crushed
Saltine Crackers	14 crackers = ½ cup finely crushed

Bananas	1 medium = ⅓ cup mashed
Lemons	1 medium = 3 tablespoons juice + 2 teaspoons grated zest
Limes	1 medium = 2 tablespoons juice + 1½ teaspoons grated zest
Oranges	1 medium = ¼-⅓ cup juice + 4 teaspoons grated zest

Cabbage	1 head = 5 cups shredded	**Green Pepper**	1 large = 1 cup chopped
Carrots	1 pound = 3 cups shredded	**Mushrooms**	½ pound = 3 cups sliced
Celery	1 rib = ½ cup chopped	**Onions**	1 medium = ½ cup chopped
Corn	1 ear fresh = ⅔ cup kernels	**Potatoes**	3 medium = 2 cups cubed

Almonds	1 pound = 3 cups chopped	**Pecan Halves**	1 pound = 4½ cups chopped
Ground Nuts	3¾ ounces = 1 cup	**Walnuts**	1 pound = 3¾ cups chopped

EASY SUBSTITUTIONS

WHEN YOU NEED...		USE...
Baking Powder	1 teaspoon	½ teaspoon cream of tartar + ¼ teaspoon baking soda
Buttermilk	1 cup	1 tablespoon lemon juice or vinegar + enough milk to measure 1 cup (let stand 5 minutes before using)
Cornstarch	1 tablespoon	2 tablespoons all-purpose flour
Honey	1 cup	1¼ cups sugar + ¼ cup water
Half-and-Half Cream	1 cup	1 tablespoon melted butter + enough whole milk to measure 1 cup
Onion	1 small chopped (⅓ cup)	1 teaspoon onion powder or 1 tablespoon dried minced onion
Tomato Juice	1 cup	½ cup tomato sauce + ½ cup water
Tomato Sauce	2 cups	¾ cup tomato paste + 1 cup water
Unsweetened Chocolate	1 square (1 ounce)	3 tablespoons baking cocoa + 1 tablespoon shortening or oil
Whole Milk	1 cup	½ cup evaporated milk + ½ cup water

Recipe Index

A

Air-Fryer Caribbean Wontons 232
Air-Fryer Chicken Parmesan.................114
Air-Fryer Crispy Chicken Wings 11
Air-Fryer Garlic-Rosemary
	Brussels Sprouts 151
Air-Fryer Smoked Pork Chops.............108
Almond Bear Claws 71
Almond Cake with
	Raspberry Sauce........................ 204
Aloha Burgers 93
Amish Sugar Cookies...........................190
Angel Biscuits 55
Antipasto Kabobs 13
Apple Dutch Baby................................34
Apple Kuchen Bars 176
Applesauce Muffins 74
Apricot Kielbasa Slices 18
Artichoke & Spinach Dip Pizza............... 8
Asian Tofu 142
Asparagus & Egg Salad with
	Walnuts & Mint..........................155
Audrey's Lemon Meringue Bars..........177

B

Back-to-School Cookies.......................184
Bacon Cheddar Potato Skins 16
Bacon Cheeseburger Buns.....................90
Bacon-Wrapped Spam Bites 25
Baked Baby Potatoes with
	Olive Pesto................................. 15
Baked Chips 27
Baked Fish & Rice 136
Balsamic Asiago Salad..........................169
Balsamic Chicken with
	Broccoli Couscous 98
Banana Crumb Pudding 219
Banana Nut Brownies 182
Bananas Foster Baked
	French Toast...............................45
Beef Braciole 104
Beefy Swiss Bundles............................114
Berry-Patch Brownie Pizza 176
Berry Puff Pancake 49
Best Banana Ice Cream.......................231
Best Bran Muffins 61
Big-Batch Bloody Marys 9
Biscuits & Sausage Gravy 42
Blackberry Apple Pie 212
Blood Orange & Goat Cheese
	Galette 198
BLT Muffins 60

BLT Waffle Sliders 37
Blue Cheese Kale Salad 160
Blue-Ribbon Beef Nachos......................99
Blueberry Pudding Cake 209
Boston Cream Cupcakes 206
Broccoli Fritters................................. 18
Broccoli-Mushroom Bubble Bake.........48
Buffalo Chicken Lettuce Wraps 78
Buffalo Wing Poppers...........................20
Burger Sliders with
	Secret Sauce 81
Butterfinger Cookies...........................172
Butternut & Portobello Lasagna 135
Buttery Cornbread 72
Buttery Crescent Rolls 75

C

Caramel Nut Crunch Pie 210
Cast-Iron Cherry-Berry
	Peach Pie 211
Cast-Iron Favorite Pizza......................111
Cheery Cherry Cookies...........................191
Cheese Enchiladas.............................127
Cheese Lover's Fondue 24
Cheeseburger Cups 106
Cheesy Summer Squash
	Casserole 165
Cheesy Vegetable Egg Dish.................50
Chicken Chorizo Posole 87
Chicken Francese 112
Chicken Pesto Sandwiches.....................95
Chicken Tikka Meatballs
	with Ginger Rice 109
Chocolate & Vanilla Creme Brulee.......219
Chocolate Chip Cheese Ball 20
Chocolate Chip Cookie Dough
	Cheesecake 233
Chocolate-Glazed Raspberry
	Eclairs.....................................227
Chocolate Marshmallow Cookies.........178
Chocolate Mayonnaise Cake 204
Chocolate Pecan Skillet Cookie 187
Chocolate-Strawberry
	Celebration Cake 210
Chocolate Zucchini Cupcakes...............213
Chorizo & Grits Breakfast Bowls...........35
Chunky Chipotle Pork Chili 91
Cinnamon Swirl Quick Bread...............64
Cinnamon Tea Rolls 67
Classic Macaroni Salad 156
Coconut Mango Bread Pudding
	with Rum Sauce..........................224

Coconut Milk Strawberry-Banana
	Pops..217
Coconut Tres Leches Cupcakes............202
Contest-Winning Hearty
	Hamburger Soup..........................89
Contest-Winning New England
	Clam Chowder.............................86
Contest-Winning Strawberry
	Pretzel Dessert.........................226
Corn Dog Casserole............................ 117
Cowboy Calico Beans 169
Creamed Peas 160
Creamy Chicken Rice Soup 94
Creamy Strawberry Crepes 43
Creamy Tomato Shrimp
	with Penne..............................134
Creamy Twice-Baked Potatoes...........157
Creole Pasta with
	Sausage & Shrimp.......................104
Crescent Turkey Casserole 101
Crumb-Coated Red Snapper 147
Crunchy Waldorf Salad 163

D

Dijon-Bacon Dip for Pretzels 8
Din Tai Fung Chilled
	Cucumber Salad 162
Dirt Dessert....................................220
Double Chocolate Espresso
	Cheesecake..............................221

E

Easy Crab Cakes..............................132
Easy Deviled Eggs 26
Easy Egg Rolls 16
Eggs Benedict Casserole 45
Falafel 141

F

Farro Salad with Charred Shishito
	Peppers & Corn........................... 161
Favorite Dutch Apple Pie.................... 209
Feta Cheese & Pomegranate
	Guacamole 26
Fiesta Corn & Beans..........................158
First-Place Coconut Macaroons...........182
Fluffy Pancakes 33
40-Minute Hamburger Buns..................58
Four-Fruit Compote............................50
Frozen Chocolate Monkey Treats.........235
Frozen Margaritas.............................. 15
Fruity Pull-Apart Bread.......................64

G

Garlic Bubble Loaf......................................67
Garlic Chicken with Maple-Chipotle
 Glaze...103
Garlic Knots..62
Garlic Tomato Bruschetta.........................21
Ginger-Glazed Grilled
 Honeydew..235
Gluten-Free Brownie Bars 175
Gooey Butter Cookies.............................183
Gooey Chocolate Caramel Bars...........190
Graham Streusel Coffee Cake.................68
Grandma Krause's Coconut
 Cookies...180
Green Chile Adobado Poutine................102
Green Chile Corn Fritters.........................54
Grilled Caesar Chicken
 Breasts...121
Grilled Huli Huli Chicken 98
Grilled Lobster Tails.................................144
Grilled Vegetable Platter.........................153
Ground Beef Gyros....................................84

H

Hash Brown Egg Bake 30
Herb-Stuffed Roasted
 Cornish Hens 111
Herbed Cheese Sticks...............................26
Herbed Onion Bagels.................................62
Homemade Honey Grahams 187
Homemade Tortillas...................................71
Honey Grilled Shrimp...............................124
Honey Lemon Meringue Pie.................206
Hot Milk Cake...202
Hot Wing Dip...23
Hummingbird Cupcakes............................20

I

Ice Cream Cone Treats 229
Incredible Coconut Cake.........................205
Irish Creme Chocolate Trifle 234
Italian Brunch Torte..................................35
Italian Meatball Buns 25
Italian-Style Drop Biscuits 75

J

Jalapeno Cheese Bread 70
Jam-Topped Mini Cheesecakes 220

K

Kentucky Coleslaw...................................167
Lean Green Smoothie 51

L

Lemon Blueberry Bread 58
Lemon Bread Pudding..............................231
Lemon Breakfast Parfaits.........................50

Lemon Dream Cheesecake...................228
Lemon-Garlic Cream
 Fettuccine...127
Lemon Lover's Cookies 184
Lemon-Rosemary Layer Cake 194
Lime & Gin Coconut
 Macaroons...191
Linguine with Herbed
 Clam Sauce...144
Loaded M&M Oreo Cookie Bars...........179
Loaded Mexican Pizza 143

M

Mad About "Meat" Loaf 141
Mandarin Orange Chicken Salad..........158
Mango Bread..57
Mango Glace with Pineapple
 Pomegranate Salsa...........................223
Mango Orange Quencher 27
Margarita Chicken Quesadillas...............23
Margarita Cupcakes 199
Marinated Cheese 12
Martha's Fish Tacos 139
Mashed Red Potatoes.............................168
Meatless Taco Salad................................146
Mediterranean Bulgur Bowl...................125
Mexican Chicken Chili 94
Mexican-Style Stuffed Peppers............107
Milk-and-Honey White Bread 61
Mini Ham Quiches 30
Mini Sweet Potato Scones with
 Rosemary & Bacon 57
Mixed Berry Shortcake...........................195
Mixed Berry Tiramisu..............................222
Moist Pineapple Banana Bread..............54
Mom's Chocolate Bread 74
Mom's Meat Loaf 112
Monte Cristo Casserole with
 Raspberry Sauce...................................38
Moussaka 113
Mushroom Panzanella.............................162

N

Navy Bean Vegetable Soup 83
Nonni's Fritole 216

O

Oatmeal Cake with Caramel Icing........197
Oh-So-Good Oatmeal.................................42
Old-Fashioned Whoopie Pies.................201
Olive & Red Pepper Linguine 166
One-Pot Black Bean Enchilada
 Pasta..132
One-Pot Spinach Beef Soup.....................95
Onion Beef au Jus 79
Orange Cream Pops 232
Orange Zucchini Muffins...........................68

Orzo Shrimp Stew....................................143
Oven Fries...154
Overnight Fruit Salad.................................40

P

Party Shrimp... 13
Patriotic Ice Cream Cupcakes 213
Peach Crumble Dessert.........................226
Peanut Butter & Jelly
 French Toast..51
Peanut Butter Chocolate Bars..............185
Peanut Butter Cookie Cups..................190
Peanut Butter Cookies...........................179
Peanut Butter Silk Pie............................201
Pear-Blackberry Crisp............................234
Peloponnesian Chicken Pasta...............117
Pepperoni Pasta Salad...........................167
Pepperoni Pizza Loaf.................................84
Pina Colada Icebox Cake........................228
Pineapple Pork Stir-Fry...........................130
Pineapple Pudding Cake.........................212
Pineapple Smoothies.................................49
Pomegranate Magic Bars 189
Portobello & Chickpea
 Sheet-Pan Supper 131
Potato-Lentil Stew...................................146
Pots de Creme..216
Power Berry Smoothie Bowl....................46
Pressure-Cooker Corn
 Chowder...81
Pressure-Cooker Hawaiian
 Breakfast Hash 38
Pressure-Cooker Shredded
 Chicken Gyros.......................................89
Prosciutto Egg Panini................................33

Q

Quick Ambrosia Fruit Salad...................169

R

Ragin' Cajun Eggplant &
 Shrimp Skillet.....................................128
Rainbow Gelatin Cubes...........................224
Rainbow Quiche..47
Ranger Cookies...188
Red Lentil Hummus with
 Brussels Sprout Hash 21
Reuben Waffle Potato
 Appetizers 11
Roast Beef with Chive
 Roasted Potatoes 120
Roasted Red Pepper Bread......................72
Rocky Road Rice Krispies
 Treats...188
Rosemary Salmon & Veggies.................146
Rustic Italian Tortellini Soup...................93
Rustic Summer Vegetable Pasta 136

S

Salmon Grilled in Foil 124
Salsa Spaghetti Squash 140
Saucy Garlic Chicken 119
Sausage & Crescent Roll
    Casserole 41
Sausage Cheese Puffs 37
Sausage Chive Pinwheels 27
Sauteed Apples 51
Savory Roasted Chicken 120
Scalloped Taters 168
Seasoned Tilapia Fillets 134
Sesame Ginger Beef Skewers 101
Shakshuka Breakfast Pizza 40
Shrimp Monterey 131
Simple Herbed Scallops 147
Sloppy Joes Sandwiches 94
Slow-Cooked Barbecued Beef
    Sandwiches 82
Slow-Cooked Sirloin 118
Slow-Cooker Pasta e Fagioli 83
Soft Garlic Breadsticks 65
Sopaipillas 223
Sour Cream Pound Cake 213
South Dakota Frito Treats 191
Southern Shrimp & Grits 137
Southwest Vegetarian Bake 139
Sparkling Red Wine Sangria 12
Special Creamed Corn 154
Special Raisin Pie 199
Special Stuffed Strawberries 234
Spicy Breakfast Lasagna 46
Spicy Flank Steak 108
Spicy Sausage Rigatoni 118
Spinach & Feta Bourekas 19
Spinach Salad with
    Hot Bacon Dressing 150
Springtime Potato Salad 153
Spritz Cookies 173
Strawberry & Peach Lime
    Custard Bars 180
Sugar Cookie Fruit Pizzas 235
Summer Orzo 165
Summer Turkey Kabobs 121
Surprise Monkey Bread 75

T

Taco Pasta Salad 157
Tacoritos 116
Tahitian Breakfast Treats 69
Tarragon Asparagus 168
Thick Sugar Cookies 175
Tilapia Florentine 128
Toffee Apple Cinnamon Buns 59
Toffee Poke Cake 212
Triple Tomato Flatbread 14
Tropical Smoothie Bowl 36
True Belgian Waffles 34
Turkey Focaccia Club 95
Two-Tone Caramel Brownies 172

U

Upside-Down Frito Pie 121

V

Vegan Quinoa Salad 147
Vegetable Pad Thai 140
Veggie Macaroni & Cheese 166
Veggie Nicoise Salad 129
Watermelon Cups 24

W

White Chocolate Fruit Tart 197
White Wine Garlic Chicken 120
Wyoming Cowboy Cookies 183

Y

Yogurt Berry Parfaits 31

Z

Zippy Turkey Zoodles 107
Zucchini & Cheese Drop Biscuits 74
Zucchini Onion Pie 150
Zucchini Walnut Cake 207